SCIENCE, ANIMALS, AND EVOLUTION

Contributions in Philosophy

CATHERINE ROBERTS

SCIENCE, ANIMALS, AND EVOLUTION

Reflections on Some Unrealized Potentials of Biology and Medicine

Foreword by
Arthur M. Young

Contributions in Philosophy, Number 14

Greenwood Press

WESTPORT, CONNECTICUT • LONDON, ENGLAND

Library of Congress Cataloging in Publication Data

Roberts, Catherine.
  Science, animals, and evolution.

  (Contributions in philosophy ; no. 14 ISSN 0084-926X)
  Bibliography: p.
  Includes index.
  1. Biology—Philosophy. 2. Science—Philosophy.
3. Humanism. I. Title.
QH331.R62   574'.01   79-52322
ISBN 0-313-21479-4

Library of Congress Catalog Card Number: 79-52322
ISBN: 0-313-21479-4
ISSN: 0084-926X

First published in 1980

Greenwood Press
A division of Congressional Information Service, Inc.
51 Riverside Avenue, Westport, Connecticut 06880

Printed in the United States of America

10 9 8 7 6 5 4 3 2 1

Copyright
Acknowledgments

That it is really the good and the right which holds and binds things together, they never reflect.

Plato, *The Phaedo,* 99c

Contents

Acknowledgments

It is a pleasure to acknowledge the help, both direct and indirect, that Richard Thorne, Harold Wakeford Cox, John Vyvyan, Basil Wrighton, Jon Wynne-Tyson, Martin Andic, and Flava have given to me in the preparation of this book.

Parts of this book have previously appeared as articles in Danish or English as follows:

Chapter 2 is based on an article orginàlly published in Danish in *Kristeligt Dagblad,* June 4, 1969.

Chapter 3 is based on an article originally published in *The Ark* 32 (1969): 98-102.

Chapter 5 was originally published in Danish in *Kristelight Dagblad,* February 24, 1971.

Chapter 6 is based on an article originally published in Danish in *Kristeligt Dagblad,* November 4, 1971, and reprinted in revised English translation in *The Aryan Path* 43 (1972): 295-99 and 342-46.

Chapter 7 is based on an article originally published in Danish in *Kristeligt Dagblad,* February 24, 1972.

Chapter 9 is based on an article originally published in *Animals' Defender* 13 (1969): 106-14.

Chapter 10 was originally published in *The American Scholar* 40 (1971): 497-512.

Chapter 12 is based on an article originally published in *The Aryan Path* 43 (1972): 8-13.

Foreword

This is a unique book. It comes at a time when we are beset with
problems—pollution, crime, nuclear and chemical waste, threat of atomic
warfare, and so on—and people are beginning to realize that the
material benefits science and industry have made available have been obtained at the cost of perhaps irreparable injury to our ecology.

Some of these problems can be solved by science, but not all. Further,
there is the unsettling thought that since many of the problems have
come about through interventions made possible by science, then something else is needed. Otherwise, we will be treating only the symptoms.
Above all, beyond the demands for more energy, more leisure, more
housing, and more productivity there is the possibility that some self-
restraint, some self-limitation, is the only salvation.

But, if so, what is to ensure this self-restraint?

Catherine Roberts does not address herself directly to this problem.
Her point of departure is cruelty to animals as practiced by biologists, an
issue that seems minor when compared with the threat of atomic warfare.
But the issue concerning animals is seminal, and, as she develops it, it becomes the basis for the important distinction that makes self-limitation
possible. If man had no other concern than his immediate self-interest,
there could be no self-limitation. Self-limitation is action directed toward

a higher goal, and the difference between immediate needs and ultimate goals is the spiritual dimension. This dimension is involved in animal experimentation because by brutally exploiting animals for our own benefit we do violence to the life force in its evolution—not only the life force of the animals, but of our own. Such unfeeling activity mars our own score. By invoking the spiritual dimension, Catherine Roberts establishes a Good higher than human needs, even if the need is to save a life.

The recognition of this higher Good enables Catherine Roberts to distinguish two sorts of humanism—anthropocentric and theocentric. The first is centered on immediate human welfare and the second on man's ultimate goals.

What makes her vision unique is that she is not misled by humanism as a substitute for religion. She perceives that humanism makes the same concessions that science does and brings us no closer to spiritual goals. Its compass is human needs, not human aspirations.

As Roberts rightly observes, the evolution of life from more primitive forms—in fact, the emergence of life itself—cannot be explained by necessity alone. Of course it is necessary that life survive, but necessity cannot account for life's continual capacity to surpass itself. What is impressive about evolution is not that some species survive and some die out, but that life evolves; it insists on surpassing itself.

This suggests that man is not the end point of evolution; Roberts joins Michael Polanyi in calling for an ultra-biology to study not just the forms leading to man, but what lies beyond man. Her thesis is that evolution moves toward the highest Good, and this, for her, *is* the spiritual dimension.

In one sense this thesis is a return to religion, but, because it is devoid of those specific characterizations of the Godhead that have always been the source of religious differences leading to wars and fanaticism, it restores the original thrust of the religious instinct, which can only be the same driving force that has activated evolution. That this is a creative force is precisely what makes it spiritual and impossible for science to manipulate. Even organized religion cannot capture or contain it.

Catherine Roberts takes us through many of the professions that administer to man's welfare—medicine, pharmacology, organ transplantation, vivisection, religion, even the humanistic efforts of Oxford philosophers—and reveals the lack of spiritual perspective in each of their otherwise well-intended arguments.

I doubt if most of us realize how far the tide of science has carried us from our true course, and it is salutary that her uncompromising argument, which meets the rational mind at every turn, leaves us no alternative but to awaken from our bedazzlement with science that Blake called Newton's Sleep.

So the question is whether, with Catherine Roberts, to accuse science of being morally wrong and under obligation to recognize spiritual origins or to wait for science to discover in its own way, the spiritual dimension. So far I have been waiting, but perhaps time is running out.

Arthur M. Young

SCIENCE,
ANIMALS,
AND EVOLUTION

Introduction

To have been opposing, for more than a decade, the increasingly retrograde relation between biologists and sentient animals without having been able to stem the tide in any way was one compelling reason for writing this book. Integrating and supplementing my arguments would, I hoped, make the whole more attractive and convincing than its parts. At the same time this book was conceived as an alternative to those contemporary systems of biological thought about evolution and ethics that fail to see that man, confronted with the reality of creatures lower than himself and the reality of the spiritual realm higher than himself, must improve both alliances if he himself is truly to evolve. Evolutionary cognizance of both the human-animal relation and the human-divine relation will, I believe, become inseparably bound to the ethical expectations of those who would create a better world.

Derived from the Latin *e* (out) and *volvere* (to roll), the basic meaning of evolve is to roll out, unfold, develop. Thus, despite the seemingly random and fortuitous nature of many of the hereditary variations that permanently alter evolving individuals and populations, the scientific age generally regards the evolution of life on earth as a continuous progression from the simple to the complex and more highly organized, which has culminated in a biosphere dominated by man. But since neither

Darwinism nor any modification of his evolutionary theory based upon newer knowledge of mendelian and non-mendelian genetics and the geological, paleontological, and anthropological record can adequately explain the origin, development, and relationships of the multitude of species now in existence, science may be far indeed from the truth about the unfolding of life on this planet. Our primary concern here, however, is not so much what has happened as what will happen to evolving life. Very apposite to the reflections that follow is a statement made by Michael Polanyi when he was envisioning the regeneration of biology, "This is the point at which the theory of evolution finally bursts through the bonds of natural science and becomes entirely an affirmation of man's ultimate aims." (*Personal Knowledge,* 1958, p. 404)

When, in this scientific age, we consider man alone as an evolved and evolving species, the word evolution may take on an ominous connotation insofar as we think of the future in terms of exploding biology and medicine lacking ethical criteria yet imposing genetic, surgical, pharmacological, or psychological directives upon the further physical and mental development of life. But in turning from the scientific to the religious perspective, we find that the word evolution acquires a different semantic flavor. In the religious sense, human evolution is a wholly positive concept envisioning the gradual unfolding of man's spiritual-ethical potentials and possessing enormous significance now when man is becoming obsessed with such things as genetic engineering, cloning, and cryonics. In my mind, there can be no question that he will soon burst through these constricting, damaging bonds of established science.

It will require an openness and a turning toward the higher spiritual reality of the universe. The more man looks in this direction, the more he sees and becomes—and optimum conditions are created for the awakening of all. Man's spiritual evolution is a religious unfolding of his highest potential for love, virtue, compassion, justice, peace, joy, harmony, and balance. Although there is no evidence that such traits are inherited, countless individuals have demonstrated that they can be permanently acquired. Man needs no further changes or enrichment of his gene complement to do so; it suffices as it is. For contemporary man, with all his genes, is also spiritually endowed. If man's biological evolution, based upon the hereditary transmission of physical and mental characters, has provided him with a body possessing a consciousness enabling him to reflect upon his thoughts and actions, he has also been given a spark of divinity, and he thus knows that his further evolution requires reaching out to that which transcends himself—to the *summum bonum,* the divine Good.

And in doing so with ever increasing intensity in the time to come, *Homo sapiens* cannot fail to help other species in their spiritual evolution, whatever their highest potentials and destiny may be. The theme of this book is thus not so much life's biological past but rather what appears to be intuitive truth about its further spiritual development: Man, learning to live more righteously and nobly with himself and his living environment, will be participating more fully in divinity by helping to realize spiritual potentiality everywhere, in all.

Such a view may appear irreconcilable with the evil times and ethical chaos in which we find ourselves. It would rather seem that *Homo sapiens* has suffered a spiritual regression from which there is no hope of recovery. An optimistic evolutionary prognosis is nevertheless held by millions of contemporary minds, in particular those who accept as absolute truth the immortality of the soul, reincarnation, and karma. For them, man's spiritual evolution must be individual before it can be collective. And since each human individual, consciously or unconsciously, is making a difficult, laborious spiritual ascent because he or she has no other choice, a cumulative good will eventually prevail. All human endeavors are thus destined to become more spiritual—including biology, the study of life.

This book attempts to show what biology is and what it could be. It is basically at odds with the prevailing desire of scientists to further evolution through the attainment of more and more scientific knowledge of all forms of life by all conceivable means. It proposes, rather, that from now on one of the first evolutionary responsibilities of the biologist should be the exercise of professional self-restraint. Based upon the conviction that the essence and quality of human life are more significant than mere existence, the view is put forth here that the objective pursuit of scientific knowledge can and will become an increasingly subjective endeavor providing biologists with an opportunity to become changed in the process through the fuller realization of their own potentials. If biologists were to make the ethical choice to study human and nonhuman life in the spirit of the saints and the sages—with self-denial, self-restraint, self-sacrifice, humility, brotherhood, and love—they would be personally contributing to the human evolutionary advance, and, at the same time, transforming biology into an infinitely higher endeavor than it now is.

This book points to the prospect of creating a new science of life that is ethically self-limiting in both means and goals because moral progress would be valued more highly than the advance of traditional biology. This new science would be a study of life that recognizes that further scientific manipulation and control of life is, by any evolutionary standard, undesirable. It would recognize that kindness and justice for lower forms of sentient life are more humanly desirable than is objective knowledge of them. If, as at present, experimental biology and medicine can only advance through the continued suffering, death, and blank denial of the rights of innocent lives, then the scientific conscience must become ready and willing to admit with Bernard Shaw that for the sake of evolving life as a whole, there are some things men must not know—and some things they must not do. Already moral philosophers are becoming uneasy about the human-animal relation in science, and within those fields of experimental research where biology's most flagrant misdeeds are being perpetrated upon captive animals, there are signs among the younger biologists of pangs of conscience and open revolt against the established system.

A radical change in the scientific conscience is bound to come. Without it, there can be no permanent betterment of man's relation to either the animal kingdom or the source of his being, and the world will at last become spiritually uninhabitable. With it, right relations among the sentient creatures of the earth can gradually be established, permitting man to look forward optimistically to the evolution of all animate nature as an increasingly harmonious whole.

One of the basic postulates of this book is that the new biology cannot fully emerge out of the anthropocentric limitations of secular and scientific humanism. The humaneness of humanists is too narrow a moral vision for that. The growing rational opposition of anthropocentric humanists to scientific methodology is a wholly necessary, but as yet inadequate, beginning of the orientation of man toward the divine Good. Any renewal of the scientific conscience that is radical and permanent enough to create a spiritualized biology must arise out of a humanism that recognizes the dictates of the spiritual realm. Evolution and ethics must again be seen from the high perspective. In returning to its source, evolving human life is compelled to ascend toward the Good—and to become progressively better as it moves upwards. Biology, the study of life, and biologists, the students of life, are both deeply involved in this spiritual ascent.

Spiritual is an infinitely elastic word. When we use it to designate that which is conceptually distinguishable from the material and has objective existence quite independent of human thought, we point beyond the purely intellectual toward the mysterious reciprocal relation between the human and the divine, as well as toward the equally obscure reciprocation between immanent and transcendent divinity. Man, it has repeatedly been said, is a spiritual being; throughout his evolutionary journey, be it in the body here on earth or in periods of pre- and post-earthly existence, he possesses some kind of divine spark within that is ever seeking its source. In this view, to which I adhere, human spirituality has its origin in ultimate divinity. Human spirituality thus cannot be divorced from religion, which is man's concern with his relation to the divine. But since religious faith may be restricted to passive submission to dogma and authority, the spiritual will be used here in a wider, more mystical and metaphysical sense to denote any religious manifestation of, or striving toward, a transcendent reality recognized as the ultimate Good existing beyond the apprehension of the intellect and the senses alone. Spiritual experience, whether called faith or perception, is thus in part supra-rational, intuitive, and extrasensory. Its acquisition, so the spiritually enlightened tell us, depends upon the proper orientation of our inner spark of divinity, or eye of the soul, toward the divine light of the spiritual realm which, in turn, enhances the ethical purity of our being by imparting to our conscience a growing knowledge of transcendent love, will, and eternal values. This is not to say that the emanative spiritual energy of the divine embraces only ethical criteria or that evolving man will never reach a state beyond ethics. Rather, the ethical aspect of the spiritual is stressed throughout this book to emphasize that *at this stage in evolutionary history* the greatest human question confronting the species remains how man can learn to choose between good and evil.

Since spiritual knowledge thus refers, in what follows, to different degrees of awareness of the divine Good, I must at the outset emphatically disclaim possession of transcendent truths acquired through the higher forms of spiritual experience. On the contrary, this book has been written in full recognition of the great distance separating the spiritual aspirants high up on the mountain from the dark and difficult foothills where most of us find ourselves. Those above are closer to the light of truth; these lower regions, dimly illuminated, seem still darker by our own confusion and imperfection. All that I can claim is to see the direction of the path ahead more clearly than those about me who, in the name of science, are vehemently denying that it leads toward the source of all light.

On the basis of this claim *Science, Animals, and Evolution* indicts the scientific conscience for monstrously unethical choices in the pursuit of the life sciences, and it attempts to envisage a new biology that is in harmony with the evolution of man into a truly spiritual-ethical reality. To do justice to this dual theme is admittedly beyond the powers of any one mind. Yet the attempt, however groping and incomplete, may help to persuade others that the gradual emergence of a spiritualized biology is neither wishful thinking nor a utopian dream but an inevitable evolutionary step forward in the realization of the human potential.

_1_

Two Kinds of
Humanism and the Good

Humanism has to do with the realization of the human potential. A deep-rooted concern for what man can do to better himself must have been present in all stages of human evolution. Today anyone who has devoted any part of his life and thoughts to the amelioration of the human condition can be called a humanist, and that includes nearly all of us. But what kind of humanists are we?

Underlying the theme of this book is recognition of two kinds of humanism, "anthropocentric" and "theocentric," and the present tensions between them.[1] Since the one designation may sound tautological and the other self-contradictory, it is first of all necessary to justify the use of these terms.

In California there has long existed a remarkable weekly journal called *Manas,* which is devoted to the support of "intelligent idealism under the conditions of life in the twentieth century." In 1972 *Manas* called attention to a dismaying array of new biological visions of the future of man. In rightly deploring the ethical confusion of those biologists who would improve human life by its further scientific manipulation, the anonymous author contrasted their "mechanistic" approach with various "humanistic" views, including my own, and pointed to the great difficulty in establishing fruitful interchange between the two groups:

The origin of the virtues is not a problem in the biological universe of discourse, and when biologists speak of improving man, they mean improving the human organism. As biologists, they think themselves entitled to ask: What else is there to man? We have specific evidence to support what we say and propose.

Dr. Roberts suggests that biological considerations alone do not really touch the essential nature of man, nor do they take any cognizance of essentially human problems. And if the molecular biologists say to Dr. Roberts, Show us your experiments, she can only reply that her evidence lies in her and others' efforts to think wisely and well, as human beings should, and to take into account the full spectrum of human reality and experience.[2]

In expressing grateful appreciation of this sympathetic interest in my views, I am compelled to add that if my previous book conveyed the impression that virtue concerns human reality alone, this impression resulted from imperfect expression, inadequate knowledge, or both.[3] More convinced that ever before that man's further ethical development will need a humanism that is oriented toward divine reality, I hope to revise the earlier impression by emphasizing the possibilities of meaningful communication between contemporary biologists and the particular group of humanists to which I aspire to belong. If spiritualized biology is to become more than a concept in the mind, it must begin with an interchange of opposing ideas.

A rigorous characterization of the fundamental difference between the two groups is necessary. Since both are earnestly interested in the evolutionary progress of man, let us call them both humanists but distinguish them as follows:

The evolutionary visions of the biologists are based upon the conviction that the objective knowledge of science is the only reliable source of truth. In refusing to allow spiritual knowledge to contaminate their rational *Weltbild,* they deny the existence of a divine reality and a divine ethic. Seeing the human-divine relation as an illusion, they are forced to see man evolving autonomously by his own unaided powers. The other group, while accepting scientific knowledge as a source of truth, rejects the belief that "man, when he acts sensibly, has only one mode of knowing: the scientific."[4] It sees the divine as the supreme reality, which evolving man, in enforced self-transcendence, is approaching through progressive acquisition of spiritual-ethical knowledge.

The two groups can thus be broadly differentiated in terms of science and religion, but I prefer the designations anthropocentricity and theocentricity, which point connotatively to the teleological difference between the groups. Where is man going? How far can he go? Has he an ultimate destiny? Anthropocentric and theocentric humanists are in fundamental disagreement on these questions; it cannot be otherwise when they look upon human potential from such radically opposed perspectives.

The anthropocentric humanist sees the realization of the individual's potential in terms of life on earth. The concepts of the immortal soul and metempsychosis, he believes, are wishful thinking, since individual death is synonymous with extinction. But since *Homo sapiens* as a species continues to evolve, the anthropocentric humanist sees its potential as realizable through further acquisition of scientific truths that can improve the body and mind. Despite all attempts, he cannot, however, reasonably see "godlike" qualities in man. By flatly denying the existence of any higher reality than the human, the anthropocentric humanist acknowledges no divine source to which man can return, and from which man can receive divine light and wisdom on his way. When divinity is wholly denied, the adjectival prefix "theo-" has no meaning except illusion. Anthropocentrically speaking, evolving man must remain man so long as he survives. The human potential is, and always will be, strictly human in nature.

The theocentric humanist has a fundamentally different approach to the mysteries of life, death, and evolution. He recognizes first of all in the universe a divine reality whose existence preceded life on earth and was responsible for its origin. Whether he ponders the fate of the individual soul after death or the evolutionary destiny of the human race as a whole, the theocentric humanist thinks in terms of the compulsory approach of the human back to the divine from which it originated. Human life, he sees, possesses a divine spark and thus must strive to return to its divine source to complete its cycle. In this cyclic view evolving man, in one sense, is always approaching the divine, ever making a spiritual ascent to that which transcends the human. Teleologically, man cannot remain man, for he must at last be reunited with the spiritual from which he came. Nor can evolving man ever be wholly independent (as so many now imagine) of divinity. In its farthest reaches, theocentric humanism views evolving man as embarked upon the inconceivably slow and difficult development that is leading to what may be called his own deification.

Deification is admittedly a dangerous word to employ at present, since it can, quite rightly, bring to mind the blasphemous arrogance with which scientific hubris operates in our time. It must be emphasized, therefore, that nothing could be further from my thoughts than to equate deification with the contemporary illusion that modern men are already deified because of their godlike skill in manipulating their lives and directing their evolution. Such humanistic thinking is spiritually and ethically contemptible. In this work, deification, so far as the individual is concerned, refers to man's attempt to realize his highest potential through an act, seemingly best known to mystics, by which the human soul becomes one with the divine reality. This union, they tell us, may be likened to the sudden transformation of the divine spark into flame and involves the loss of human identity. Obviously, however, the loss can only be a temporary one, for the mystical experience does not make the mystic a god. He undergoes a permanent inner transformation, but after the experience he is still a human being living in the body. The individual human soul, as Zaehner expresses it, survives the mystical encounter with the divine.[5] Thus, on earth, the potential of deification is only incompletely realized. How far it is realized after our death we do not know. But from an evolutionary viewpoint, in terms of the spiritual ascent of the human race, deification is a potential whose complete realization must be the final destiny of human life: the spiritualization of matter through the final return of the created to the uncreated Good from which it came. Theocentrically speaking, evolving man is undergoing the experience of self-transcendence—destined, after untold eons, to become something more than man. Still human, his realizable potential is, in truth, divine.

This teleological distinction between anthropocentricity and theocentricity brings into relief their opposing world views. The one is centered upon evolving human reality; the other upon divine reality, which intervenes in human evolution by imparting to it the power of self-transcendence. This does not mean that theocentric humanism is restricted to a God in anthropomorphic image; it is rather the soul's recognition of, and turning toward, the divine, in the conviction that whatever its ultimate essence, it is a supreme Good that can make us better than we are. Theocentric humanists are those who seek knowledge of this Good, already knowing that spiritual-ethical truths are supremely desirable in human evolution. Regardless of their religious faith, these humanists do not forget (as some religions seem to have done) that the transcendent nature of the human-divine relation requires spiritual striving toward the Good. Nonspiritual forms of religion have in fact ravaged the world with immorality of varying kinds and degrees. Yet, one must remember that the religions of the world are never static enterprises but are constantly evolving toward an enhancement of their spiritual nature. Possessing an infinitude of as yet unrealized potentialities, world religions cannot fail to become more truly spiritual and theocentric with the passage of time.

Modern science is also in a state of evolution toward a realization of its true nature. At present, seeing itself ideally as an activity arising out of human search for truth that can benefit mankind, science is predominantly anthropocentric. Yet a small minority of contemporary scientists, including some biologists, are guided by the religious-spiritual perspectives of theocentric humanism, although they rarely express themselves about the relation of science to the divine. Nor is anthropocentric humanism, be it agnostic or atheistic, restricted to members of the scientific profession. The growing critique and mistrust of established science, which comes largely from without, is predominantly anthropocentric in nature.

Earnest concern about biology and the future of man and about the scientist's responsibility is expressed in various anthropocentric ways within and without scientific circles. Some are working out admirable plans, often of great intellectual complexity, for directing science and technology into new channels to ensure survival and well-being. Others are advocating the transformation of modern science into a more critical endeavor to diminish ecological damage caused by scientific and technological development. Still others, wholly distrusting the scientific conscience, hope that science will be brought to a permanent standstill. Such antiscientific activity has resulted in numerous encounters with scientific defenders of the status quo. But in all cases the interchanges are between anthropocentric groups radically divided as to what is best for evolving man but tacitly agreed that what is best for him does not concern his relation to a divine ethic. Participators in these confrontations are not concerned with the relations between science and religion. Most of them would no doubt agree with the conclusions of J. R. Ravetz:

> The obsolescence of the conception of science as the pursuit
> of truth results from several changes in the social activity of
> science. First, the heavy warfare with "theology and meta-
> physics" is over. Although a few sharp skirmishes still occur,
> the attacks on the freedom of science from this quarter are no
> longer significant. This is not so much because of the undoubted

victory of science over its ancient contenders as for the deeper
reason that the conclusions of natural science are no longer
ideologically sensitive. What people, either the masses or the
educated, believe about the inanimate universe or the biological
aspects of humanity is not relevant to the stability of society,
as it was once thought to be. The focus of sensitivity is now
in the social sciences; and the techniques of control by those in
authority vary in subtlety in accordance with local requirements
and traditions. Hence the leaders of the community of natural
science no longer need to hold and proclaim this sort of ideological commitment as a rallying slogan for their followers and potential recruits. Also, the experience of modern scientists in their
work, seeing the rapid rate of obsolescence of scientific results,
makes the vision of the pursuit of truth not so much wrong as
irrelevant. But, more important, the attention of the general
educated public has shifted away from the problem of the nature
of pure science and its relation to philosophy and religion.[6]

While the fact that modern preoccupation with science, technology, and
the future generally neglects the religious-spiritual perspective is undeniable, there is no reason to suppose that this state of affairs is permanent.
On the contrary, there are signs all around us that purely anthropocentric
interest in science is a temporary phenomenon which may soon pass
away. The conviction that (1) there has been no final victory of science
over "its ancient contenders," and (2) the conclusions of contemporary
biology and biomedicine are highly relevant to all religious ideologies
that are spiritually concerned with human evolution, fosters the belief
that the attention of society will again be directed to the relations between science and religion and to the as yet unrealized spiritual potentials
of each.

An interchange of thought between anthropocentric and theocentric
humanists would necessarily take a quite different form from those encounters in which all the participants belong to the former group. Interest
would be focused upon individual moral responsibility and ethical choice
rather than upon critical analysis of social problems and responsibility.
The theocentric approach to a better world stems from the view that
evolving life on this planet is an approach to the divine Good and that
contemporary biologists, as amoral or immoral students of life, will be

forced to turn their attention to its spiritual-ethical aspects. Although the arguments of the theocentric humanists would derive from confident expectation of ultimate victory, they would avoid that aggressive, polemical, egoistic attitude which insists that "I am right, and you are wrong." Fully enlightened theocentric humanists do not point triumphantly to the spiritual truth within them. Humble before it, they point away from themselves to the source of truth. Their purpose in confronting the biologists would be to widen the perspective of their opponents by opening for them a new direction of thought. This is in admirable agreement with T. F. Torrance's elegant definition of persuasion, "In persuasion we seek to direct the mind of another to something in such a way that it falls under the compulsion of its reality and cannot but assent to it."[7]

Yet the phrase "in such a way" serves as a reminder that this kind of persuasion is a most difficult art. In the arguments to follow, no claim is made to have mastered the art: my experience of theocentricity is too limited. What I have experienced nevertheless compels me to offer these arguments to biologists as a new source of the truths of life.

"When you talk to scientists," Jung once remarked, "you cannot begin with a religious creed. You have to show the facts and let them draw their own conclusions."[8] This book, written from the religious-spiritual perspective, is concerned with the fact that the practices of modern biology are a flagrant violation of the divine ethic. Its indictment of biological means and goals, however necessary at present, may also be psychologically incompatible with persuasion. Negative criticism tends to arouse indignant self-defense, and when it is further combined with scientifically unprovable assertions about the spiritual direction of evolution, the whole attempt runs the risk of scornful rejection as the bigoted utterances of religious illusion.

The risk is being taken without hesitation. With the world on the threshold of a spiritual awakening, this seems a wholly propitious moment for theocentric humanists, whatever their stage of enlightenment, to engage biologists in an evolutionary-ethical dialogue. Scientific pressure may give way to sacred pressure much sooner than expected. The tangible realities provided by the traditional *Weltbild* of established science constitute only a very small part of reality. Already there are signs of rapprochement between theoretical physics and mysticism; some physicists are listening with earnest attention to a more spiritual view of matter, energy, and potentiality than most contemporary biologists would dream

of entertaining. No biologist worthy of the name should, however, belittle
the significance of the religious revival that life is now experiencing. The
scientific age is, in fact, being confronted on all sides by a new theocentricity emerging out of the reality of the human-divine relation. And
since the sum total of biological knowledge in the traditional sense cannot
prove that there is no higher reality than man, it would be supremely
sensible for biologists to accept with an open mind the possibility that
a divine reality exists and that man's progressive knowledge of it is essential to his further evolution. That the blatant atheism of established biology
will gradually give way to a quieter agnosticism appears already as an
evolutionary inevitability—a necessary development in the expansion of
the theocentric *Weltbild*.

More than fifty years ago A. N. Whitehead made a prophetic statement, "When we consider what religion is for mankind and what science
is, it is no exaggeration to say that the future course of history depends
upon the decision of this generation as to the relations between
them."[9] Although religion in the West, at that time, was well into a
period of decline, Whitehead's generation decided to sever the relationship as completely as possible by choosing to acquire scientific truths
and to neglect religious truths. The subsequent course of history under
the domination of scientific and technological authority reveals that the
decision was faulty. Modern man, in a scientific age divorced from the
divine ethic, continues to place his hopes on his own rational powers,
but he does so in mounting hesitancy, doubt, and fear. In the face of
endless crises, the scientific age flounders in ethical confusion. Rejecting
the divine, it does not know how to choose between good and evil. Contemporary religions, overwhelmed by scientific and technological progress,
have little to offer a sick world except humble submission to scientific
truths. As a result, the world knows neither how to surmount its crises
nor how to prevent them. The scientific age is best characterized by its
ignorance of man's true potential. The spiritual awakening, now only
beginning, has not yet made a deep mark on world conscience.

We are still floundering in an ethical confusion unknown to any true
spiritual leader, past or present. Refusing to acknowledge divine reality,
and at the same time unable to make an ethical choice, our vaunted
reason should tell us that the nature of the divine must include an absolute
and unchanging ethic by which all men can be directed toward righteousness. It is this religious-spiritual awareness of our ethical potentiality and

its realization as a function of divine activity that is missing in the anthropocentric world view. For we live in a scientific age and there is no *good* in science. Science, the leading anthropocentric endeavor of our times, cannot, by its own admission, make an ethical choice. In contrast, theocentric humanism provides the moral vision without which no human endeavor can long survive. Science must either acquire this moral vision or face the consequences of gradual decline and disappearance in a spiritually awakened world. In the 1920s Whitehead suggested that the clash between religion and science is "a sign that there are wider truths and finer perspectives within which a reconciliation of a deeper religion and a more subtle science will be found." He saw that both science and religion, still highly imperfect endeavors, possess vast spiritual potentials destined to be realized.

As a platonist convinced that evolving human life on this planet is an approach to the divine Good, and as a biologist convinced that our study of evolving life must continue, I believe that both religion and science will become increasingly spiritualized, and that a new relation will be established between them whereby they will renew and purify themselves in conscious orientation toward the divine ethic.

It hardly needs saying that this belief bears little resemblance to the beliefs of those anthropocentric humanists who foresee renewal and betterment of all human endeavors as accompaniments to the increasing secular denial of the divine. Even the humanism of Abraham Maslow, which expresses a most commendable idealism seeking to promote the spiritual transcendence of the human condition through the progressive realization of man's potential for good, is based upon a conviction that sharply diverges from the theme of this book.[10] Precisely because Maslow steadfastly refused to admit the theoretical possibility that a human-divine relation exists, his vision of "transhumanistic" psychology and potentiality appears both obscure and unplatonic.

Plato never founded an institutional religion, and his views are held in little esteem by contemporary scientists and are often disregarded by those participating in the spiritual awakening. Yet his religious-spiritual perspective could well serve to direct the intellectual energy of contemporary science and religion into the channel of ethical potentiality whereby men would desire more spiritual knowledge to realize themselves—not anthropocentrically for their own sake—but theocentrically for the sake of the cosmic Good.

It would be presumptive to attempt here or elsewhere a concise, straightforward definition of Plato's concept of the Good. Plato never made more than veiled allusions to its nature, although it was both the summit of his hierarchy of ideas and the spiritual reality to which he was irresistibly drawn throughout his life. For 2300 years men have speculated about the Good, but despite all attempts to conceptualize supreme virtue, let alone that which transcends it, the nature of the Good has remained essentially indefinable. It could not have been otherwise. Plato and later Plotinus, who expounded the concept at greater length, saw that the Good, this divine perfection and transcendent source of all else, is fully knowable only to itself and thus beyond evolving man's power of rational understanding. Yet they also saw that knowledge of the Good is attainable through becoming good, and that this progressive approach to perfection through participation is man's inevitable destiny.

In a discussion of the religion of Plotinus, a contemporary scholar, A. H. Armstrong, has attempted to elucidate the compulsory ascent toward the Good in this thought-provoking passage:

> The Good is above virtue, as he is above everything: and on the
> level of Intellect the virtues exist archetypally but there is no
> virtuous action because there is no action at all. The life and
> activity of the intelligible world is all contemplation. But, for
> Plotinus, to pass beyond virtue does not mean any repudiation
> of virtue or any denial of the continued obligation of virtuous
> conduct on the level on which it is possible. Plotinus is no anti-
> nomian Gnostic. There is no break in his system between the
> higher world of spiritual liberty and the lower world of moral
> law. The perfectly good and wise man, the sage, only passes be-
> yond virtue to reach the source of virtue, the Good who makes
> good actions good. And, just because he has reached the Good,
> his actions on the lower level where virtue and vice are possible,
> on which his soul must continue to operate as long as it is in
> this world, must be morally better, not worse, than before.[11]

There have been many other attempts, but what seems most important is the idea, so beautifully elaborated by Werner Jaeger, that the Good is a divine center leading the human race upward.[12] And as spiritual aspirants with mystical intuition and experience, both Plato and Plotinus knew that the human soul, possessing a divine spark which seeks its source, strives toward goodness, righteousness, beauty, and truth, and that this act toward the Good is the highest form of human love. Whether we today can unequivocally equate the Good with the Christian God is a moot question which makes no easier our understanding of the concept. What is important to remember is that both Plato and Plotinus—by any standard two of the greatest intellects the world has ever known—were theocentric philosophers who spoke of the Good both as a human thought and as a divine reality without which the thought could not be. As a concept the Good thus arose out of man's active participation in the human-divine relation or, to use another terminology, out of man's confrontation with the "numinous," which Rudolf Otto used to denote a part of the reality of the divine presence which arouses awareness of itself in human thought and emotion.[13]

The Good can be viewed in quite another light, as evidenced by Iris Murdoch's fascinating lecture, *The Sovereignty of Good over other Concepts*.[14] Here an atheistic philosopher casts overboard the whole theistic foundation of the platonic Good, apparently considering it as merely a projection of the human mind without any external counterpart of existent divinity. Yet fully cognizant of the supremacy of the concept, Murdoch appeals to modern man to look toward this "distant transcendent perfection" as a source of new energy and virtue and as a means of overcoming the bondage of self.

Splendid as this appeal is to a scientific age forgetful of Plato and enmeshed in self-love, if the concept of the Good is to assume its rightful place in human evolution, it needs to be considered as an expression of platonic theocentricity as originally intended. Plato, and Plotinus with him, saw the Good teleologically, as the divine goal to which human life must aspire—not in the sense of Teilhard de Chardin's amoral Omega point (with which it admittedly has evolutionary and spiritual affinities)— but as a true Good demanding the progressive improvement of the human conscience. Submission to the moral authority of a noble human thought is an admirable act. Yet submission to the moral authority of a divine reality and will infinitely higher than any human thought seems to be the only means by which evolving man can truly surpass himself.

The human potentials recognized by anthropocentric humanists are strictly limited to human reality; those of theocentric humanism are as unlimited as the divine reality itself. In a spiritually evolving world falling under the compulsion of the Good, need one doubt whose will be the final victory?

Notes

1. Since this book was written, I have recognized the existence of a variant form of anthropocentric humanism which has been designated "biocentric." Interested readers are referred to my papers, "The Three Faces of Humanism," published in 1975 as Tract 14 by the Gryphon Press, Lewes, Sussex, an Occasional Paper with the same title published in 1976 by the Farmington Institute for Christian Studies at Oxford, and "The Three Faces of Humanism and Their Relation to Problems of Science and Education," *Teachers College Record* 80, no. 3 (February 1979): 564-86.

2. "Two Views of Man," *Manas* 25, no. 19 (May 10, 1972): 1-2, 7-8.

3. C. Roberts, *The Scientific Conscience: Reflections on the Modern Biologist and Humanism* (New York: George Braziller, 1967).

4. Malaoni Martin, "The Scientist as Shaman," *Harper's* (March 1972).

5. R. C. Zaehner, *Mysticism, Sacred and Profane: An Inquiry into Some Varieties of Praeternatural Experience* (London: Oxford University Press, 1957), pp. 29, 160.

6. J. R. Ravetz, *Scientific Knowledge and Its Social Problems* (Oxford: Clarendon Press, 1971), pp. 20-21.

7. T. F. Torrance, *God and Rationality* (London: Oxford University Press, 1971), p. 199.

8. C. G. Jung as quoted in V. White, *God and the Unconscious* (London: Collins, 1952), p. 92.

9. A. N. Whitehead, *Science and the Modern World* (Cambridge: Cambridge University Press, 1926), p. 224.

10. A. H. Maslow, *Religions, Values, and Peak-Experiences* (Columbus: Ohio State University Press, 1964); "Farther Reaches of Human Nature," Lecture, First Unitarian Church (San Francisco, September 14, 1967); "Various Meanings of 'Transcendence,' " 17 pp., n.d.

11. A. H. Armstrong, ed., *The Cambridge History of Later Greek and Early Medieval Philosophy*. Part III. *Plotinus*, by A. H. Armstrong (Cambridge: University Press, 1967), p. 259.

12. W. Jaeger, *Paideia: The Ideals of Greek Culture*, vol. 2, *In Search of the Divine Centre*. Trans. Gilbert Highet (Oxford: Basil Blackwell, 1957).

13. R. Otto, *The Idea of the Holy: An Inquiry into the Non-Rational Factor in the Idea of the Divine and its Relation to the Rational* (London: Oxford University Press, 1923).

14. I. Murdoch, *The Sovereignty of Good* (London: Routledge & Kegan Paul, 1970).

2

Good, Evil, and Ethical Confusion

Conscience is the recognition that one can distinguish between good and evil and is thereby obliged to make moral choices. Since the emergence of civilizations, and probably long before, the most common criteria for moral choice have been various forms of secular and sacred authority which men could fall back upon or which they were forced to respect. In the Age of Enlightenment, when all Europe was activated by thoughts about democratic freedom and scientific advance, the Western mind became increasingly independent of these traditional norms, welcoming its liberation as a great blessing and an indisputable sign of evolutionary progress. Man's newly found pride and self-respect supported the view that a free conscience, continually nourished by new scientific truths about sensible reality, was eminently suited for making the right choice. *Homo sapiens,* rational to his fingertips and alone in a universe without enduring norms, was at last guiding his development toward change as his unknown, but only possible, goal. This scientific outlook is still one of the foundations of twentieth-century humanism. It is not yet generally recognized that the edifice is beginning to totter.

Today, when the world is in explosive development and when many, in teleological uncertainty, find their greatest delight in rejecting long-established ideals and norms, there are others who openly admit that a

seemingly free conscience no longer permits them to distinguish good
from evil. The severance of individuals from traditional aims and values
is everywhere accompanied by some form of moral insecurity. An increasing number of contemporary men and women, confused and helpless
in the face of what the world calls progress, dare not choose. Their conscience is unequal to the task.

Why does modern man find the moral, the amoral, and the immoral
so difficult to distinguish? What is wrong with the contemporary conscience? One possible answer lies in the fact that the world conscience,
ostensibly free, is in fact so greatly dominated by the scientific outlook
that it has become a kind of scientific conscience.

Some assert that scientists have a purely objective attitude toward the
reality they investigate, and that this objectivity toward scientific truth
separates their work from distinctions between good and evil. In other
words, since science is not concerned with morals and ethics, there can
be no scientific conscience. This assertion is untenable. For more than
five hundred years scientists have made choices concerning those things
and those relations they wished to investigate, and why and how it should
be done. Nor have they failed to make suggestions as to how their results
should be utilized. Science, they have said, must advance; ergo, all scientific activity is morally defensible. Scientists, like all others, have chosen
with their own conscience to do what they have done. And the advance
of the life sciences has been based upon a deplorable insensitivity to good
and evil.

No one can deny that scientists have made great contributions toward
improving the human environment and ameliorating human suffering and
that many of them have devoted their lives to idealistic efforts to help
their fellow creatures. But let us look more closely at the present state
of the scientific conscience. There is no need to list the so-called triumphs
of the biologists in their ever increasing interference with evolving life,
nor the many examples of their belief that life's future evolution must
keep pace with scientific advance: others have done this most thoroughly.
Nor is there any need to cite the never ending examples of increasing
cruelty with which biologists carry on experiments on nonhuman forms
of life: animal welfare societies all over the world are becoming increasingly active, and many condemnatory books are appearing. Those outside
science who know about these degrading scientific activities do not want
biologists to continue to do all that they can do. But there is need to

stress the fact that the present scientific conscience refuses to admit that it has erred. The prestige of science must be maintained. Biologists who may be uneasy about the present scientific conscience usually express their uneasiness by giving the accelerating rate of modern progress (which they themselves have helped to bring about) the blame for contemporary moral uncertainty. To admit to being unable to differentiate good from evil is more than an expression of an uncertain, helpless condition—it is an expression of moral and spiritual bankruptcy.

The situation seems to be different with regard to the younger generation. They possess much more optimism than uncertainty. Dissenting, rebellious youths have demanded an equal say in the problems of both universities and society at large because they believe they can solve the problems better than anyone else. This conviction is due not only to youthful idealism, courage, and need for active participation—it stems also from the frustrating influence of the daily deterioration of the world conscience and upon current ideological and philosophical thought. Young rebels, for example, readily accept the modern existentialist craving for self-knowledge that so optimistically places the "free individual conscience" higher than any traditional, established authority. Here there can be no striving after eternal values or ideals to satisfy human frustration. If there is belief in authoritative norms and goals, they must be dynamic, flexible, and impermanent—well suited to the changing situations that arise out of unrestrained scientific progress. Such an autonomous conscience, which welcomes demonstration and dissent, is as a rule hypercritical of the permanency of all established norms, and in some cases, the criticism is admittedly justified. But such a conscience also leads the young and the immature to the false assumption that their own conscience is infallible and therefore the only thing in the world that is uncriticizable. They are so certain of its infallibility that they have repeatedly tried to force others to submit to its decisions. The frequent use of physical violence against those who disagree clearly reveals that many of the dissenting young are spiritually immature. A conscience that egotistically denies the existence of any external authority, and at the same time fails to repudiate the doctrine that the ends justify the means, cannot cope with the essential problems of evolution.

Even if the academic protest succeeded in arousing society to the need for world renewal and reform, and even if the protesters were sincerely seeking life's meaning, no essential contribution to the solution of our present dilemma was made. Despite much talk about purposeful activities, the ultimate goal of the protesting youths was not clearly formulated. They did not tell us how they would use the freedom and the power they demanded nor how they would diminish suffering, fear, violence, and destruction. Despite their love of liberty and their hatred of authority, they did not realize that they were in subjection to the scientific outlook. Their wishes seemed largely identical with that of the rest of our scientifically minded world: a more perfect democratic state on earth where freedom and knowledge will continually be acquired to increase understanding.

Is it not time to ask, Understanding of what? Contemporary human progress, which keeps pace with man's growing scientific understanding, is daily becoming more chaotic and immoral. Dependence upon a so-called free individual conscience nourished by new scientific discoveries without end is not the way out of our dilemma. Should we not begin instead to think about the possibility of a progressive development of conscience toward a state of changelessness?

This new orientation will require knowledge and understanding essentially different from the kind we now seek. We cannot, for example, distinguish good from evil by asserting that human strength, dignity, and maturity depend upon man's total freedom to choose values he has invented himself. Nor can we learn to make a moral choice on the basis of biological knowledge acquired through the brutal study of sentient organisms made in the delusion that a living animal is primarily an object to be studied and exploited for the sake of humanity. To know the difference between righteousness and unrighteousness, we must also renounce all forms of anthropocentric self-knowledge which delight in their total independence of everything except the lower egoistic self.

Something quite different is required: the theocentric self-knowledge of the spiritual élite, which is always with us. Even in the darkest periods of history, there have always been spiritual leaders, living and dead, to whom people could go to become enlightened. The message of Socrates, Plato, Plotinus, and many others, Christian and non-Christian, was basically an ethical one: the human conscience can best develop by recognizing the authority of a divine reality immeasurably higher and purer than man. Anthropocentric striving for a "free" conscience liberated from traditional authority and restraint should be replaced by a loving submission to that which is superior to the purely human. Even the teachings of the Buddha, which, according to some schools of Buddhist philosophy, deny the existence of any authority higher than the human mind, exhort the spiritual aspirant to rise above egoistic preoccupation and to live by an ethical system, which, in itself, is so wonderful as to suggest, if not strongly indicate, its divine origin. Be that as it may, the progressive acquisition of theocentric wisdom seems to satisfy one of man's deepest desires: to love and be loved by that which is higher and purer than himself. Consciously or unconsciously, the human conscience desires to be possessed, and it shall be.

We are to come higher yet! But we need to begin thinking about the future in more positive terms. Our further ascent requires a new approach— a more truly evolutionary approach. When we look upon human progress merely in terms of a never ending stream of biological, medical, and technological breakthroughs leading toward unknown goals through the alteration of bodies and environment, we are envisaging evolution through a dense fog. Let us try to see it another way: *Human evolution is proceeding toward the divine Good, and no power on earth can stop its ascent.*

If this be true, how can we then explain the spectacular advance of atheistic science, to say nothing of the ethical chaos and intellectual unrest that accompany it?

In posing the question in this way, I am not blaming science for all the world's ills nor advocating the abolition of scientific inquiry. Seeking biological truths about both evolving man in the body and his living environment should obviously continue. What I am advocating is that contemporary scientists open their minds to a neglected perspective. Only the minutest fraction of the potentials of science has so far been realized, because scientists, with few exceptions, are not yet thinking of their endeavors in spiritual terms. The atheistic, materialistic, amoral, and immoral mentality that characterizes twentieth-century science is so inimical to the ethical evolution of man that it actually promotes human unrest, together with widespread misery to man and beast. A profound regeneration of the scientific conscience is bound to come.

It may well be darkest before dawn. If human evolution is cyclic, then we may be at the lowest and darkest point of our particular cycle, just rounding the turn that will lead us more rapidly and joyously to the light. Yet the conditions of our present existence indicate that pain and self-sacrifice and joylessness will be with us for some time to come, especially if we continue atheistically, or even agnostically, toward what we consider to be an unknown and shifting goal. Another choice remains: to admit and repent the tragic ethical errors of the recent past and to realize that the path of theocentric humanism, which alone can lead us where we are destined to go, has been there all the time. In refusing to open our eyes to these spiritual facts of our evolutionary situation, we deny and smother our sparks of divinity and prolong and intensify the fear and doubt of suffering creation.

Of course, at any one stage of evolutionary history, the world's human population shows an enormous range of spiritual-ethical diversity. With the species having still so far to go, there can be no spiritual equality among the living but rather a hierarchy of goodness with a spiritual élite at the summit. Yet, to repeat, despite all signs to the contrary, we are all on our way to the Good. Whether we approve or not, it is our predestined fate to approach the Good. What will happen when an ever increasing number of human minds find that their glimpse into the future is one of joyous expectancy? No doubt it will mean that the species is acquiring a more perfect understanding of human conscience and its right and proper degree of freedom.

The contemporary conscience desperately needs to be liberated from the authority of contemporary science. Equally, if not more importantly, it needs to become free from egoistic preoccupation, which is the greatest tyranny known to any of us, scientists and nonscientists alike. So long as we are enslaved by egoistic fear and desire, we possess neither ethical criteria nor peace of mind. A conscience liberated from egoism tends to see more clearly that which is infinitely and eternally good as the final goal. How far from the self-centered goals of our times! The evolving human conscience has indeed an enormous potential of freedom to realize. Yet, in the final sense, the conscience of evolving man can never become wholly free, since it is duty-bound to choose, as far as possible, that course of thought and action which is in most perfect agreement with the Good to which it is being drawn.

Since the world has become smaller through improved means of communication, it may not be long before all the peoples of the earth become acquainted with an evolutionary perspective based upon Plotinus's teleological doctrine that the human intellect *needs* the Good. Five hundred years ago the West chose to submit to an anthropocentric authority which asserted that human reason alone was sufficient to guide human evolution. The result of this erroneous judgment is now evident all about us.

We no longer believe that what is human needs what is divine. In our doubt and uncertainty we are most prone to believe that our best choices must be in step with scientific advance. We literally surrender ourselves, body and mind, to science. We decide, for example, to prolong our life spans artificially, whatever the cost, even by receiving organs from dying individuals. We decide also to deep-freeze bodies upon death in hope of future resuscitation, to undertake painful experiments of all kinds on sentient beings, to become dependent for our well-being on various drugs, and to investigate the possibility of cloning individuals. The list is much longer. We should vehemently protest, but we do not, because our conscience is impaired and knows not what to say.

The young people, who are now eager to change the world but do not know how to do so, may become the chosen generation. Perhaps their world and their conscience will indict science on the gravest of all charges—of ethical confusion so great that it is hindering the true evolution of *Homo sapiens.* They may charge contemporary biologists with defending the immorality of scientific means and goals and with lack of repentance for the outrages that have been committed upon life by students of life. An attack of this kind would be more constructive than destructive. It might well be the first step in the renewal of the scientific conscience and the spiritualization of biology.

3

Space Travel and Faith

The journeys to the moon, those latest and greatest scientific triumphs of our so-called Christian society, have not aroused unqualified praise and admiration. The consummate elegance and fantastic precision with which men have been sent to the moon and brought back again to the earth have naturally impressed and fascinated all of us. At the same time enthusiastic voices laud the accompanying technical and medical advances that are to raise our standard of living and improve our daily life. But no amount of pride or jubilation in these achievements and their concomitant benefits can wholly dispel the growing ethical opposition to space research as a priority in a world still unable to eliminate unnecessary hunger, suffering, violence, and death.

One of the leading figures in space research sought, with unlimited optimism, to break down this opposition. To judge from the press, Wernher von Braun had no ethical problems. Elated and triumphant over the nearly faultless moon journeys, he looked forward to new landings and prophesied, within a relatively short time, space travel to all the planets of the solar system. To aspire to still greater results is a scientist's natural reaction to successful experiments, but in contrast to most of his colleagues, von Braun based his optimism upon Christian faith.[1] He further disclosed that through his prayers he had been guided and strengthened in the view that man's continued exploration of space is an expression of God's will and that it is through Jesus Christ that man attempts to master his physical surroundings. Wernher von Braun's religious views must, of course, be respected. But since modern humanism is replete with agnosticism and atheism, it is not to be expected that many scientists or humanists will share his views. It can, however, be expected that at least some scientists will welcome his statements as a convenient justification for their activities in a society calling itself Christian.

Among Christians, von Braun's religious legitimation of space travel evoked widely different responses. Some share his views completely; they regard the exploration of the universe as support for the belief that man must do what he is able to do because God has provided him with the requisite facilities. Other Christians feel that even if space exploration is God's will, the growing problems here on earth should first be solved. Still others do not relate space exploration to Christianity at all but only to the explosive advance of science and technology. But common to nearly all is the underlying view that *in itself* the exploration of the universe is neither good nor bad but merely a part of evolutionary development, which cannot and should not, be stopped. They believe that man must subdue nature with all the scientific knowledge and technological skill at his disposal. In other words, many Christians, including theologians, consider space travel and exploration as an amoral or ethically neutral enterprise quite unrelated to Christian morality. For them, space exploration is above all a necessary and inevitable realization of the human potential. Speaking shortly after the moon landing, with much authority and certainty about man's conquest of the world of matter that makes up his physical environment, a Danish theologian stated, ". . . there have been set no limits to the task of conquering it. It is a Christian task to push on to the moon."[2]

The problem can, however, be seen with Christian eyes from a completely different perspective. For the indisputable fact remains that some Christians already have set a limit to the Judaeo-Christian view that man shall subdue the world. Through their thoughts and deeds these spiritually mature individuals, be they hermits, mystics, saints, or quite ordinary Christians, have demonstrated two things: (1) that the Old Testament's statement concerning man's dominion over the earth and the life belonging to it (Genesis 1: 26 and 28) cannot be separated and isolated from the New Testament's message of divine love, compassion, and justice, to which man shall conform, and (2) that this message is valid for man's dealing with all living creatures which are able to experience pain, fear, and other forms of suffering.*

These two demonstrations have set a moral, and extremely Christian, limit to man's conquest of his physical environment; the conquest must not go so far that it includes the maltreatment of the world's sentient beings. As one of these exceptional Christians expressed it not so many years ago:

> ... the Creator, who by making His creatures sentient, and giving us dominion over them, thereby binds us to use them in accordance with their nature and with the divine attributes of justice and benevolence. There must be an *objective* right and justice with regard to the animals, founded on the order of creation, independent of human interests and for the sake of the animals themselves, *because they can feel.*[3]

The world owes much to these Christians. Their interpretation of Christianity has deeply penetrated its moral core to give the evolution of life a more divine perspective. Obviously there can be no human evolutionary progress if the end is held to justify any means. Yet most contemporary Christians are inclined to sanction the conquest of nature by all conceivable means. It is thus becoming increasingly necessary for Christians everywhere to realize that man's conquest of his environment is taking place with methods which are a scandalous affront to Christianity.

I am speaking now about the fact that science and technology, in their efforts to expand life's environment and enlarge man's knowledge of the forces of nature about him, have profaned sentient beings through the

---

*While it is true that the Bible itself is often silent or ambiguous about man's ethical behavior toward nonhuman life, what is claimed to be an early Essene version of the Gospel depicts Jesus as a strict vegetarian who repeatedly exhorts his followers to treat all sentient animals with the utmost kindness, mercy, and compassion. The work was found in a Tibetan monastery and translated from Aramaic into English in the last century by The Reverend J. G. Ouseley, who apparently believed it to be the original Gospel.[4] Some today agree; others consider it wholly spurious. Whatever the truth about its origin, it is a work of great ethical purity and beauty which enormously strengthens the view that Jesus preached a doctrine of universal love and nonviolence for the whole of creation.[5]

infliction of suffering and death to such an extent that it comprises the grossest kind of cruelty. For more than twenty years space research scientists have been intensively studying the biological and medical aspects of human space travel, and in this time they have violently abused a large number of higher animals. Although these deeds have taken place in a so-called Christian society, the scientists responsible for them have completely ignored the rights of the experimental animals—not least their right to be treated by more highly developed creatures with Christian justice and mercy. In regarding experimental animals as objects—a kind of inexhaustible gift from nature which can and shall be used at will— the present scientific conscience suffers from a sickness unto death.

These remarks must not be considered as a fanatic cry of antivivisectionism. Regardless of what scientists, humanists, theologians, and ordinary Christians now believe, the problem of animal experimentation is of the greatest significance for the true evolution of life. Before me is an American publication dealing with experimental animals which describes, among other things, some experiments that were carried out by the Northrup Space Laboratories under contract from the United States Air Force School of Aerospace Medicine in Texas. If nothing else, these experiments show how worthless is the claim that anaesthesia is the panacea for the suffering of experimental animals. The purpose of the experiments was to carry out a scientific analysis and evaluation of different types of restraining devices. For this purpose twenty-three chimpanzees were subjected to impacts that caused minor injury, disability, or death. In addition, some unexpected results occurred, including injury to the animals' faces due to broken and torn off muzzles, asphyxiation due to the improper placing of the muzzle, and internal hemorrhage. The animals that survived these treatments were kept alive with the help of narcotics, artificial respiration, and oxygen. Each injury was carefully described, and the publication calls some of them "revolting."[6]

No Christian should tolerate these acts. No Christian should maintain that the exploration of space, which for many years has openly sanctioned the use of these and similar methods, is neither good nor bad. No Christian should express his unconditional pride and joy in each new triumph of space research. Yet despite opposition to the priority given to the moon journeys, many Christians seem to be doing just these things. As a personal acquaintance in Washington, D.C., wrote in a letter dated July 27, 1969, "I have felt very depressed and hopeless in face of the almost obscene euphoria in this country over the moon landing."[7]

Homo sapiens, life's highest species, can never improve itself by committing sins against life's lower species. If it is absolutely necessary to continue to explore the universe, it is a Christian duty to condemn the animal experiments that have already been carried out toward this end and to demand the total abolition of this kind of scientific methodology. And if the result is that further space exploration be delayed or restricted through lack of biological and medical knowledge, then all the greater would be life's true evolutionary progress. The Greek word *sophrosyne* meant, among other things, restraint, and it is my deepest conviction that science will soon be compelled to admit that biological sophrosyne is much more closely bound to human evolution than is space travel. Of course a limit has been set to man's conquest of the world; although it has long since been overstepped, the limit can be found once again in theocentric humanism.

The evolution of life cannot be separated from man's relation to the divine realm. Man, the summit of life, has now reached an evolutionary stage where his greatest need is for the moral values and laws with which he can continue his ascent toward the Good, which is drawing him upward. The gratification of this need surpasses all other human efforts, including the exploration of outer space, and renders them quite insignificant. The true evolution of life is becoming increasingly dependent upon its approach and submission to the final authority of faith.

Belief in a divine authority gives man an enormous ethical responsibility. When we are prepared to use our reason, conscience, and will theocentrically in making choices between good and evil, we will have become a more active part of that spiritual ascent that constitutes the true evolution of life. Our participation and engagement in this ascent demands that the exploration and exploitation of our physical surroundings take place through human thoughts and deeds in harmonious accord with the divine Good to which we are all proceeding. Any evolutionary development that erroneously chooses to disregard this submission to the Good is an expression of man's spiritual ignorance and immaturity.

Not surprisingly in this age of science, those humanists who oppose space research have not condemned the abuse of animals that has accompanied it. Modern humanists are, as a rule, so preoccupied with the anthropocentric view of life that they often forget to look either higher or lower than man himself. On the other hand, it is both surprising and distressing that so many theocentric humanists who call themselves Christians sanction, without any semblance of protest, their fellow creatures' abuse of

lower forms of life. In remaining silent they further man's immorality
and creation's unnecessary suffering and thereby place themselves in
direct opposition to the true evolutionary development of life. This fact
is all the more distressing because men of faith should be able to view
and evaluate all contemporary events from the highest perspective.

We all know that the moon is no more than a satellite of the earth
and that its distance from us shrinks to insignificance in comparison with
the magnitude of the solar system. Further, we all know that the solar
system is only as a grain of sand in the universe. The successful journey
to the moon has not changed the fact that man is still earth-bound. And
even if the space explorers' plans to travel to the planets are realized, and
even if these trips greatly advance our scientific knowledge of our surroundings and their origin, we all know that in outer space human possibilities are, and will remain, extremely limited. Our age is nevertheless
possessed with a desire to go farther and farther away from the earth to
examine more distant physical realities.

Many who believe in a divine authority are carried along with this
stream of thought. Yet they know that modern man's true development
cannot lie in this kind of lunar or planetary contact. They know, or should
know, that man's evolution lies here on earth in his striving for divine con-
tacts by which life is slowly being brought under the eternal moral laws.
And in this striving here on earth, where man now belongs, the potentials
of life are unlimited.

How can modern man best acquaint himself with these unlimited
potentials? The most certain way is through the ancient theocentric
outlook which proclaimed that life is approaching the Good. Such a theocentric humanism can only oppose any space exploration that pushes on
toward the moon at the cost of the suffering and want of innumerable
human beings on earth. But with equal certainty it opposes any scientific
authority that profanes living, sentient, lower forms of life by the infliction of physical and mental anguish. These scientifically approved means
toward an end are in glaring disharmony with love, righteousness, and
compassion and thus in flagrant opposition to the revealed nature of the
Christian God. We are now witnessing an intellectual and moral revolution of the younger generation, whose burning desire is to change the
established order, but does not yet know how it can be done. It is
time for Christians, and all other theocentric humanists, to form a strong
and vital counterbalance to the immoral advance of science. Those who

have faith are able to hasten the true evolution of life, and in an age of space travel it is their evolutionary responsibility to do so.

Notes

1. A. Taft, "Why Has God Allowed Us Into Space?" Interview with Wernher von Braun, *Christian Life* (July 1969): 18-21, 42-43.

2. Interview with Johannes Sløk, "Maanen og Kristne Mennesker" [The Moon and Christians], *Kristeligt Dagblad* (Copenhagen), 23 July 1969.

3. B. Wrighton, "Justice and the Animals," *The Ark* 45 (April 1952): 4-15.

4. *Evangeliet om det Fuldkomne Liv eller de Tolv Helliges Evangelium.* Danish translation by Erna Frislev of J. G. Ouseley's *The Gospel of the Holy Twelve.* (G1. Viby, Sjælland: Strubes Forlag, 1971).

5. C. Roberts, "On Christian Ethics and Abstinence from Animal Food: A Reply to Helena Sanders," *The Anglican Society for the Welfare of Animals,* Bulletin 7 (1976): 12-15.

6. "Substitution Exhibit No. 3: Experimental Trauma," Part I, United Action for Animals Report (New York, n.d.), 10 pp.

7. Frances Shibley, personal correspondence, July 27, 1969.

4

Pharmacology and the Numinous

Pharmacology is a branch of science concerned with drugs useful to man, chiefly because of their remedial and healing properties. It is an entirely respectable word, without any odious connotation. It is well to remember, however, that the Greek word from which pharmacology is derived, φάρμακον, denoted not only a medicinal remedy but also a bewitching potion or a toxic or fatal drug. Thus the verb φαρμάττω had three meanings: to medicate, to enchant, and to poison. The Greeks knew a good deal about the nature and properties of the natural substances producing these effects, but all their knowledge is but a drop in the overflowing bucket of twentieth-century knowledge of drugs, both natural and synthetic.

Pharmacology is indeed a flourishing branch of modern science. The esteem it enjoys is related to the accepted view that the rapid advance of our knowledge of drugs is, in itself, inherently good. Whether this scientific knowledge concerns prophylactic, healing, intoxicating, injurious, or deadly chemical compounds, it is generally believed that the use to which they are put is not the concern of the scientist. For science, as Aldous Huxley once said, is generally held to be "divinely impartial."

It is true that scientific knowledge per se is objective factual information about the world; but science, the organized and orderly striving

after this knowledge, is no more impartial than are the scientists who
pursue it. And scientists, being human beings, pursue science from a
variety of motives ranging from pecuniary considerations and desire for
power, prestige, and social standing to intellectual passion for the truth
and philanthropic aims to use the truth to help their fellow men. The
twentieth century is an age of science because society is favorably disposed to science and willing to support it. It is so disposed for two main
reasons. One is that society has become convinced that pure science is a
necessary and inevitable part of human progress—a kind of amoral development of nature by which our understanding of the world is ever increased
by a dispassionate search for scientific truths, whatever they may be. The
other reason is the conviction that as our understanding of the world and
ourselves increases, we are better able to employ the findings of science
for the alleviation of the miseries of human existence. Thus, since man's
continued progress and welfare is believed to depend upon the advance
of science, society continues to give unhesitating support to the unrestricted expansion of scientific endeavor.

This scientific outlook still dominates the world. It has already led to
what Lewis Mumford so rightly described as the "automation of knowledge"—this unbridled, compulsive desire of the twentieth century for
the unceasing accumulation of objective facts as welcome contributions
to our storehouse of scientific knowledge. And as man is naturally best
served by that branch of science that deals with life, funds for all kinds
of biological investigations labeled "fundamental research" are as a rule
readily on hand, so far as our straitened economic circumstances permit.

In a discussion of the present nature and extent of biological research,
an anonymous reviewer has written:

> But people have a right to ask why biologists should tinker with
> these things at all. Well, we all want to have our cancers cured,
> our diseased organs replaced, our congenital deformities pre-
> vented, our food supplies assured, our epidemics controlled, our
> nerves soothed; and if we want these things we shall simply
> have to take the risk of scientists doing the experiments they
> need to do to achieve these ends. Society cannot, and should
> not try to, decide what a man may discover, but society can
> and does decide how any discovery is to be applied. . . . In all
> highly developed communities elaborate machinery exists to

determine and control expenditure on scientific research; and
even the smallest projects are carefully scrutinized by competent
and socially responsible bodies before they are accepted. There
is not the slightest chance of any biological discovery being applied to society as a whole unless society wants it to be
applied.[1]

This particular expression of a common viewpoint seems inexcusably misleading. It attempts to show that the primary motivation behind scientific
progress is the scientists' disinterested idealism in complying with the demands of society for specific beneficial applications of research. This argument is unfair. Biologists do not "tinker" for years with animal hearts
because society has demanded that human hearts become replaceable.
Nor did Alexis Carrel begin his animal transplants at the beginning of the
century because of directives issued by the society in which he lived.

The fact is that society, dominated by the scientific outlook, allows
science to advance in the hope of benefiting by it, but the scientist, not
society, determines the rate and direction of the advance and is thus in-
extricably implicated in, and responsible for, the use to which his results
are put. The scientist possesses the expert knowledge to decide which
kinds of investigations stand the best chance of yielding fruitful results
and to foresee the possible applications of the results he expects to obtain. The scientist points out to society what can be done and what should
be done. The scientist assumes the leading role by advising and persuading
society that the panacea for the human condition lies in further scientific
progress. And since the increasing applications of advancing scientific
knowledge have convinced the world that his claim is justified, he continues his extravagant demands for increasing support and, more often
than not, for completely free hands to pursue his work. Outside interference and control, he says, would hinder the uninterrupted progress
of science—an intolerable state of affairs.

Biologists are not amoral puppets, so subservient to the desires of
society that they are wholly without responsibility for the work they do.
Our gratitude to them for having carried out investigations which have
led to enormous material benefits does not permit us to exonerate them
from blame for the dehumanizing and despiritualizing consequences of
their activities. Scientists have always had a responsibility to the world,
and for contemporary biologists that responsibility is enormous.

Many biologists are trying to meet it. But in doing so, they have not given sufficient thought to the possibility of restraining their demands and their efforts or questioning the dictum that scientific progress is synonymous with human progress. Some scientists behave as though their scientific knowledge entitles them to act not only as responsible advisors, but as natural leaders who must convince society that what man can do, he must do. This is shown in their increasing predilection for visionary schemes for man's future based upon the application of the newest scientific truths. Although such visions of human improvement are to be expected in a scientific age, it is remarkable that they have extended so far beyond the alleviation of human misery. For scientists no longer abandon their laboratories for the sole purpose of suggesting ways and means to replace hunger, disease, and ignorance by food, health, and understanding. Modern scientific prophecy is not content with negative to positive visions. Now it starts with the positive and looks forward to what it thinks transcends the positive. What has happened is that many biologists have proclaimed that scientific knowledge, rationally applied under their expert direction and control, can make normal, healthy human beings "better." This trend is particularly evident in scientific thought about the possible applications of pharmacological research.

In 1957 a member of the medical profession, speaking about "psychic energizers" (those pharmacological products which, in contrast to the "tranquilizers," reduce and alleviate abnormal states of apathy) stressed that such drugs, by increasing the amount of psychic energy, can be of great value in psychiatry when applied under strict medical supervision. Then he continued:

> Perhaps it is in this direction that we may be able to transcend ourselves upward instead of downward. It is not beyond the realm of possibility that, after concentrating on correcting the aberrations of thinking, feeling, and acting, man is capable of focussing his attention firmly on the achievement of something more than mere surcease of sorrow. The exaltation of heightened awareness, strong positive affective relationships and the pride of useful accomplishments may, at this moment, lie within our grasp.[2]

These words, written shortly after the publication of *The Doors of Perception*[3] and *Heaven and Hell*,[4] seem to echo Aldous Huxley's view that treatment of the healthy is a natural and desirable extension of treatment of the sick. Although Huxley was one of the first to perceive the possible disasters of a scientifically controlled world, in the field of pharmacology he appeared to be awaiting the discovery of the ideal drug and thus welcomed each new advance. His factual and fanciful eulogistic descriptions of the effects of drugs on the human mind may have had a greater influence upon the minds of biologists than is generally supposed. They have, at least, called him the "prophet of the chemopsychiatric age." This epithet is, however, a misnomer. Our age is not content with the cure of sick minds as the word chemopsychiatry implies. Nor was Huxley, with his imaginary "soma" drug, thinking primarily of helping the mentally ill. He, and others with him, was thinking of drug consumption for the healthy who wish to create a better world. It would be more correct to designate Huxley as the prophet of the psychochemical age, which is a more adequate term for an era in which biomedicine has extended into realms beyond its field of competence. Already biomedicine has seriously suggested that the pursuit of science, as it is now conceived and practiced, may give man the spiritual maturity he lacks.

In the first chapter of *Drugs and the Mind* Robert S. De Ropp recognized some of the moral objections of philosophic and religious thinkers to the idea of attaining spiritual insight through pills or injections but pointed out that the moral aspect of drug consumption was not the subject of his book.[5] In the last chapter, however, he answered those who protest against scientific interference with spiritual life by the biochemists' best retort: that their primary concern is not for those who are "masters of their souls" but for those who are mentally ill, and therefore they do what they do. Following up the argument, De Ropp then spoke ironically of the "lucky neurotics" and pointed, as did Huxley, to the dangers of an overtranquilized world. But, he continued, our world is in such a disturbed, anxious state, ever confronted with the threat of a new outbreak of atomic warfare, that to keep it in equilibrium, we need steady, well-balanced men. And although he lets the reader decide for himself in this matter, he states that the perfect euphoriant may soon be discovered and that such a "happiness drug" would at least be preferable to the toxic effects of ethyl alcohol.

He concludes with the wise statement that we must "face the supreme task which confronts our age: how to reach spiritual maturity before we destroy ourselves." Without specifically committing himself on this issue, he makes it clear that the real frontiers of biological research lie with the brain and its extended network of nerve cells, since it is here that "those processes take place which lead to the ultimate choice between good and evil."

De Ropp's book seems an admirable presentation of the facts then known about drugs and a fair treatment of the divergent opinions regarding their use. But his unwillingness to take a personal stand on the moral choice involved in the consumption of drugs for the attainment of spiritual insight reflects the dilemma of the scientific age. Rational, anthropocentric humanism cannot be expected to take a decisive stand on this issue; having no criterion other than human nature and scientific progress, it cannot cope with this particular moral choice. All it can do is to hope that the increase of scientific knowledge about the function of the brain and the effect of new drugs upon the nervous system may gradually be applied to the permanent spiritual improvement of the human race. In the twenty-one years since publication of De Ropp's book, biologists, medical scientists, and physicians have had an opportunity to witness many tragic consequences of the unrestricted use of available drugs and can hardly condone the further spread of this practice. But until there are definite signs of restraining scientific investigation on the hallucinogens and other psychopharmacological agents, it can be assumed that at least some members of the biomedical profession are tacitly following Huxley in looking forward to the discovery of a chemical shortcut to spiritual maturity.

In doing so, scientific and secular humanists reveal their lack of spiritual consciousness. Denying the supreme importance, or even the existence, of the human-divine relation, and being unable to separate mind from matter and soul from body, many biologists equate the brain—this "real," tangible, visible brain together with its connected network of nerves—with mind and with what others would call soul. And with the help of untold numbers of experimental animals their investigations of the somatic nature of man goes on day after day, year after year. In speaking of the brain and nervous system, De Ropp expressed the scientific viewpoint explicitly: "Nothing, therefore, that a human being possesses is more precious than this mass of nerve cells, for every aspect of his physical, mental, and emotional life depends on their well-being."[6] If evolving man is to attain spiritual maturity, he will have to replace such a belief with the certitude that mankind possesses something infinitely more precious than its mass of nerve cells.

It is true, of course, that our spiritual life can express itself in mental operations which arise in a tangible organ. It is also true that moral choice is accompanied by physical and chemical changes in the brain and nerves and that if these parts of the body are diseased or defective, our mental and emotional life is deranged. This must be so, for we are in the body. But this is not the whole truth of the matter, and certainly not the most essential part. If our supreme task as human beings is the attainment of spiritual maturity, then the fundamental question becomes, What sets the processes in action which make us choose between good and evil?

The anthropocentric humanist, denying the existence of man's immortal soul and divine spark, has no certain answer to this question but believes that the answer will come with the advance of science. The theocentric humanist, in contrast, can point to some kind of answer. It bears upon the numinous, that sacred reality which induces in man a state of suprarational, intuitive, and often emotive knowledge about itself. During his evolution, man seems to have equated the numinous with divine love and goodness, and this concept endures. All the anthropocentric rationality of the scientific age cannot demolish it. And throughout recorded history those individuals who were deeply conscious of the numinous were best able to choose the good. They had, in fact, no choice but to choose rightly. Plotinus, in speaking about the entry of souls into bodies, expressed a point of view which bears directly upon this kind of choice:

The souls go forth neither under compulsion nor of freewill; or, at least, freedom, here, is not to be regarded as action upon preference; it is more like such a leap of the nature as moves men to the instinctive desire of sexual union, or, in the case of some, to fine conduct; the motive lies elsewhere than in the reason: like is destined unfailingly to like, and each moves hither or thither at its fixed moment.[7]

Intuitive choice of the good instead of the evil reflects man's awareness that the highest part of himself—the best he has within him— is divine. He knows that in his soul he has a spark of supernatural reality, and he desires above all things to make it glow and grow. Light seeks light. Love seeks love. He aspires toward the infinite goodness of the numinous, and, slowly and with great effort, he ascends to realize his potential. Such instinctive thoughts and actions point to the divine origin of moral choice. Man's most precious possession is spiritual, not material.

Now if this were only idle speculation or wishful thinking about the numinous and its relation to the nature of the human potential, one might be able to look with more tolerance and goodwill upon the anthropocentricity of the scientific age. If one were filled with doubt and uncertainty about these matters, one might listen with some sympathy to those who, having participated in a psychedelic experience, maintain that since "there is no clear dividing line between mystical experience induced by sanctity, mental sickness, and hallucinogenic drugs," we may be heading either to a "debunking" of religion and religious mysticism or to the "deification of mysticism-by-chemistry."[8] One might even be able to read without indignation the statement, "It seems to me that only special pleading can maintain that the graces mediated through mushrooms, cactus plants, and scientists are artificial and spurious in contrast with those which come through religious discipline."[9] One might even be attracted to the views of those who, while not actually encouraging the use of drugs for the attainment of spiritual insight and the concomitant ability to make the right choice, are at least sufficiently tolerant to wait and see what science can do— and if the "perfect" spiritual drug were to be discovered, to be prepared to give it a fair try.

But the fact is that knowledge of the sacred reality of the numinous is not idle talk at all. If it were, the fairest and noblest representatives of the human race have all been hopelessly deluded. Either those individuals who have been most profoundly conscious of the numinous, those who understood the meaning of holiness and *areté*, those who expressed the loftiest soarings of the human spirit, those whose radiant spiritual insight caused them never to be forgotten—either they thought and acted in a state of ignorance and delusion far greater than ours, or they participated in the human-divine relation and knew that they did. There is no other alternative.

If the progressive realization of the human potential is to be equated, as it must be, with the attainment of spiritual insight sufficient to choose good rather than evil, then the frontiers of human research are not the anatomy and physiology of the brain and nervous system nor the body's response to its uptake of various chemical substances of our environment. The frontiers of human research are rather with the spiritual knowledge that man has already attained about the divine Good and the thoughts he has already uttered about aspiration toward it. The frontiers of research are thus with those spiritually enlightened individuals who, in complete ignorance of LSD, mescaline, frontal lobes, tranquilizers, and ataraxics, struggled throughout their lives to come higher up the mountain, and, in doing so, partook of the divine fire which descended to meet them. In them supernal light and love coalesced with divine immanence, and their inner fire still burns for us to see. It is our proof of the reality of the numinous.

To travel the spiritual path requires efforts of widely different character. It is enlightening to compare, for example, Nikos Kazantzakis's novel about St. Francis[10] with Father Déchanet's treatise on Christian yoga.[11] The Greek man of letters believes that God is to be found not only through complete disregard for the body but through its deliberate mortification as well; the French Benedictine monk believes that God is to be found by keeping the body glowing with health in order to make it a perfect instrument of the soul. Yet as far as we know, saints, ascetics, and mystics of all kinds always find some degree of the spiritual maturity for which they strive. At the one extreme their "mass of nerve cells" must be shattered and ragged almost beyond repair from the agony or self-inflicted pain which seems to be a constant accompaniment of their ascent. At the other extreme their nerves must be in a state of well-being reflecting the inner peace and harmony that is attained through years of self-discipline dispensing as far as possible with mental and physical suffering. Bodily instruments of many kinds facilitate the soul's encounter with the numinous.

If biomedicine continues, as it surely will, the chemical and physical investigation of the brain, nerves, and consciousness, it should also admit the possibility that the numinous—this divine reality which imparts spiritual knowledge of itself to the soul—may be responsible for changes in somatic cells and tissues and in the accompanying mental operations and physical actions that reflect the soul's attainment of, and response to, such knowledge. Until the minds of anthropocentric scientists are open to this theocentric view, their research on the central nervous system and states of the consciousness, however valuable some of it may be for the alleviation of the suffering of the mentally ill, cannot enhance the spiritual insight of the healthy.

The apparent similarity of the experiences of neurotics, drug consumers, and mystics is a problem of great difficulty and complexity. In a brilliant and scholarly work, R. C. Zaehner challenged from the Catholic point of view Aldous Huxley's contention that a religious experience can be obtained from drugs, since he believed that what Huxley called religion "is simply another word for the manic-depressive psychosis." With admirable clarity Zaehner then went straight to the heart of the matter:

> [Huxley] draws the conclusion that mescalin is potentially a cure for the egocentricity of modern man just as religion was the recognized cure in the past. Obviously, if mescalin can produce the Beatific Vision here on earth,—a state that we had hitherto believed to have been the reward for much earnest striving after good,—the Christian emphasis on morality is not only all wrong but also a little naive.[12]

And further:

> On Huxley's premisses [*sic*], then, we are forced to the uncomfortable conclusion that both mescalin and mania are capable of producing the Beatific Vision and of enabling us to realize ourselves as the threefold Absolute of Being-Awareness-Bliss. This is to reduce all meditative and contemplative religion to pure lunacy.[13]

Zaehner maintained that the ecstasy of manics and mescalin consumers, being by their own admission beyond moral choice and good and evil, cannot be divine. Accordingly, he concluded that the final criterion for distinguishing sacred from profane mysticism must be the effect it has upon the individual. A divine experience, he says, invariably leads to a transformation or sanctification of character:

> . . . the mystic who is genuinely inspired by the divine love,
> will show this to the world by the holiness of his life and by
> an abiding humility in face of the immense favours bestowed
> which always he will see to be God's doing, not his own.[14]

Enlarging upon this criterion might be profitable. Motives and will need to be mentioned. A true seeker of the divine reality is motivated by a passion for it, a passion which guides and controls his will, and this aspiration seems to separate him from those who lack it. A manic-depressive is rarely a seeker of the divine and thus cannot be characterized as a spiritual aspirant. Nor can he be expected to will his state or to have aspired to it; on the contrary, he most probably directs his efforts towards alleviating or curing his abnormal mental condition. A healthy person who participates in a psychedelic experience does so from different motives, depending upon whether he is an atheist or a theist or an agnostic. He desires either an experience of nature or an experience of God, but in either case, will not be bothered with any ascetic or moral effort to attain his goal. But a true spiritual aspirant, whose love of the divine reality is so great that he wills the struggle of asceticism and self-discipline to attain it, is at once in a different category. By his uncompromising love of the Good he is forced into active participation in self-improvement.

Possibly the chemical and physical processes going on in the brain of the neurotic, the drug-user, or the mystic during their praeternatural experiences are similar or identical. It probably does not matter very much. Instruments can be made to resound in various ways without their highest potentialities ever being realized. And we know that even the true spiritual ascent abounds in pitfalls and snares which affect the somatic potential. It is enlightening to compare the experiences of two theistic mystics separated in time by nine hundred years.

From Zaehner we learn that the eleventh-century Muslim mystic, Abu'l-Qasim al-Qushayri, spoke of the "expansion" and "contraction" of the soul, that is, of periods of mental exaltation and depression which, in modern terms, would be called the poles of manic-depressive psychosis.[15] Qushayri described a spiritual aspirant in this condition as being a prisoner of an obsession and wisely recommended that he wait quietly until the mood passed: "Both conditions, that of expansion as well as contraction, have been considered . . . to be a poor thing and a harmful one if compared with the [spiritual states] which are above them. . . ."[16] Zaehner concludes that the Muslim mystic regarded the state of expansion as a "trap set by God in the path of the aspirant Sufi through which He can sift the wheat from the chaff,"[17] a kind of divine testing, since the expanded state could easily be mistaken for something higher. In other words, it was a temporary mental derangement sent to test those engaged in the spiritual quest.

Thomas Merton, a twentieth-century contemplative, while probably not speaking specifically about the manic-depressive psychosis, nevertheless had some very relevant thoughts about the possible delusion which may confront those who are seeking God:

> In any degree of the spiritual life, and even where there is
> no spiritual life at all, it can happen that a man will feel
> himself caught up in an emotional religious ferment in which
> he overflows with sensible, and even sentimental movements of
> love for God and other people. If he is completely inexperienced
> he will get the idea that he is very holy because of the holy
> feelings that are teeming in his heart. All these things mean very
> little or nothing at all. They are a kind of sensible intoxication
> produced by some pleasure or other, and there is only an acci-
> dental difference between them and the tears that children some-
> times shed when they go to the movies. . . . The whole spirit
> is rocked and reels in an explosion of drunken joy or a storm
> of compunction which may be good and healthy, but which
> is still more or less animal, even though the spark that started
> the fire may have had a supernatural origin. . . . A burst of
> spiritual exuberance can tone you up on a feast day, after
> weeks of struggle and labour. But generally the effect of
> this commotion is no better than natural. When it is all over
> you have no more profit than you might have from a couple
> of glasses of champagne or a good swim. So to that extent
> it is a good thing.
>
> But the danger is that you will attach the wrong kind of
> importance to these manifestations of religious emotion.
> . . . For anyone who is really called to infused contemplation
> this taste for "experience" can be one of the most danger-
> ous obstacles in his interior life. It is the rock on which many

who might have become contemplatives have ended in ship-
wreck. And it is all the more dangerous because even in the
houses of contemplative orders people do not always clearly
understand the difference between mystical contemplation in
the proper sense and all these accidentals, these experiences,
these manifestations and curiosities, which may or may not be
supernatural, and which have no essential connection with
sanctity or with the pure love which is at the heart of true
contemplation. . . . Passion and emotion certainly have
their place in the life of prayer—but they must be purified,
ordered, brought into submission to the highest love.[18]

Such are the warnings of two spiritual aspirants who speak from personal experience on the changes in mental states to which they are ex-
posed. Both admit that such unpredictable, spontaneous, unsought
changes may be of supernatural origin but that they are in themselves of
little importance in the spiritual quest.

In turning to the changed mental states induced by pharmaceuticals,
it should be stressed that the use of a drug to induce a religious experience is a deliberate act of will, an effect upon the mind which is sought
and found by the spiritual aspirant at any time he desires. Does participation in the human-divine relation take place at the express command of
the human member of the relation? Does the numinous impart knowledge of itself merely at our bidding? It verges upon the grotesque to
suppose that the minds of twentieth-century anthropocentric biologists
who have denied their God and who pursue their work without any
thought of their own spiritual-ethical improvement should nevertheless
be able to devise ways of purifying or combining natural substances
from the environment into pharmacological products which enable any
spiritual aspirant at will to enter into an active relation with the divine
reality.

We cannot suppose that a drug such as LSD, which only belatedly has
been shown to have damaging effects upon the mind and upon the genes,
is at the same time our chief hope of attaining spiritual maturity. As J. R.
Elkinton has so well stated, "Such a danger seems a large price to pay for
artistic and spiritual insights that apparently have produced as yet no
recognizable masterpieces."[19]

It is, of course, conceivable that an individual who uses any kind of

drug for a religious experience chooses to do so through a divine injunc-
tion or will working within himself. But does it appear even remotely conceivable that the spiritual awareness of a genuine religious experience could
depend upon the intake of drugs whose production has been based upon
the deliberate torture of sentient animals? When Alan Watts, in his unrestrained enthusiasm for chemical-induced "spirituality," wrote, "The
pharmacologist . . . may be doing us the extraordinary service of rescuing
religious experience from the obscurantists,"[20] had he ever stopped to
consider how drug testing is carried out? Did either Aldous Huxley or the
hippies ever stop to consider how science actually investigates the nature
and properties of drugs? Did the psychologists who tried to guide people
in the wonders of psychedelic experiences know that in a book of 626
pages on the hallucinogens, a whole chapter is devoted to animal studies,
including sections on the effect of hallucinogenic drugs introduced intra-
systemically and on their intracerebral effects?[21]

De Ropp, in discussing the purification of mescalin from peyotl, writes:

> The chemists, ever on the lookout for new worlds to conquer,
> had taken the divine plant into their laboratories, bent on deter-
> mining the nature of those substances that endow it with its
> vision-provoking properties. The brown malodorous decoction
> of the mescal buttons was progressively purified and one crystal-
> line compound after another was separated from the crude
> material. No less than nine alkaloids were finally crystallized,
> several of which influenced the behaviour of experimental
> animals. Most poisonous of these alkaloids was lopophorine,
> which, in doses of about 12 milligrams per kilogram body
> weight, would produce in rabbits violent convulsions of the
> type seen in sufferers from tetanus or strychnine poison-
> ing.[22]

And further:

> F. M. Sturtevant and V. A. Drill, who injected mescaline
> directly into the brains of cats, thus forcing the drug past the
> blood-brain barrier, have shown that it produces dramatic
> effects on the animal's behaviour. The cats began a loud con-

tinuous yowling which was unlike any normal cat sound.
They retched, they salivated, they defecated, and their
breath came in short gasps.[23]

Rabbits in convulsions and cats behaving "dramatically." Should these
things be tolerated by any scientist?

In 1968 De Ropp published a new work entitled *The Master Game:
Pathways to Higher Consciousness Beyond the Drug Experience.*[24] In
contrast to *Drugs and the Mind* of more than a decade earlier, De Ropp
now reveals himself as a scientist who truly aspires to realize his potential
through knowledge and insights unattainable by the pursuit of established science. Combining an imposing array of chemical, physiological,
and psychological facts with a wide knowledge of religious and spiritual
writings of East and West, he erects a system of scientific mysticism,
which he calls creative psychology and by which he reinterprets the
beliefs and convictions of the theists. His system is designed to enable
man to "create by his own efforts a new being within himself" by reaching higher levels of consciousness. The ultimate state is union with the
universal consciousness, which is a conceptual entity to replace God.
The Master Game discloses the wisdom of an enlightened man who is ever
aspiring to come higher and who obviously has already experienced a con-
siderable measure of success. Yet quite apart from the sweeping, scornful
condemnation of Christianity and the clergy so characteristic of our
scientific age, the Way of creative psychology diverges in other important
respects from the path of theocentric humanism. This divergence is most
clearly brought out in De Ropp's attitude toward the drug experience.
Granted, he maintains that the psychedelic drugs can only reveal higher
states of consciousness without ever making them realities, and he warns
that their continued use for this purpose is both physically harmful and
a false substitute for the inner effort required of a spiritual aspirant.
Nevertheless, he regards the taking of drugs under scientifically controlled
conditions as a necessary source of chemical, psysiological, and psychological information about the human body and as a desirable source of
evidence for the existence of higher levels of awareness. This leads him
to advocate an "enlightened legislation" to provide, under proper care
and facilities, the opportunity to participate in the psychedelic experience for anyone who desires to do so. He says, "carefully controlled

experiments with drugs are justified if they lead to the conclusion that the fourth and fifth states of consciousness are possible for man."[25] The rules of the creative psychology game thus have an exaggerated dependence upon scientific knowledge, even mistaking it for final authority in matters of conduct. Although De Ropp states that "it is not spiritually lawful to take psychedelics merely for 'kicks' or to use them as substitutes for the special kind of inner work that alone can produce lasting results,"[26] he is equally insistent that "it is *physiologically* lawful to obtain information about the workings of one's own organism by any means that does not damage the organism or render its possessor a slave to the procedure in question (physically dependent on a drug, for example),"[27] and that "it is *psychologically* (or spiritually) lawful to obtain such information as part of a life game, the aim of which is realization of higher states of awareness."[28]

Since the end can never justify all conceivable means, both views are morally unacceptable, especially when the means involve harm to *other* organisms. Creative psychology, unlike theocentric humanism, sees the exploitation of lower forms of life in the laboratory as a biological necessity; the use of experimental animals for drug testing or for attaining biological information of any kind whatever is never once condemned in *The Master Game*. On the contrary, in discussing the activity of the hypothalmus region of the brain, De Ropp states, "we are forced to rely for this information mainly on data obtained from monkeys."[29] We are not forced to do anything of the kind: such information is in no way essential to our spiritual evolution but instead actually retards it. An attitude toward sentient nonhuman creatures which is devoid of compassion and a sense of *their* rights is a blind acceptance of the immoral scientific dogma that the attainment of scientific knowledge justifies any scientific methodology. It is also a reminder that an expanding consciousness is not necessarily accompanied by a proportional expansion of the conscience.

The mistreatment of lower forms of life, which even the noble aim of treating mental diseases cannot wholly justify, seems to me to constitute part of the incontrovertible evidence for the utter impossibility of pharmacology being a stepping stone to spiritual maturity. For if pharmacology could provide us with the means of active participation at will in the human-divine relation, then we are forced to admit that man's path to the realm of the spirit is besmeared with atrocious acts of cruelty to other sentient beings and the mortification of their flesh. The very idea that the end could justify such means is an ethical absurdity, since the end of spiritual aspiration must necessarily include compassion for other sentient beings.

Notes

1. Review of G. R. Taylor, *The Biological Time-Bomb, Times Literary Supplement,* 25 April 1968.

2. N. S. Kline, "Foreword," in *Drugs and the Mind,* by R. S. De Ropp (New York: Grove Press, 1957), p. x.

3. A. Huxley, *The Doors of Perception* (London: Chatto & Windus, 1954).

4. A. Huxley, *Heaven and Hell* (London: Chatto & Windus, 1956).

5. De Ropp, *Drugs and the Mind* (New York: Grove Press, 1957).

6. *Ibid.,* pp. 286-87.

7. Plotinus, *The Enneads,* bk. 4, parts 3, 13, trans. Stephen MacKenna (London: Faber & Faber, 1956).

8. C. Mayhew, "Letter to the editor," *Times* (London), 25 July 1967.

9. A. W. Watts, *The Joyous Cosmology: Adventures in the Chemistry of Consciousness* (New York: Vintage Books, 1962), p. 19.

10. N. Kazantzakis, *God's Pauper: St. Francis of Assisi,* trans. P. A. Bien (Oxford: Bruno Cassirer, 1962).

11. J.-M. Déchanet, *Christian Yoga,* trans. R. Hindmarsh (London: Burns & Oates, 1960).

12. R. C. Zaehner, *Mysticism, Sacred and Profane: An Inquiry into Some Varieties of Praeternatural Experience* (London: Oxford University Press, 1957), p. 13.

13. *Ibid.,* p. 84.

14. *Ibid.,* p. 193.

15. R. C. Zaehner, *Hindu and Muslim Mysticism* (London: Athlone Press, 1960), p. 118.

16. R. C. Zaehner, *Mysticism, Sacred and Profane,* p. 86.

17. *Ibid.,* p. 87.

18. T. Merton, *New Seeds of Contemplation* (London: Burns & Oates, 1961), pp. 190-191.

19. J. R. Elkinton, "Beards, Flowers, Drugs, and Love," *Annals of Internal Medicine* 67 (1967): 1342.

20. A. W. Watts, *The Joyous Cosmology,* p. xviii.

21. A. Hoffer and H. Osmund, *The Hallucinogens* (New York: Academic Press, 1967).
22. De Ropp, *Drugs and the Mind,* pp. 48-49.
23. *Ibid.,* p. 60.
24. R. S. De Ropp, *The Master Game: Pathways to Higher Consciousness Beyond the Drug Experience* (New York: Delta, 1968).
25. *Ibid.,* p. 48.
26. *Ibid.,* p. 44.
27. *Ibid.,* p. 43.
28. *Ibid.,* pp. 43-44.
29. *Ibid.,* p. 45.

5

Life, Death, and Medical Science

During the more than 300 years that the Society of Friends has existed, Quakers have openly opposed war, slavery, capital punishment, and other kinds of physical force and violence and have given both philanthropic aid to the chronically destitute and immediate relief to victims of war and catastrophe. Through the years the many humanitarian problems that have been wholly or partially solved by these peace-loving, sober-minded, quiet Christians have impressed the world again and again. Notwithstanding, the peculiar form of faith upon which their activity depends has never had great appeal; today the international membership of the Society of Freinds is only about 200,000. And today, as in other active groups, there are among their members new, critical voices demanding profound introspection and renewal to make possible a greater and more effective Quaker engagement in this world of crises. Quakers, they say, can no longer act only as benevolent spectators. They need to engage themselves actively in the advance of science as well as in all secular progress and the new radicalism, which are guiding political, economic, and theological development. Their basic principles must be clarified and made relevant.[1]

What is the basis of Quaker Christianity? To one who is not a member of their society, it seems to be the assertion that the Christian God is a

living reality who can be experienced, and therefore Christianity is more
personal experience than submission to religious dogmas and conventions.
In addition, Quaker Christianity seems to be based upon two essential
points: (1) the belief that each human individual has within himself an
inner light—a divine spark and potential force—which is related to the
highest Good, and (2) the belief that through the gradual realization
and liberation of this force the world shall be transformed into a spiritual
kingdom which has vanquished fear, ignorance, and sin. On the basis of
these assertions Quakers cannot help thinking and acting in an evolutionary manner. Human life is considered to be an unavoidable spiritual
growth toward the Good. And in virtue of their unceasing differentiation
between what exists and what should be, these theocentric humanists
are attempting to improve the quality of life. They seem, thus, to be
under compulsion to better the evolutionary stage in which they find
themselves. Their concomitant views on both the sacred and the profane
and the eternal and the impermanent have much relevance for a world
in revolution. One of their most relevant views deals with the democracy
of the future, which they see from a perspective that puts narrow contemporary views to shame. According to the Quakers, true democracy is
neither submission to the will of the majority (which can be ethically inadequate) nor disregard for the will of the minority (which can be ethically
correct). True democracy is instead a collective spiritual striving after
God's will. This is not merely Christian theory. The Friends are speaking
here out of experience, but without attempting to hide that their striving
often demands greater tolerance, self-control, understanding, and sincerity than they possess. When their small groups, after repeated unsuccessful attempts, continue to strive for spiritual agreement in difficult
problems, they may in certain cases experience a "creative and dynamic"
reality, which gives them greater intellectual and spiritual insight than
normal democratic procedures can ever provide. For Friends know that
an inner light can be strengthened and become a source of light for others
whenever the human will makes a sincere attempt to subordinate itself
to the divine will.

   A recently published Quaker book entitled *Who Shall Live?* is an
attempt to conform to this principle.[2] It deals with the enormously difficult ethical problems that have arisen within modern biology and medical
science; it was written by an American "Working Party," which for several
years concerned itself with "the religious and moral issues posed by

scientific advances in the control of death as well as in the control of birth." The committee consisted of eight professionally qualified members from biology, medicine, and theology. That the book as a whole should be considered no more than a preliminary attempt to deal with ethical issues is made clear in the authors' preface, which states that they are unable to answer many of the questions raised and that they do not presume to speak for all Quakers. In the Introduction also appears the admirable Quaker thought that the whole attempt is not so much concerned with what man in his present situation *can* do but with what he *ought* to do.

Who Shall Live? deals with a series of related topics: population growth, scientific control of life and death, the quality of life, and the choice of priorities. It also contains useful appendices on population data, reproductive processes, fertility control, religious and medical views on abortion and abortion laws, new definitions of death, and laws on the donation of tissues and organs, together with valuable bibliographic notes.

Assuming that the quality of life cannot be significantly improved so long as millions of despairing persons suffer from poverty, hunger, disease, and ignorance, the authors, from the first chapter, make a strong exhortation to reduce birthrates, not because they are increasing but because death rates, thanks to biomedical research and technology, are falling. Nevertheless, about 10,000 persons on an average die every day of malnutrition, and about half the population of the world is on the brink of starvation because we cannot bring our natural resources and our growing population into equilibrium. Closely associated with this fact is the increasing pollution of the earth which arises out of reckless technological exploitation and misuse of nature in the name of humanity. Were we fewer individuals, the Quakers say, there would be less suffering and less pollution. Since a voluntary increase in death rates is out of the question, we must learn to control our fertility. The great question is how?

The Quakers' answer is brief and to the point: our desperate situation demands more sexual education, greater access to contraceptives, and the legalization of abortion. But the story does not end there; they make clear that all their answers, although arrived at in unanimous agreement as the well-considered opinions of the working committee at the time, may possibly need future revision as a result of new and better insights.

The enormous difficulties associated with fertility control are not concealed. Family planning by sexual education and contraceptives has so far not been able to bring birthrates into balance with death rates. The authors further emphasize that even if universal access to birth control aid existed, it alone could not solve the population problem. They believe that first of all the proper motivation for limiting the size of families must be established, and to expect that this motivation can come about before economic and cultural conditions are significantly improved on a worldwide scale is unrealistic.

The Quakers propose abortion only as the lesser of two evils, since they hold that no woman shall be forced to give birth to an unwanted child. At the same time they hold that no doctor shall perform an abortion against his conscience, and, in general, they favor a gradual decrease in abortions. That a noticeable decline in births has taken place in those countries (Hungary, Rumania, and Japan) in which abortion is legal is to be seen in relation to the fact that the number of abortions decreases as the use of contraceptives increases. The Quakers believe that this development is good; they have no objections to contraception and prefer it to abortion. As they do not wish to recommend a standard of chastity based upon fear of the physical and social consequences of the common practice of premarital sexual intercourse, they intimate that if we are to improve the quality of life for our descendants, our simple biological duty is to make use of the artificial means that science has developed for controlling fertility.

Various methods of contraception are described and evaluated, but the conclusion is that scientific research has not yet produced the ideal contraceptive. Both the IUD (intrauterine device) and the pill are recommended as much more effective than the natural methods based upon self-control. Like so many others, these Quakers believe that some form of chemical or mechanical control of the sexual process is a necessity, since *Homo sapiens,* despite the threat of continual suffering and possible extinction as a result of its uncontrolled sexual instinct, seems unable to practice the voluntary continence which could ensure its welfare and survival.

What is noteworthy about these views, which do not significantly deviate from the prevalent liberal and "realistic" opinions about fertility control, is that they arise directly out of theocentric humanism. By relating the divine and the human in their belief in the inner light of Christ, Quakers regard evolutionary development as a realization of spiritual potentials. At the same time our physical being and its potentials must also be understood. The book describes in detail the sexual process, including the various forms of natural contraception, through which nature allows only about one-half of all fertilized eggs to develop into viable individuals. The authors maintain that biologists cannot say with certainty just when a new life begins, since they regard life as a continuous whole (that is, alternating between haploid and diploid cells)—an assertion which is a little misleading, since, as is also pointed out, only the (diploid) fertilized egg, and not the (haploid) sex cells, has the possibility to develop into a human being. More important, however, is the committee's recognition of the fact that in our present crisis, biological knowledge alone is inadequate and that the solution to our problems must be sought elsewhere.

According to their belief in an inner light, Quakers are compelled to consider abortion, for example, as a moral and theological question which concerns the sanctity of the individual life. The question is not so much when a developing new life acquires self-consciousness or soul, but whether it is ever morally defensible to destroy a potential human being. Has a fetus an absolute right to live? Following a discussion of the various religious views on this subject, the Quakers say that killing is immoral because (1) it destroys the divine ("that of God") in the victim, and (2) the killer violates his own divine potential. But, it is added, to be bound by absolute moral criteria is not consistent either with Quaker views about traditional religious authority or with contemporary liberal views on the best life for the individual, the family, and society. One can almost feel the spiritual anguish with which these gifted Quakers ask, "How do we decide which moral values should have priority?" The impression is clearly made that their final choices were the result of many, many difficult attempts to come closer to spiritual democracy.

The authors' moral difficulties are again revealed when they turn to the problems associated with control over death. Moral uncertainty is only a recognition of the fact that striving after supreme moral values must continue. Is it mercy or murder to turn off the respirator? The authors say that some doctors desire to maintain life as long as possible in the hope of some miraculous recovery or out of respect for the sanctity of life, while others believe it is God's will and an act of love to destroy a life that no longer has any meaning as a human being. The working committee's belief is that when the brain is so injured that the patient can never regain consciousness, then the quality of life is so reduced that it

must be ethically right to withhold therapy in order to help the patient
to die—not least when the patient is a potential donor of an organ. They
say that brain death is possibly more satisfactory than the present criteria
of death, but that the final definition of death which is to be accepted
by medical science must be acceptable to the legal profession as well in
order to avoid criminal acts. On the justification of euthanasia in general,
the working committee frankly states that it is not yet able to take a
stand. But they have sufficient wisdom and insight to state that from the
standpoint of evolution death is a good and a natural thing, whereby
those who have made their contributions to human development make
room for those who have not yet done so. It is also a pleasure to find
that these Quakers lack any kind of enthusiasm for expensive transplants
carried out at the cost of other kinds of medical aid, and that they are
basically opposed to the proposals of some geneticists to "improve" man
scientifically by manipulation of his genes. Toward the end of the chapter
on control over death a fundamental question is posed: What are we prolonging life for? And they believe rightly that the essential problem is to
improve it.

Who Shall Live? ends with the wise thought that our future depends
upon the choices we now make. Even though the Quakers mention that
choices concerning life and death are usually made on the basis of compassion for the weak, they will not make a definite statement about
priority. It is, however, clear that some of their own decisions are in
greater accord with "situation ethics" than with moral absolutes. They
believe, for example, that the imminent danger of starvation, suffering,
and death justifies the increasing use of the best contraceptives scientific
research can supply. Furthermore, they justify abortion by evaluating
an embryo's potential life lower than the quality of the life of the family
and society.

Are these choices in accord with the divine will? As the authors themselves stress, no one knows for certain, but I believe there are many who
do not think they are. Is situation ethics, supported by unrestricted scientific advance, the final moral word? Does there not exist a loftier ethic—
one that is eternal and unchanging—leading *Homo sapiens* upward toward
the Good? We all know intuitively that compassion for the weak is in
harmony with the divine. But can there be anything weaker or more defenseless than a living embryo? Should we completely disregard the statement on abortion issued in 1970 by the Catholic bishops of England and

Wales, which maintains that neither before nor after birth is the child the property of the parents, since only God is the master of life?[3] Should we wholly neglect the thought that the criterion of brain death has nothing whatever to do with soul or spirit or inner light? Nor should the working committee forget that the biomedical triumphs that have given us so much control over life were attained through the suffering and death of millions of defenseless experimental animals. Our ecological crisis makes it imperative that we establish as soon as possible a healthy and harmonious relation between humans and other living organisms. This can never come to pass so long as research workers in biomedicine regard highly developed, sentient animals as nothing more than scientific objects of investigation. We cannot come closer to the Good by choosing methods which are in disharmony with the goal. The prevailing authority of science, many of whose decisions have revealed a sick conscience, is no sacred authority.

Fortunately some are awake to these facts, and they are openly attacking established biology and medicine. Were Quakers to listen to their voices, they would discover that they have allies who also desire to find out what man ought to do. Through collaboration they might help each other to throw off the scientific yoke which so often restricts man's true evolution. Quaker efforts to improve the quality of life still pay too much regard to contemporary scientific directives and too little regard to the spiritual leaders and the sacrosanct traditions of the past. When new critical Quaker voices declare that one should think more scientifically and rationally, they mean, apparently, that science and the scientific world picture cannot be in opposition to a religion bent on the realization of man's spiritual potentials. Sooner or later they may be forced to rethink their argument. They have not yet realized that science has already been compelled to take up a defensive position. From different quarters demands have been made for a scientific moratorium to give scientists time to think about what they are doing and why. We stand at the threshhold of a spiritual revolution. From now on, everything is possible. Who knows? Perhaps human development is leading to a consideration of the possibility of a voluntary sexual moratorium which would solve the population problem and raise the quality of life to a heretofore undreamed niveau.

Dear Friends! Your basic beliefs and principles and your conviction that life shall be improved are a part of the most significant insights of our times. It was inevitable that this first Quaker attempt to throw light upon the relation between life, death, and modern biology is in many ways intellectually and spiritually satisfying. But, as you yourselves state, the enormous problems of human development require much more spiritual maturity than we now possess. Try, try again and again to come closer to the divine will. Make your methods and experiences relevant in a world confronted with ethical choices. All of us have great need of the evolutionary help you can give.

Notes

1. P. A. Lacey, "Quakerism looks to the future," in *Break the New Ground: Seven Essays by Contemporary Quakers,* Friends World Committee for Consultation (Birmingham, England, 1969).

2. *Who Shall Live? Man's Control Over Birth and Death,* report prepared for the American Friends Service Committee (New York, 1970).

3. Bishops' Conference of England and Wales, *Statement Concerning Moral Questions* (London: Catholic Truth Society, 1970); *Times* (London); 31 December 1970.

6

Organ Transplantation and the Brain-Death Criterion

For some years the Scandinavian countries have been engrossed in discussion of contemporary medical attitudes toward human life and death. To facilitate organ transplantation, health authorities in Finland have made brain death a valid criterion of death for donors, and many Scandinavians believe that Denmark, Norway, and Sweden should follow suit. Death, they say, *is* the death of the brain, and worldwide legal acceptance of this definition will not only save lives and further the advance of medical science but will also make it easier for doctors to solve their ethical problems. At the same time a mounting resistance to the brain-death criterion, arising from widely different ethical concepts of life and death, has appeared in the Danish press, and at least one group protest against revising the traditional death criterion has been delivered to the minister of justice. The following reflections, originally intended to help swell the tide of resistance in Scandinavia, may also serve to bring international thought to bear upon one of the most urgent problems of our times.

Scientific literature pertaining to the ethical problems confronting modern medicine has grown to an almost insurmountable size without having reached any general agreement as to the best solutions. In 1970, a distinguished American physician, Dr. J. R. Elkinton, published a survey of the most significant statements made by his colleagues on life, death, and ethical choice.[1] The section on transplantation concludes:

In the literature delineated above are discussed in detail a
great many ethical problems deriving from the use of artificial and transplanted organs in man. The least attention seems
to have been paid to the most fundamental ethical problem of
all: to what extent is it right or desirable for the future of the
human species, as well as for the welfare and autonomy of
specific individuals, to carry out these biomedical procedures
by which more and more members of the species are kept alive
at the expense of the organs, efforts, and resources of the rest of
the population. The question is not likely to be asked by the
patient who benefits nor by his individual physician. Yet the
question is there. Perhaps we need to hear more from the
philosophers.

Elkinton is completely right. Despite many admirable contributions
to the literature, the medical profession as a whole has not penetrated
to the root of the problem. Society needs to hear not only philosophers'
views on organ transplantation but also those of spokesmen for the
world's religions and all others who, unlike the anthropocentric humanists,
believe that evolution is being guided by superhuman authority. The
need seems to be especially great in Denmark, where the problems concerning transplantation and the criteria of death may possibly be solved
by a small group of enthusiastic medical scientists and politicians who
have been trying, in the name of science and humanism, to convince the
people that transplanted organs are a good and natural thing and a great
step forward. Surprisingly many Christians have accepted the evolutionary
illusion that unimpeded scientific advance is necessary on the grounds
that it must be God's will that man does everything he can. According to
a newspaper report, the chairman of a Christian political party in Denmark, himself a doctor, once expressed the view, "There can be no such
things as 'hands off God's sovereign field of activity'," partly because
"God has no limits to his field of activity, and partly because God has
commanded us to form, develop, and create"—after which he mentioned
the possibility that one day the process by which a fertilized egg becomes
a fully developed child may take place outside the mother.
    Such blind confidence in the unrestrained advance of biomedical re-
search and its practical application seems so un-Christian, unethical, and
immature that it cannot go unchallenged. Our staggering world has a
desperate need to think and act on a wholly different plane. At the

moment nothing could benefit biology and medicine more than a self-imposed moratorium whereby research workers would find time and peace to think through their means and goals with juridical, philosophical, and theological assistance. Society's enthusiastic acceptance of the scientific claim that all research is beneficial has brought us all nearer disaster. We need to stop and cool down the gigantic, white-hot activity of biomedical research. Transplantation surgery is certainly one of the runaway fields. It must be brought to a halt.

Some of Christiaan Barnard's heart and lung transplantations have aroused consternation and indignation around the world because of their relation to South Africa's explosive racial question. Many of Dr. Barnard's enthusiastic colleagues have no doubt sincerely hoped that he would stop dragging apartheid into the field of transplantation surgery. But whether the transplantation of organs is carried out on dark-skinned or light-skinned individuals is not the main question; that issue may help to illuminate unhealthy, immoral conditions but can hardly lead to the final solution.

The solution comprises an ethical choice seen in a higher, evolutionary perspective. The question is simply whether the transplantation of organs is in any way desirable, necessary, or inevitable for our future. Must medical science continue in this direction merely because it is possible to do so? Must patients with defective organs be provided with viable organs taken from the living, dying, or dead? Or shall the human race slowly begin to conform to the divine will by recognizing that our further evolution is a spiritual ascent demanding moderation, self-restraint, and self-sacrifice, not least by medical science?

This ethical choice will require, among other things, knowledge of the best arguments for and against organ transplantation and the accompanying demand for a new death criterion—that is, the transplantation of indispensable organs, the removal of which would mean certain death to the donor and which therefore can only be removed from a corpse. Although scientific power, prestige, and ambition must decidedly play a role in transplantation surgery, as well as in all other fields of science, it would be unjust to conclude that the work of the surgeon is entirely due to these factors. He must be given the benefit of the doubt; we shall assume that he does what he does first and foremost to lengthen his sick patient's life. A Norwegian doctor, Ole Jacob Broch, has excellently described in a few words both the activity and motivation of transplantation surgeons:

The instant death is declared according to the valid rules,
a team which is prepared for action can begin. The dead
person can then be attached to various apparatuses which ensure
the continuance of respiration and circulation so that the viability of the organs which are to be removed can be maintained as long as possible. When the organ has been removed,
the weapons are put down and death can take the remains of its
victim. This may seem macabre, but it is a fight against time and
the prize can be life to another person.[2]

To save a life! Once this thought is uttered, any discussion of medical
ethics may come rapidly to a standstill. For most people, to save a life
seems so fine, so noble, so ethically right that there can be nothing more
to discuss. Is not a doctor's duty according to the international code of
medical ethics to preserve life from conception to death? Some merely
express gratitude that there are "teams prepared for action," who so un-
tiringly fight against time to maintain life. Others, who are breaking
away from habitual scientism, have reached quite different conclusions.
They declare that the transplantation surgeon's fight against time is, in
truth, a fight against nature, man, and God. The bases for their declaration are two: (1) the medical profession's neglect or ignorance of life and
death concepts which deviate from the scientific-humanistic view, and
(2) the medical profession's lack of compassion for lower animals.

Our age has accustomed itself to see the course of life against a scientific-
humanistic background. God, if not dead, in any case no longer plays a
role in human behavior or evolution. Progress is guided not by divine
ethics but by new scientific knowledge. The idea of a divine spark or immortal soul is an old-fashioned, untenable moral invention. Emotion,
sensation, thought, and conscience, being dependent upon the physical
and chemical activity of the brain and nervous system, are wholly amenable to scientific explanation. The highest reality is man and his potential.
So long as there is life, there is hope. Death is the definitive end whereby
life's activity is forever finished. Since death is our last and greatest enemy,
we must seek as best we can to maintain life's physical existence. This
goal justifies all conceivable means.

Therefore, continues medical science, we take organs from the dead to
help the dying to live longer. The traditional death criterion based upon
cessation of circulation and respiration is no longer valid, since it is now

possible to restore and maintain these functions artificially, and since it does not give us sufficient time to remove viable organs for transplantation. The present criterion must therefore be revised in step with the times. We are aware that the precise moment of death is difficult to define, because death is a slow, complicated biological process involving organs, tissues, and cells that die at different rates. Electroencephalograms (EEGs), supported by clinical evaluations can, however, establish the point in time when the cessation of cerebral function is definitive and irreversible, and this criterion of death we believe to be final. Here we come closer to the true nature of death—the physical destruction of brain cells and tissues together with the cessation of cerebral function and the total extinction of consciousness. At the same time this criterion provides us with a precise moment of death that may be in advance of the cessation of heart and lung function. Thus, when two consecutive EEG measurements, separated by a standard time interval, fail to register any electrical activity in the brain, the patient can be declared dead, and we believe it is then ethically defensible to maintain circulation and respiration by artificial means and to remove the organ for which another patient is waiting.

It is not wholly inconveivable that there might be something ethically defensible in this conclusion, provided it were an expression of a concept of life and death which had universal validity. But it is no such thing. It merely represents a scientific-humanistic view of life and death that is limited to those who deny the religious perspective toward which human evolution, despite all signs to the contrary, is proceeding. In contrast to modern humanism, religion in its broadest sense denotes recognition of the existence of a superhuman reality, which necessitates a human-divine relation. Not surprisingly, therefore, religious concepts of life and death differ radically from that of the transplantation surgeon. According to the religious outlook, life is more than physical and psychical existence; it is also an opportunity for spiritual improvement. And death is much more than the physical destruction of the brain and the disappearance of all its measurable activity; it is also a sacred initiation into a new state of reality. In contrast to the negative attitude of scientific humanism, religion looks upon death as something immeasurably positive. It is not the end of life, but its culmination. The difference is enormous. Death becomes the highest point of earthly life, because it leads to a closer approach to the divine.

A visible result of death is the destruction of the physical body and its functions, but other profound changes, invisible and immeasurable, must also take place. We know very little about the commencement and duration of these changes. No transplantation surgeon should maintain that the cessation of the brain's electrical activity is identical with the moment of death or is even an adequate definition of death. Quite apart from the fact that instruments are fallible and that brains registering flat EEGs for various periods of time have later begun to function normally,[3] it is a logical absurdity to use scientific measurements as the last word about a human phenomenon whose true nature is unknown and which, since time immemorial, has been regarded as something more than a biological process. The declining electrical activity of the brain of a dying person in a hospital is a measurable biological phenomenon which is also encountered in isolated mammalian brains and in mammalian cerebral tissue cultures in the laboratory—a fact which permits no authoritative scientific pronouncement about the state of consciousness of intact human brains or of isolated brains and cerebral tissue cultures of animals. In human life and death, in particular, consciousness, subconsciousness, unconsciousness, and the collective unconscious are mysteries not now amenable to biomedical explanation, since they point beyond the limits of conventional science.

Neither the cessation of the brain's measurable activity nor any other medical signs of irreversible coma[4] can reveal whether the unconscious dying patient at that particular moment lacks all power of awareness and is devoid of soul and spirit. If transplantation surgeons and other adherents of electroencephalographic thanatopsis believe the immortal soul and the divine spark to be illusions with which death cannot be concerned, they have no scientific proof in support of their contentions. Most of us know next to nothing about the changes in the states of consciousness during the death process. Our ignorance of the psychical and spiritual changes that take place in the dying is, in fact, boundless. We cannot define death in any wholly adequate terms, and without definition there can be no wholly adequate criteria, medical or otherwise. In the face of such a mystery, we need to tread gently and respectfully. Transplantation surgeons nevertheless lay hands upon a dying patient as though they were thoroughly grounded in every aspect of his death. They have no ethical right to do so, not even with the permission of the dying.

As far as is humanly possible, it is the business of the living to help the dying to die a natural death in a way that is in keeping with death's beauty and grandeur. Every dying hospital patient should have the inalienable right to the time and the peace which a natural death requires. This is wholly denied a patient who is attached to a machine which measures the declining electrical activity of his brain, when his circulation and respiration are artificially maintained by other machines, and when his organs are removed by hurried surgical operations. The medical profession must not consider man's relation to the divine as irrelevant. Socrates did not know what death's nature was or where death would lead him; yet his own voluntary death was in full agreement with his religious concept of death as the noble culmination of life. In dying, he had no need for the help of his fellow men. Most of us will have much need of it, and no atheistic or agnostic scientific humanist has the right to decide that spiritual aid during the death process in a hospital is out of the question because there is immediate need for organs to be taken out of the dying person's body.

Medical and clerical duties must not be confused, but the medical profession could enlarge its knowledge of both life and death (and thereby solve the ethical dilemmas brought about by organ transplantation and the excessive use of heart and lung machines) if it were to turn to a study of the different kinds of care for the dying. These range from silent presence to unceasing words. Roman Catholics, with extreme unction and special prayers, attempt to lead the dying closer to the divine light. C. G. Jung held that the Catholic masses for the soul, which are "expressly intended for the psychic welfare of the deceased," are on a higher level than the Protestant death rites, which he felt to be limited by a "world-affirming optimism." Eastern care for the dying naturally differs widely from that of Western countries. Tibetan Buddhists, with their own particular concept of the superhuman, do not try to benumb the mind with drugs but rather to keep it clear so they can communicate to the dying words of spiritual truth. When the physical signs of death are visible, a white cloth is laid over the face of the corpse, and no one may touch the body for three to four days, a period deemed necessary for the separation of the "consciousness-principle" from the body. During this period chanting and prayers are supposed to lead the changed state of consciousness into more enlightened paths believed to be in harmony with spiritual development toward the highest reality. W. Y. Evans-Wentz's classic edition of the *Tibetan Book of the Dead*,[5] supplied with Jung's brilliant psychological commentary, should be obligatory reading for every transplantation surgeon. For without knowledge of religious views of life and death, the surgeon sees the donor's dying body before him as a lifeless object without the possibility of aid—a rapidly perishing source of organs— and nothing more.

Maintaining this outlook it is not strange that transplantation research looks upon sentient animals merely as objects of scientific investigation. The atrocities experimental animals have experienced in transplantation laboratories since the days of Alexis Carrel and C. C. Guthrie are not mentioned by supporters of transplantation surgery, but biomedical research of this kind continues. In hundreds of laboratories throughout the world merciless research workers are inflicting suffering and death upon defenseless animals. Recent transplantation research has comprised among other things living two-headed dogs, monkeys reduced to body-less functional brains, and mice forced to live out their lives sewn together in pairs. These biological acts of violence are not due to sadism. They are due to spiritual immaturity and ethical apathy. Can transplantation surgeons or anyone else seriously believe that such means hasten the true progress of man?

Nor should we forget what animal experimentation of this kind may lead to:

> A hopeful and completely practical goal for future research is isolation of the human brain. There are no outstanding engineering problems, since the same mechanical support systems used for the monkey brain could be scaled up and employed. Even brains harboring known diseases could be studied profitably under similar laboratory conditions after the donor's death. Just as with heart transplantation—and to an even greater extent—it would be imperative to remove the organ immediately after death, since extensive deterioration would make the brain worthless for study.[6]

This is a nightmarish prospect. The electrical activity of a living, isolated monkey brain, implanted with electrodes, cannot only be measured, but scientists can also indirectly communicate with the brain by using one of the electrodes as a point of stimulation when current is applied. They state, further, that the isolated monkey brain "displays a remarkable retention of inherent electrical rhythmicity that strongly suggests it may retain some semblance of 'consciousness.' "[7] This is no authoritative scientific pronouncement about mammalian consciousness; it is something worse. It is a scientist's suspicion that the monkey brain he isolated and kept artificially alive in the laboratory was in a partially conscious state for the duration of the experiment. It implies, as well, that such extraordinarily interesting and fruitful neurological research must be continued by all means at his disposal. The modern scientific conscience, choosing to carry out such experiments on animals, would hardly be expected to show much restraint in studies of isolated human brains. Into what monstrous ethical apathy contemporary students of life have lapsed!

In an attempt to think through the ethical problems of modern medicine, one searches for a key word or phrase that might attract general ethical attention. I believe Dr. Elkinton has found something significant when he speaks of the relation of the medical profession to the "quality of Life."[8] With special reference to kidney transplantation, he advocates as an alternative, preventive medicine, which might give the medical profession a new orientation toward the spiritual life. But their obsession about prolonging physical life makes transplantation surgeons forget that life has a spiritual dimension. Through techniques that have caused countless thousands of animals injury, suffering, and death, and through violations of the culmination of human lives, they continue to transplant living organs from one person to another. Neither the recipient, the donor, nor the transplantor gains any spiritual benefit from the act. On the contrary, the whole act is not only inhuman but it disturbs the natural evolutionary rhythm between life and death. Flesh is kept forcibly alive in an unfavorable and inharmonious alien environment. From the standpoint of evolution, transplantation surgery is a shortsighted, life-inimical error.

Transplantation surgeons have not yet understood that the growing revolt against the establishment is primarily a spiritual revolt against the unnatural, the inharmonious, the ungraceful, and the unethical which the scientific age is directing against nature, man, and God. They have not realized that a new epoch is already dawning, in which man will learn to live and die in quiet harmony with the superhuman will which is guiding his true evolution.

Dr. Elkinton concluded his examination of the literature of medical ethics with a familiar quotation: There is "a time to be born and a time to die. . . ." But, he adds, "how to know when is the time?"

With respect to the transplantation of organs, I would say that the time to die has come when a dying person, young or old, can be kept alive only by means that have arisen out of scientific violation of both human and animal creatures.

We have no need to change the traditional death criterion in order to promote contemporary transplantation madness. We need to change our attitude toward the mystery and sanctity of death to elevate the spiritual quality of life. We need a religious perspective of evolution that will slow down biology's insane drive and thereby hasten man's ascent toward the divine Good. This ethical choice, involving voluntary renunciation of the unnatural and immoral prolongation of a life already ordained to death, is a basic condition of the new epoch we are entering.

Notes

1. J. R. Elkinton, "The Literature of Ethical Problems in Medicine. I-III," *Annals of Internal Medicine* 73 (1970): 495-98, 662-66, 863-70.

2. J. O. Broch, *Det kunstige Menneske* [The Artificial Human Being] (Oslo: Minerva Forlag, 1969).

3. "What and When Is Death?" *Journal of the American Medical Association* 204 (May 1968): 219.

4. Ad Hoc Committee of the Harvard Medical School to Examine the Definition of Brain Death, "A Definition of Irreversible Coma," *Journal of the American Medical Association* 205 (August 1968): 337.

5. W. Y. Evans-Wentz, ed. and comp., *The Tibetan Book of the Dead,* with a psychological commentary by C. G. Jung (London: Oxford University Press, 1960).

6. R. J. White, *Industrial Research* 10, no. 4 (April 1968).

7. *Ibid.*

8. J. R. Elkinton, "Medicine and the Quality of Life," *Annals of Internal Medicine* 64 (1966): 711-14.

7

Humanism in the Churches

On a January evening in 1972 a discussion of death criteria, including the related subjects of organ transplantation and the artificial maintenance of respiration and circulation, took place in Filips Church in Copenhagen. The large church could barely accommodate the great number of people attending. Toward the close of the meeting the hope was expressed that no one present took it amiss that such a discussion had been held within a church, and then, after the audience had been reminded that approximately 95 percent of the Danish population were members of the Folkekirke (the established Lutheran church), the meeting was brought to a final close with psalms and prayer. Even though its aim was quite understandable—to procure and disseminate information about a global problem—several grounds for criticism of this meeting come to mind.

In the first place, the majority of those present seemed to have forgotten that they were gathered together in a place where man's relation to the divine is to be preached and strengthened. With the exception of a few unsuccessful attempts to turn the discussion toward the central problem, there was no sign that evening of any orientation toward the divine. For two hours men and women communicated with one another in a way that revealed only a humanistic conviction that the problem of death criteria revolves about the question of how modern medicine can best save and prolong human life.

Any discussion of death criteria that neglects the religious aspects of the problem seems to be highly out of place in a church. Religion, regardless of whether it is Christianity or not, is no synonym for modern humanism or philanthropy. Religions' singular concern is the divine, regardless of how differently it may be conceived and interpreted. The basic religious world view is thus theocentric; religion strives to see the divine at the cosmic center, and the religious person attempts to live a spiritual and ethical life. But the discussion in Filips Church that evening was based on an anthropocentric world view which sees at the center of the universe only man. The meeting did in fact express a humanism so strongly secular that the concluding psalms and prayers seemed misplaced.

Four experts led the discussion: a senior physician, a senior nurse, a clergyman, and a headmaster. The latter two were, in addition, members of the Danish Parliament. All four seemed to agree that organ transplantation is both desirable and indispensable, and none seemed to have any ethical objections to the introduction of the brain-death criterion in transplantation surgery.

The physician admitted that contemporary medical control of life and death may in certain cases give rise to ethical doubt, but he was convinced that doctors can now determine the time of brain death with certainty. He stated that since electroencephalographic examinations are not always dependable, they can be replaced by roentgenological and other kinds of examinations of cerebral circulation; he maintained that if the patient is in a hospital that possesses modern equipment and the necessary scientific and technical expertise, this new method is wholly reliable. In emphasizing that he did not want in any way to be thought cynical, he also said that a person with a dead brain was nothing more than a physiological preparation. There is no doubt that he was sincere and honest; like so many contemporary humanists, the physician obviously believed that death is only a physiological phenomenon, whose nature is best understood by physiologists. The thought was not expressed—although it was supposedly implied—that in the name of medical science, one has the right to do what one will with a preparation that is no longer a human being.

The nurse's few remarks about transplantation included her approval of the practice of supplying both the donor and the recipient with separate medical teams—a viewpoint based upon the failure to recognize that this practice reveals a double morality not at all flattering to the contemporary medical conscience.

The clergyman, who, in agreement with the physician, admitted that the problems under discussion were ethically difficult, had apparently solved some of them to his own satisfaction. He hoped that Christian love of one's neighbor would embrace the dying person's willingness to donate his organs to anyone who had need of them. But his kind and pious manner of speaking underwent a rapid change when a rather ironical interrogator began, to use the clergyman's own expression, to tread on his toes. At this moment both the clergyman and the headmaster became angry and excited and resorted to highly unchristian phrases which encouraged the assembly to try to hiss the interrogator out. It was, in truth, an unseemly affair before an altar. The church seemed to be used that evening as a convenient meeting place and discussion club for humanists who were more concerned with scientific and technological progress than with life's true evolution. Otherwise, they could hardly have failed at a church meeting on life and death to speak about the progressive realization of life through its search for religious-spiritual truths.

It is especially regrettable that Christian congregations have been so little influenced by the spirit of the Gospel that they allow themselves to be led by modern humanism's inadequate views of man's spiritual development. At present the different religions of the world tend to nod in silent approval to all biological and medical statements about life and death as though they were the whole truth. The meeting in Filips Church fully supported this tendency. The religious background for the problem of death criteria seemed to escape the notice of the congregation. Most weight was laid upon medical definitions of life and death and how the one can be prolonged and the other delayed. Surely the matter concerns much more than this. It concerns an ethical choice between: (1) submitting to a medical authority, which already is impoverishing the quality of life and violating the dignity of death, or (2) refusing to do so in the name of a higher authority.

In order to come to a decision about the advisability of introducing the brain-death criterion as an aid in solving the problems of life and death, it is quite wrong by any standard to regard medical science as the final authority in this matter. Death, as well as life, is both a physical and a spiritual mystery which medical science, despite centuries of experience and research, by no means fully understands. From the standpoint of evolution the problems associated with death criteria are immeasurably great. It is time that the religious *Weltbild* asserts itself to expand the narrow evolutionary perspective of our times. This picture possesses unlimited possibilities for helping and guiding evolving man in his present difficulties.

The authentic religious attitude must necessarily oppose the scientific assertion that a patient whose brain is dead is a preparation lacking all powers of perception and comprehension. Religion cannot sanction the view that the physical destruction of the brain is synonymous with the total extinction of the mind, the personality, the spirit, and the soul. The religious world picture considers a dying person's gradual physical and spiritual transformation as a necessary preparation for consciousness and existence on a new plane. No one can fully explain the nature and course of the transformation, but religion, in contrast to science, finds it right to look upon the whole death process as a sacred phenomenon— as part of the individual's evolution toward the divine light. Any belief in resurrection, reincarnation, or the immortality of the soul demands respect for the mystery of death and for the patient's right to a natural death without physical or spiritual disturbances of any kind. Belief in existence after death is incompatible with the desire to delay death in all conceivable ways. A Christian should not fear death so much that he is willing to sanction all medical profanations of this sacred phenomenon. Nor should he condone medicine's unbridled exploitation of experimental animals, which overtly profanes any form of Christian love and compassion. But that evening in Filips Church in Copenhagen, as in many other places in the world where ethical discussions of life and death are taking place, there was no more thought about animals than about the divine. Only man and his physical survival were in focus.

The problems associated with death criteria, transplantation surgery, and the artificial maintenance of respiration and circulation, comprise an ethical challenge which the contemporary scientific conscience is unable to meet. Anthropocentric humanists nevertheless believe that we must follow along with scientific progress in order to solve the problems of life and death. They even believe that unaided man is capable of finding the solutions and must do so, because there is no other way open. They are mistaken.

Guided by the religious world picture, we could try to orient our souls toward the divine light that is responsible for the true evolution of life. In this way we could begin to liberate ourselves from the tyranny of modern science, whose limited perspectives and knowledge are leading mankind toward the absurd frontiers of anthropocentric humanism. We need to guard ourselves against this evolutionary and ethical error of judgment. We must not forget that the spiritual evolution of life is based upon the human-divine relation, whereby man can learn to live in ethical harmony with himself and other creatures.

8

The Revolt
of the Philosophers

The revolt was long in coming, but was inevitable. Contemporary moral philosophers could not remain silent indefinitely before the increasingly immoral activities of contemporary scientists. In a scathing denunciation of man's present relation to sentient animals, a group of Oxford philosophers, with some sympathizers, have written a book called *Animals, Men and Morals.*[1] Although the scope of their argument includes the use of animals for food, sport, and personal indulgence, as well as experiment, the book is in no uncertain terms a revolt against the methodology of modern biology and medicine. Here, at last, moral philosophers have left their ivory towers to oppose actively the grim immorality of the scientific age because their conscience obviously compelled them to do so. "We have not assembled this book to provide the reader with yet another manual on how to make brutalities less brutal," the Introduction states.[2] And as Patrick Corbett says in his postscript, "We make no bones about our object in contributing to this book: we want to change the world. Our view as to how men should see and treat animals is at present the view of a minority, but we believe that this minority is growing and we want to make it grow faster."[3]

The vigor, novelty, and scope of this outlook presents a striking contrast to some of the exasperatingly static views of animal welfare societies whose only objective is to eliminate animal suffering. Here is something incomparably better and stronger. Here is the philosophical foundation of man's relation to animals, forcing the reader to consider the rights of animals and to compare them with the rights of men. In doing so we are also forced to recognize that the human destruction of animal life is a moral problem which humanitarians can no longer blithely disregard. As one of the philosophers expresses it:

> Progress in animal welfare has come to mean the adoption of more painless methods of slaughtering animals, and it is not thought absurd that the R.S.P.C.A. spends a considerable amount of time and effort killing unwanted but perfectly healthy cats and dogs "to prevent cruelty."[4]

This is an admirable point of view that needs, again and again, to be driven home to those animal welfare workers who, because they quite understandably cannot bear the thought or sight of suffering, choose to eliminate it by the most rapid and efficient means at their disposal.

We must, nevertheless, be grateful for all well-meaning attempts to improve the plight of animals. Men respond in widely different ways to inhumane treatment of nonhuman life, and every new statement of the problem, regardless of whether it comes from anti-vivisectionists or moral philosophers, is a potential source of ethical stimulation. All who are actively opposing the cruelties and injustices to which sentient animals are being subjected, especially in scientific laboratories, are fighting the good fight. Any words of criticism of their efforts may therefore seem highly out of place. The theme of this book nevertheless requires the most careful appraisal of whatever is most relevant to it.

Generally, *Animals, Men and Morals* fails to satisfy because the contributors lack the spiritual vision that extends to the ultimate reality beyond the two classes of beings with which they are concerned. Their gaze is centered upon the sensible world alone. More is required to change it permanently.

The contributors to *Animals, Men and Morals* quite naturally attack the scientific exploitation of animals with the most effective weapons they possess—logic, reason, and facts. Assiduously avoiding any religious-ethical overtones, except for condemnatory purposes in line with Lynn White's contention that Christianity is largely responsible for our ecological

crises,[5] they call upon science in support of a view of evolution that
stresses the similarities between man and animals. "Science," they say,
" . . . produces progressively more evidence each year to suggest that the
differences between man and the other animals are smaller than were
once imagined. . . ."[6] In other words, since we are not essentially different from animals, it is biologically reasonable and desirable to narrow
further the gulf between us and them by showing moral consideration to
all. As another contributor says, "The necessity and the possibility for
enforcing an absolute categorical distinction between man and animals
have been exhausted."[7]

Not all the contributors take such an extreme position. Some hold that
rationality and/or morality does truly distinguish men from animals, but
nowhere in the book is there evidence of a rationality or morality extending beyond the limitations of modern anthropocentric humanism.

> Reason [it is stated] is necessarily the language of moral,
> political, and scientific argument: not because reason is holy or
> on some elevated plane, but because it *isn't;* because it is acces-
> sible to all humans; because, as well as working, it can be seen
> to work.[8]

This implies that morality cannot by any stretch of the imagination or reason be considered holy or elevated either. Since they claim a sacred basis
for morality to be nonexistent, we must therefore turn to science for
our ethical foundation—a perfectly rational choice in a scientific age where
scientific knowledge has replaced the divine ethic as our moral guide.

> The gap between men and other animals [writes another con-
> tributor] now appears smaller than ever, although, indeed, sci-
> entists have agreed since the days of Darwin in principle that
> there is no essential difference biologically. Why then do we
> still make an almost total distinction morally? If all organisms
> are on the same physical continuum then surely it cannot even
> be argued that we should be on a different moral continuum.
> Man is, after all, just one species in the Primate order.[9]

Ergo, as human beings, we must treat our kin well.

Yes, we must, but for more compelling reasons than those put forward by philosophers, biologists, and humanists who have lost sight of the spiritual realm as the ultimate source of moral enlightenment. *Animals, Men and Morals* is characterized by this loss of vision. Its scrupulous adherence to the scientific fact that man and animals are biologically similar leads, for example, to an imperfect and inadequate picture of modern medicine. It is, of course, the undeniable fact of biological kinship that compels experimental scientists to regard animals as an unsurpassed source of medical knowledge about human physiology, pathology, emotion, behavior, injury, illness, and death and to use them to safeguard health and prolong lives. And we must in fairness admit that these *are* the primary goals of medicine, not scientific curiosity, ambition, and prestige. But *Animals, Men and Morals* omits the fact that these medical goals, oriented more and more toward the mere fact of physical well-being and survival, are becoming less and less concerned with the quality of human life. As a consequence, many of the goals are nothing more than scientific manipulation of lives, which from the standpoint of man's spiritual evolution, is morally outrageous. The unending stream of breakthroughs in medical research, followed up by instantaneous practical application, has become a tyranny creating ethical dilemmas in every field of medicine. From the standpoint of health and survival, should medical science do everything it can do? Here *Animals, Men and Morals* seems to acquiesce in amoral submission.

The authors take no moral stand, for example, against prolonging a life by the transplantation of organs taken from the dying. The triumphs of transplantation surgery have been based upon atrocious experiments on dogs and monkeys, but even if they had not been, organ transplantation, as considered elsewhere in this book, is an expression of evolutionary madness and spiritual regression. Transplantation per se is an ethical dilemma of first magnitude. All such medical goals, being a matter of the scientific conscience, are indissolubly bound to the ethical dilemma of scientific methodology. It follows that the most meaningful arguments against animal experimentation must include the goals of the experiments. Demolish the goals and the means will gradually fall into disuse. The reverse is not, however, equally true. Encouraging alternative methods to animal experimentation both for the sake of animals *and* because they are more rapid and reliable can hardly be expected to restrain the automation of biological progress or to create a biology progressing toward spiritual goals.

The rational contributors to *Animals, Men and Morals,* failing to see
the light which is drawing man upward, fail also to see that many of the
goals of contemporary medicine violate man's spiritual nature just as much
as do the means. An unquestioning acceptance of an exclusively biological
concept of life and death springs from a narrow perspective. While men
and animals are biologically similar, the very fact that evolving man is a
moral agent responsible to the dictates of the spiritual realm is gradually
compelling him to learn to make ethical choices which are in harmony
with the divine ethic. In this evolutionary perspective contemporary
medical goals and means will be replaced by those more worthy of the
human-divine relation. The world is already beginning to see clearly that
rational humanism cannot be the whole answer to our problems. Some
are already refusing to realize their biological potentials of physical well-
being and survival if this end means lessening the spiritual quality of their
lives. The man-animal relation can never be put right with total neglect of
the human-divine relation.

Some of the difficulty seems to arise from the contributors' apparent
misunderstanding of the true religious-spiritual attitude toward animals.
For most of them, any religious belief that sees man as a unique being,
superior to all other forms of life, merely justifies his doing to animals
what he will. They seem to agree that the *only* Christian message about
animals is that God has given man dominion over them. This is to forget
that religion means rebinding or binding back or binding together—binding man to the divine source from which he came. It is also to forget that
the authentic spirit of Christianity sees the Godhead as the source of love
and goodness whereby man is exhorted to show compassion and righteousness to all forms of sentient life. St. Francis, as Lynn White recognized,
wholly grasped this inviolable essence of Christianity, but there have been
many other Christian and non-Christian interpreters of the divine ethic
besides St. Francis who have also insisted that man's relation to other
sentient creatures be guided by mercy, compassion, and love.

Perhaps here, in its disregard of love as a religious-ethical force,
Animals, Men and Morals most fails to satisfy. In it the hierarchy of
animate nature is demolished, man is reduced to an animal, and human
love tacitly becomes anthropoid emotion. The word "love" appears once
near the end in the postscript, but, as far as I know, no other place in
the text. That man's ability to love the divine Good with all his heart
could be one of the basic distinctions between him and the lower animals

is not considered by any of the contributors. This omission is serious.
When man is ethically conscious of his relation to the divine Good, he is
able to discern the unlimited scope of his evolutionary potential. This,
as far as we know, requires a knowledge and experience of love different
from the love of which nonhuman creatures are capable. To know and
experience this higher love, the individual must try to master his egoism
and to be conscious of making an ethical choice. He must deliberately
choose to transmute the integrity and identity of his lower egoistic self
into, and for the sake of, something higher. Love consciously bound to
ethics and recognized as a means of evolutionary self-transcendence is
beyond the reach of the nonhuman. While the spiritual life of animals
certainly includes love and devotion, only man knows that in the dying
of his lower self, he is reborn in a higher love. Only man is aware that his
evolutionary potential, being divine, embraces the spiritual-ethical ascent—
and he is, accordingly, far more than "just one species in the Primate
order."

To conceive of morality as something exclusively rational, wholly
apart from love and the spiritual realm, may seem natural to philosophers
and humanists in an age which likes to consider the religious perspective
merely as an object of scientific study. Yet it has long been known that
reason is by no means the only language of moral argument. It may be
well to remind contemporary humanists of the lovely expressions of
spiritual-ethical awareness which were possible in an age when poets,
philosophers, and scientists were all directly concerned with the human-
divine relation.

The English clergyman, George Herbert, born in 1593, once envisioned
an encounter with divine love, but painfully aware of his imperfections,
dared not look directly upon love until compelled to do so:

> Love bade me welcome; yet my soul drew back,
> > Guilty of dust and sin.
> But quick-eyed Love, observing me grow slack
> > From my first entrance in,
> Drew nearer to me, sweetly questioning
> > If I lack'd anything.
> "A guest," I answer'd, "worthy to be here."
> > Love said, "You shall be he."
> "I, the unkind, ungrateful? Ah, my dear,
> > I cannot look on Thee."

Love took my hand and smiling did reply,
"Who made the eyes but I?"
"Truth, Lord; but I have marr'd them: let my shame
Go where it doth deserve."
"And know you not," says Love, "Who bore the blame?"
"My dear, then I will serve."
"You must sit down," says Love, "and taste my meat."
So I did sit and eat.[10]

This vision is for man. Animals, being innocent life, have no covering of dust and sin. It is we who are guilty. The difference is qualitative, categorical, and absolute.

George Herbert must not be regarded as a spiritual visionary out of touch with secular realities. On the contrary, he practiced what he preached. Izaak Walton, his biographer, has given us many insights into this part of his character, as in the following incident, so relevant to this discussion.

Herbert's chief recreation was music, which he called his heaven on earth, and from his home in Bemerton walked twice a week to Salisbury for "cathedral musick" and for private playing on his lute or viol with fellow musicians. On one of his walks to Salisbury, says Walton:

He saw a poor man, with a poorer horse, that was fall'n
under his Load; they were both in distress, and needed present
help; which Mr. Herbert perceiving, put off his Canonical Coat,
and help'd the poor man to unload, and after, to load his
horse: The poor man blest him for it: and he blest the poor man;
and was so like the good Samaritan, that he gave him money to
refresh both himself and his horse; and told him, That if he lov'd
himself, he should be merciful to his Beast.—Thus he left the
poor man, and at his coming to his musical friends at Salisbury,
they began to wonder that Mr. George Herbert which us'd to
be so trim and clean, came into that company so soyl'd and dis-
compos'd; but he told them the occasion: And when one of the
company told him, He had disparag'd himself by so dirty an
employment; his answer was, That the thought of what he had
done, would prove Musick to him at Midnight; and that the omission of it, would have upbraided and made discord in his Conscience, whensoever he should pass by that place; for, if I be
bound to pray for all that be in distress, I am sure that I am

bound so far as it is in my power to practice what I pray for. And though I do not wish for the like occasion every day, yet let me tell you, I would not willingly pass one day of my life without comforting a sad soul, or shewing mercy; and I praise God for this occasion: And now let's tune our Instruments.[11]

The infinite scope of the human potential and man's recognition of it can also be illustrated by the thoughts and deeds of a contemporary figure, Mother Teresa, who has been made known to the western world largely through the efforts of Malcolm Muggeridge.[12] Her humanitarian work in the slums of Calcutta has been possible because of love and strength coming to her from a supernal source. It is not she that works, but the divine that works within her. Through personal experience she knows that humanitarian efforts can, and should, transcend mere altruistic, charitable, and moral aid to the suffering. Her acts of love to the destitute and dying are more than an expression of the highest form of rational relation between man and man. The divine has entered her life to give not only a wholly new perspective to her work but also to give spiritual energy to her and to the world—energy that has already become a source of light in our contemporary darkness.

The spiritual fire of a George Herbert or a Mother Teresa is what is needed to change a world searching for a spiritual-ethical vision of evolution. Evolution, it must be remembered, means unfolding, an unfolding toward the Good through the progressive realization of life's spiritual potential. We unfold by becoming good. Evolution thus means that the scientist must renounce his present *mésalliance* with animals not only because of his kinship with them but also because science is destined to become spiritualized. And as it moves in this direction, the scientist will have to look upon other sentient beings with increasing compassion and love. Evolving man, being a moral agent, must make the ethical choice to refrain from killing and exploiting other animals. In doing so, his moral argument and language will become lovelier and lovelier until at last it will, in truth, become holy and elevated, in accordance with his growing participation in the human-divine relation.

To sum up, the rational humanism on which *Animals, Men and Morals* is based seems too narrow an evolutionary perspective to bring about a permanent betterment of the man-animal relation. This conviction does not in any way imply a wholly negative evaluation of the book. As mentioned at the beginning of this chapter, *Animals, Men and Morals* is a philosophical revolt against the immoral actions of modern biology and medicine, and that, by any standard, is a long step forward. Scathing rational critique of this kind is perhaps what is first required to rouse animal experimenters out of their ethical apathy and the world out of its unthinking submission to the tyranny of biological progress. In an age which has little use for the divine, rational humanists who are concerned with the moral problem of experimental animals see as the ultimate solution their replacement by alternative methods of biological research. They are of course doing their bit to reduce the unnecessary suffering of creation. Yet as a friend, commenting upon their solution, wisely remarked:

> Perhaps its value lies in the fact that it helps to erode the
> false viewpoints and to drive out the worst experimenters, by
> speaking more in their own language, so to say, thus taking
> them forward one step at a time. They could not jump
> straightaway from the attitude to which they have been conditioned, the "reification" of living beings, to use Erich Fromm's
> term, to the idea of a spiritual ascent, and the fact that the underlying reality of life is divine. In time they will have to come to it,
> so those ideas have to be held out for those who can reach up
> to them.[13]

Let us hope that the revolt of the philosophers will help to make the world, themselves included, more open to the spiritual forces impinging upon us, so that all of us may more clearly perceive what there is to reach for.

Notes

1. S. Godlovitch, R. Godlovitch, and J. Harris, eds., *Animals, Men and Morals: An Enquiry into the Maltreatment of Non-Humans* (London: Victor Gollancz, 1971).

2. *Ibid.*, Introduction, p. 7.

3. P. Corbett, "Postscript," in *Animals, Men and Morals*, p. 232.

4. R. Godlovitch, "Animals and Morals," in *Animals, Men and Morals*, p. 172.

5. L. White, "The Historical Roots of Our Ecologic Crisis," *Science* 155 (1967): 1203-07.

6. R. Ryder, "Experiments on Animals," in *Animals, Men and Morals*, p. 79.

7. M. Peters, "Nature and Culture," in *Animals, Men and Morals*, p. 230.

8. B. Brophy, "In Pursuit of a Fantasy," in *Animals, Men and Morals*, p. 126.

9. R. Ryder, "Experiments on Animals," in *Animals, Men and Morals*, p. 80.

10. A. Quiller-Couch, ed., *The Oxford Book of English Verse, 1250-1918*, new ed. (Oxford: Clarendon Press, 1939), p. 303.

11. I. Walton, *The Lives of John Donne, Sir Henry Wotton, Richard Hooker, George Herbert, and Robert Sandersen,* World's Classics (London: Oxford University Press, 1927), p. 305.

12. M. Muggeridge, *Noget Skønt for Gud* [Something Beautiful for God], trans. G. Egebjerg (Copenhagen: Kristeligt Dagblads Forlag, 1971).

13. Winifred E. Whiteman, personal correspondence.

9

A New Approach to Animal Experimentation

There seems to be a real need to take stock of the opposing forces at work in animal welfare circles. If the problem of animal experimentation is to be satisfactorily solved, these diverging lines of thought must be brought into harmonious accord. Although European and American animal welfare societies basically agree that animal experimentation is immoral and defies the ethical teaching of Christian doctrine, most of them have little faith in the dissemination of religious sentiment or the efficacy of prayer. The spiritual character and the quiet, gentle idealism of the purely religious attitude seems to them inadequate. In their burning idealism to right a terrible wrong, nonreligious societies advocate what they believe to be more active, realistic measures. In doing so, their joint efforts are weakened by internal strife—the natural consequence of seeing the problem of animal experimentation from widely different perspectives. In this attempt to elucidate the problem from still another perspective, I wish in no way to disparage their idealistic and untiring efforts to eliminate animal suffering in the laboratory. I wish rather to persuade all animal protection societies, religious and nonreligious alike, that at this particular moment in human history they have a rare opportunity not only to further the cause but to do good over and beyond it, and that it would be folly to pass it by.

There are three conflicting views about animal experimentation. Anti-vivisectionists are split into two main camps engaged in a raging controversy over the best means to bring about enactment of legislation to protect the increasing number of sentient animals used in the laboratory. One group hopes to awaken public opinion to the necessity of immediate and total abolition of animal experimentation, while the other group, believing that realization of this proposal is hopeless, advocates a policy of partial reform in the hope that enactment of piecemeal legislation will result in total abolition at some later period. A third group is basing its appeal directly to scientists in the hope of persuading them to replace the laboratory animal by a more exact methodology involving the use of tissue and organ cultures, mathematical models, and computers. Although these groups are by no means mutually exclusive, their views as to the most effective measures are so fundamentally distinct that their members may be characterized respectively as "inflexible," "piecemeal," and "scientific" abolitionists.

It must be remembered that both the inflexible and the piecemeal abolitionists, while also promoting alternative methods of research, depend primarily upon arousing public opinion to bring about enactment of the desired legislation, while the scientific abolitionists, working more directly with scientists, are far less dependent upon the public and wholly independent of lawmaking. There is another fundamental difference. The inflexible and piecemeal abolitionists are not officially concerned with the fate of biological or medical research but only with the fate of the animals that research employs; their goal is to eliminate the sufferings of the laboratory animal, preferably by making it obsolete. The goal of the scientific abolitionists is more inclusive: they aim both to eliminate animal experimentation and to facilitate scientific progress. Therefore, they appeal to the highly developed competitive spirit of the scientist to persuade him to "upgrade and update his activities" by new methods, lest his more progressive colleagues come first with new discoveries. Their persuasion is thus scientific, their support of scientific advance by new methods is unconditional, and their chance of reducing the number of laboratory animals is excellent. In a scientific age, in which the world is still very much under the spell of the never ending stream of scientific and technological triumphs, animal welfare societies who work to foster still bigger and better research projects are obviously much more likely to succeed than those who center their efforts upon the enactment of

legislation restricting the activities of the scientists. Organized biology
and medicine seem to have no choice but (1) to enter into friendly
cooperation with those who favor the expansion and speeding up of research, (2) to be on guard against those who, indifferent to the further
progress of biology and medicine, try to persuade the public that the
scientific methodology which has been responsible for the amazing
biological and medical breakthroughs of the past decade be condemned
and outlawed, and (3) to regard as a kind of joke, hardly to be taken
seriously, the intrusion into their domain of religious and spiritual
authority.

If, then, scientific abolition has the best chance of succeeding—and
to judge from its recent reports there is a growing interest among biologists
and medical scientists in more exact and reliable methods—should not all
those who are fighting animal experimentation follow the lead of the
scientific abolitionists?

I do not think so. However sincere and well-meaning they are, and
however great their immediate chances of helping animals, their program
is based upon a failure to recognize the basic issue at stake and will thus
not bring lasting benefit either to animals or man. It cannot be right by
any standard to give our unconditional blessing to the unrestricted advance
of biology and medicine when we know what biologists and medical scientists have already accomplished and what they are planning. In an age
that has witnessed such life-degrading scientific achievements as organ
transplantation, the artificial postponement of death by deep-freezing,
and biological warfare, and which contemplates such horrors as the
biological control of human breeding and behavior and a pharmacological
shortcut to spiritual maturity, it seems incredible that anyone working
for a better world should give a carte blanche to biology and medicine to
continue to do all they can do. What is called for is surely the exact antithesis: to convince the biologist and medical scientist of the necessity of
self-restraint in his methods and his aims and of knowing when to stop.
No one actively fighting animal experimentation can any longer afford
to shut his eyes to the direction that biology and medicine are taking.
Indifference as well as support will only retard the renewal of the scientific conscience which is bound to come. The present scientific conscience, this ultimate development of anthropocentric humanism, must
give way to a humanism which allows the scientific age to become moral.
We cannot attempt to spare animals by encouraging man's present un-

righteousness and immorality to run riot. We must attempt to spare animals by helping scientists and ourselves—and all humanity with us—to at least some semblance of spiritual maturity. What can human evolution otherwise mean?

Consider the much publicized research on the disembodied brains of dogs and monkeys being carried out in the United States by Robert White. As most of us know, the details of his experiments are so horrifying that they seem to reach the limits of scientific depravity. It is not only the spectacle of a man deliberately reducing a living animal first to a clean skull on a body and then to a detached brain, but also his statement that so long as he maintains the isolated brain alive, it "displays a remarkable retention of inherent electrical rhythmicity that strongly suggests it may retain some semblance of 'consciousness'."[1] Let us relate these experiments to the conflicting views of the animal welfare societies.

They show first of all that a valid criterion for pain and suffering in the laboratory animal no longer exists. There can presumably be no physical pain in White's reduced creatures, since their nerves have been severed, but no one knows what kind of mental pain they may experience. As has been rightly asked, "What dreams may come to a disembodied brain, and what pain, that the mute organ is unable to express?" Robert White would like to discover the answer. He has not yet learned that there are some things a man ought not to know. His experiments also necessitate a revision of our ideas about anesthesia as a panacea for the laboratory animal. Electrical measurements of brain activity can be made at all degrees of anesthesia. Such experiments will continue, regardless of what legislation relating to anesthesia is enacted, for these scientists, it must be remembered, are out to study consciousness. Why? Ultimately, so they tell us, to improve human well-being. But let no one be deluded into believing that brain research is carried out only for the idealistic purpose of healing the mentally and physically ill. It is also carried out to "improve" the healthy.

While it is probably gross exaggeration to speak, as has Gordon Rattray Taylor,[2] of the possibility that improved tissue culture techniques will one day allow us to communicate with a brain grown from a fragment of nervous tissue, contemporary scientists, in supporting the activities of the International Brain Research Organization, tell us that the study of the brain "is central to the scientific investigation of the nature of man," since its functioning "gives us all that matters in life. . . ."[3] This outlook fails to recognize that the scientific study of man being carried out by contemporary biology and medicine is not research into final causes and therefore cannot give us what matters most—help in our moral and spiritual ascent.

Yet despite the present desire of scientists to extend the application of brain research beyond the treatment of the ill to the improvement of the healthy, the scientific abolitionists, in their condemnation of the experiments on disembodied brains, also expressed the hope that Robert White and his staff will continue their research by employing mathematical models. We should not hope anything of the kind. Men who are guilty of abominable acts which degrade the human race are hardly worthy of being encouraged to pursue their activities by other means, regardless of whether they lead to new kinds of scientifically correct medical treatment or beyond. Can anyone seriously suppose that their further scientific discoveries, made easier by our encouragement, would lead to ethically defensible applications? Can anyone seriously desire that such men, who set about "improving" the human condition on the basis of their new scientific knowledge, become our leaders? It is time for the scientific age to begin to challenge the authority of science; it is time we recognized that even the most thorough scientific investigation of man would not teach us how to choose between good and evil.

The primary duty of those who desire a better world is to try to make it moral. Animal welfare workers, in unison, have a role to play in the inevitable spiritual awakening. This will require discarding some of their cherished viewpoints and accepting others. First of all, they will have to see the problem of animal experimentation in its true perspective—the perspective of man's evolutionary ascent—and restrict their primary efforts to bringing about a moral renewal of the scientific conscience. They must strive to be completely fair and just in all of their arguments. They will have to admit, for example, that what is morally wrong can, unfortunately, be scientifically correct. They will have to admit that the suffering of laboratory animals has often led to the amelioration of human suffering, and that scientists have often acted out of idealistic desires to benefit their fellow men. But these admissions will in no way invalidate their basic claim that the human race has reached the stage where it can no longer sanction the doctrine that the ends justify the means. They will also have to renounce their unrestricted support of scientific research in any direction so long as it spares sentient animals.

In the final analysis, they will have to fight animal experimentation because they will know that life must ascend toward the Good.

Here there is need for much more positive thinking about morality. All of us must replace our negative thoughts, our ideas of fighting evil by regarding the perpetrators as criminals for whom new restrictive laws are urgently necessary. Instead we need to see them as persons who need to be awakened from their moral apathy by other means. Restrictive legislation would only prevent scientists from doing what they now want to do. Viewed from the evolutionary perspective, this is simply not good enough. In fact, it is not progress at all. What is now called for is not external restriction, but self-restriction that comes from within. The only truly desirable change for animals as well as men will be a permanent change in the mind and the heart of the scientist toward a greater compassion for life. As a very enlightened spokesman for a religious animal welfare society has said,

> It is impossible for a religious animal welfare society such as
> ours to designate itself specifically as an anti-vivisection society
> or anti-whatever it may be. We are ready to fight all abuse,
> all cruelty; but we are a society "for" more than a society
> "against"—for God and for his creatures.[4]

Not all animal welfare societies can be expected to subscribe wholly to this specifically Christian view, but all without exception can subscribe to the closely related view that their aim must be to fight *for* a moral renewal of the scientific age.

What should they then call themselves? "Moral" abolitionists? "Evolutionary" abolitionists? It does not really matter. What matters is that they will succeed. Already they have before them a rare opportunity, as yet hardly recognized: the recent development known as the academic revolt, which swept over the world questioning, challenging, and trying to transform not only the educational establishments but the whole status of modern society as well. Our social, political, economic, cultural, and religious beliefs and institutions are being subjected to intellectual cross-examination mostly (but not entirely) by those much younger than ourselves. While most of our traditional way of life and thought is surviving the attack intact, a great deal of it is being modified or totally replaced. Yet, no matter how much we are disturbed by these changes, and no matter how much we fear and condemn the violence and the arrogant and militant means that the revolutionary forces have often employed, none of us in this monstrously immoral world can condemn their goal of renewal and reform. There is too much good in it. Those who are engaged in animal welfare work must approach and ally themselves with this good.

It may be difficult to reach at once. It often lies deeply embedded in a chaotic welter of confused thinking and questionable activity. Despite the reformers' recognition of many of the evils of modern society, they have not yet agreed on their ultimate goal. They often believe protest, demonstration, or change will suffice, regardless of its direction. Others wish specifically political, social, economic, or educational gains. One of the prime goals is to make all aspects of society more democratic; this is to forget that a still higher goal than the democratic right to choose is learning how to make the right choice. Everyone who has read even a portion of the flood of angry protests from American students against George Kennan's address "Rebels Without a Program"[5] knows that protesting students are very much concerned with moral problems, but it would be a mistake to maintain that the academic revolt is primarily a demand for moral improvement. For all its intrinsic worth, it still remains an intellectual revolt based on moral uncertainty. The result is intellectual unrest in the absence of a unifying aim.

I believe animal welfare workers could, and should, help to bring the academic revolution to what must be its ultimate conclusion: the spiritual awakening that will make the world moral. This is no hopeless dream. In our day events surprise us less and less because we all know that anything can happen, and the waxing immorality of our age makes some kind of reaction seem imminent. The answer is not an antivivisection campaign employing slogans designed to appeal to those unthinking hordes of immature youths who delight in jumping on the band wagon of academic protest to experience a bit of physical violence and intellectual or moral hysteria in company with their fellow students. Animal welfare workers should instead seek out those serious, idealistic rebels and tell them that they have, in truth, a problem for university debate on the highest academic level. They have the problem of scientific authority, as exemplified in university animal experimentation and in the increasing domination of world thought by the scientific outlook, and in the name of human evolutionary progress, they should be heard. The time could not be more opportune for them to take part in a dialogue with scientists. The teaching and research staffs of academic institutions all over the world have been bombarded by student demands for educational reforms. Professional biologists and medical scientists have been forced to consider—often for the first time—the ultimate goals and aims of their profession. An exchange of thought between those who torture animals in the name of progress and those who condemn such acts in the same name could not fail to interest the student idealist, who likes to question all kinds of authority. The animal welfare worker, who questions scientific authority, has, however, a more definite, positive goal than has the student: He desires the moral renewal of the scientific conscience and the subordination of scientific authority to that which is higher. University discussions as here envisaged could lead to the general acceptance of the view that both the scientific exploitation of sentient animals and the increasing domination of the world by the scientific outlook are morally and spiritually incompatible with the evolutionary ascent of man.

Notes

1. R. J. White, *Industrial Research* 10, no. 4 (April 1968).
2. G. R. Taylor, *The Biological Time Bomb* (London: Thames and Hudson, 1968).
3. J. C. Eccles, "The Importance of Brain Research for the Educational, Cultural, and Scientific Future of Mankind," *Perspectives in Biology and Medicine* 12, no. 1 (1968): 61-68.
4. B. Wrighton, "Au début de la societé française, à Lourdes en aôut 1968," *The Ark* 31, no. 3 (1968): 443-44.
5. G. Kennan, *Democracy and the Student Left* (London: Hutchinson, 1968).

_10

A Debate with
an Animal Experimenter

In 1969, shortly after "A New Approach to Animal Experimentation" had been published in England,[1] it came to the attention of Robert J. White, the American neurosurgeon whose experimental work on animals I had condemned in my article. He wrote at once to say among other things that he could not understand how anyone could assume that animal research is an ethical or moral problem as defined under Judaeo-Christian doctrine. In the correspondence that ensued Dr. White accepted with alacrity a proposal to publish in the United States an exchange of ideas on animal experimentation, adding that he felt "it would be wrong to limit such a discussion and presentation to just our work but that rather our purpose should be to examine in a larger sense many of the issues that you have already considered in your own publications."[2] The following is the complete exchange of ideas as it appeared in the Summer 1971 issue of the *American Scholar*.[3]

Animal Experimentation and Evolution

I should like to thank Dr. White for accepting my proposal to debate the problem of animal experimentation in contemporary biomedicine. His acceptance is particularly gracious in view of my recent critique of the methods and goals of his current neurosurgical research. Since the value of any confrontation between two minds in radical opposition is proportional to the breadth and clarity of their respective visions, we have agreed to speak from the widest evolutionary, social, ethical and religious perspectives of which we are capable.

It would be a delusion to maintain that, since animal experimentation is apparently here to stay as an aid in saving human life and reducing human suffering, the problem under debate is really no problem at all. That one of the most distinguished neurosurgeons of our time has set aside a portion of his heavily committed schedule to justify a decade of research on animals is clear evidence to the contrary. Experimental biomedicine, already feeling the impact of an intensified attack upon its methodology, is quite aware that the problem is real and hopes to silence its adversaries by defending its actions to the intellectual and ethical satisfaction of all concerned. I am convinced that this hope is futile.

Meanwhile, the use of sentient animals in laboratory experiments continues to spread all over the civilized world. This growing practice represents inevitable human progress, so we are told, because it is carried out for the good of man and because the human, by any standard, is more important than the animal. It is undeniably true that *Homo sapiens* comes first. There are, however, compelling intellectual and ethical grounds for believing that the experimental use of highly developed forms of life is actually impeding human progress and that for the sake of men, as much as for animals, the practice must be ended. The final answer to the question of whether to retain or abolish the sentient laboratory animal may require one of the most decisive choices yet made by evolving man.

Human behavior is an elective response to alternatives. Throughout man's long evolutionary history, he has been continually confronted with choices. Prehistoric man, living with lower animals in a harsh and hostile environment, was forced to make vital decisions on which his physical survival depended. Whether, in contrast to the animals, he made moral choices between good and evil because of his religious instinct and experience, we do not know.

Some six thousand years ago, when civilizations began to emerge, the human species had long since become a fixed and recognizable physical type and was well into its psychosocial phase of evolution. Unlike the long period of slow development of body and mind that preceded it, this new evolutionary stage brought a sudden expansion of human consciousness through accelerated communication and transmission of acquired knowledge, wisdom, and experience, as well as of the religious norms of human behavior. The growth and dispersion of the three great monotheistic religions laid particular stress upon ethical conduct. Men were exhorted to make choices in conformity with moral standards of good and evil that were held to be absolute and eternal divine revelations. To a large extent the expansion of the civilized consciousness has depended upon the recognition that the conscience, guided by its traditional religious heritage, was able to distinguish between good and evil and was thus obliged to make moral choices. Civilized man, as the historical record shows, has exhibited the extremes of conformity and nonconformity to this obligation. Yet, however great his range of ethical conduct, he has, until recently, been fully aware that he had a functional conscience.

Man in the twentieth century is still very much in the psychosocial stage of human evolution, which differs, however, from all preceding periods in the nature of its interplay between consciousness and conscience. The organized acquisition of new biological knowledge and its rapid communication and application are expanding human consciousness at a breathtaking rate. The faster the pace, the greater the number of ethical choices to be made. But in a predominantly godless world where most civilizations no longer take seriously religion or the human-divine relation, the sacred criteria for choosing between good and evil are largely neglected. Although standards of decent human behavior and recognition of what are called Christian virtues have never been uprooted, the contemporary ideal is, in fact, a free conscience, where any ethical standard and conduct is as good as the next. Democracy, equality, and freedom from traditional authority at all costs! The modern conscience, breaking with the past and denying the existence of absolute and eternal criteria to guide its choices, often considers itself autonomous and infallible but is in truth pitifully immature and undernourished. Conforming mainly to the authority of expanding scientific knowledge about the reality of nature, it has increasing difficulty in function and operation. Scientists themselves are beginning to experience these difficulties. Aware of their social responsibility and not knowing how to meet it, some are working to keep society better informed of the implications of their results and, in turn, to obtain outside aid in guiding the further advance of biology and medicine. At the same time, an increasing number of men and women, bewildered by contemporary progress, are experiencing failure of conscience; they no longer dare to choose. The result is a morally chaotic world that is becoming an almost unbearable place in which to live and die.

What seems to be most lacking is a unified sense of rectitude about what we are doing and where we are going. Most of us have experienced periods of acute helplessness and frustration in the face of a seemingly uncontrollable scientific advance that is sweeping life toward an unknown goal. Our great mistake is to suppose that this biological and technological progress is synonymous with the main path of human evolution. It is not. It is only a sidepath—but one that life may have had to experience in order better to distinguish good from evil. Ever since *Homo sapiens* left the main road for the attractions of scientific knowledge and power, he has been increasingly unable to find the happiness he seeks. Nor can he ever find on a sidepath leading away from the stream of evolution to which he belongs the inner joy and peace that are his birthright.

The main path for evolving human life leads toward ultimate reality: true human evolution, regardless of what secular and scientific humanists think, is a spiritual ascent toward the Good and is based upon the interplay between consciousness and conscience. But with so much human energy being spent on expanding the consciousness alone, we obstinately maintain that this *must* be life's predestined path because there is no other. At the same time we are uneasy in the presentiment that it may be leading us to our final doom. Having lived for years with the theoretical possibility of nuclear suicide or the transformation of *Homo sapiens* into a dehumanized scientific robot, and being quite unable to prevent the horrors of unnecessary war and starvation, we cannot rid ourselves of the fear of extinction known to our primitive forefathers. Far more knowledgeable and sophisticated than they, but far less able to sense the evolutionary rhythm of life and death and to accept the natural corruption of living matter and the incorruptibility of the spirit, we have become frantically preoccupied with ensuring the physical survival of both the species and the individual. Our consternation is intensified because we are still guided by a sick scientific conscience that lacks sufficient strength and resolution to make moral choices.

Life, now faced with decisive evolutionary alternatives, has need of all its resources of mind, spirit, and intuition to make the required choices. No longer can it allow its further development to be guided by a conscience that bases its decisions solely on scientific knowledge.

Most biomedical scientists appear to be students of life who have not yet seen it whole. This implies no wholesale condemnation of their perspective. Their time-honored goals of understanding, aiding, and saving life remain noble ones, and their motives certainly include love for their fellow men and sympathy and compassion for their sufferings. Opponents of vivisection, blinded by its horrors, tend to ignore this fact, but it is unfair to scientists to do so. Modern vivisectors are not criminals for whom new restrictive laws are needed, but human beings whose conscience needs to be awakened from its moral apathy. For with their increasing power over life and death and their belief that science must do all it can, they are allowing many of their expanding goals to become as ethically shoddy as their means.

Let us first ask the biomedical scientists who depend upon laboratory animals why they consider human life so precious that it must be saved at all costs. They would better serve mankind by giving more thought to the criterion of life and less to that of death. They must tell us what all their feverish biological activity is really for. They must make absolutely clear and unambiguous why they are compelled to penetrate the secrets of life down to the minutest scientific detail and to apply their knowledge before its full implications are understood. So far their only answer seems to be that human progress demands that life's intellectual potentials be realized so that we can all live longer and suffer less. *But the realization of life's spiritual potentials, whereby the operation of a healthy conscience could place human behavior in harmonious accord with the mainstream of evolution, is ignored by these modern life specialists.* In proclaiming that the "best" state is the longest possible life of a healthy body and mind, they intensify man's unnatural fear of the struggle, suffering, and preparation for death that is necessary for the spiritual maturation of the species.

The failure of modern biomedicine to see life whole has resulted in confused goals and paradoxical behavior. We reduce life's rate of propagation by mechanical means and destroy with little compunction unwanted human embryos so that we may give better care to the fewer individuals remaining. But modern medicine is not satisfied with ensuring a minimum of medical aid to all. Medical care now embraces resuscitation by drugs and machines to delay the natural termination of aged lives, together with various kinds of euthanasia to put abrupt ends to lives of suffering. Medical care prolongs the life of a patient by replacing a defective organ

with a fresh one snatched from a dying patient regarded mainly as a donor
Medical care embraces such vast possibilities for the treatment of human
ills and the permanent alteration of the human body that we already have
plans for the surgical, pharmacological, and genetic regulation of human
behavior. No longer content with treating the sick and, in fact, often
morally at sea as how far treatment should go, some biomedical scientists
are issuing scientific directives for the ethical improvement of the healthy.

That many of the goals of contemporary science are highly questionable is already obvious to those scientists who are feeling the conscience
crisis within biology and medicine, but so far they have remained singu-
larly passive with respect to scientific methodology. There has been no
organized protest from within biomedicine against the dogma that the
advance of science justifies all conceivable means, even to the infliction
of agony upon lower forms of sentient life. In contrast, antivivisectionists, who are rightly intensifying their attack upon biomedical methodology,
remain uncritical of scientific goals. In their desire to rescue the laboratory
animal, they are now advocating more efficient alternative methods of
research and are thus indiscriminately encouraging research regardless of
its ultimate purpose. The problem of animal experimentation cannot be
satisfactorily solved by supporting means or ends of dubious morality.
Evolving life needs to be seen from a still higher perspective. Its conscience is at stake.

Animals, lacking, so far as we know, conscience and knowledge of the
Good, strive to realize their limited potentials by choosing what is best
for their survival and for a life in harmony with their environment. Men,
aware of the spiritual realm, have quite different strivings. Moral choice
between good and evil is a uniquely human responsibility that spiritually
elevates man above the rest of creation. His relation to the lower sentient
life at his mercy then becomes vital for his further ascent. So far his
enormous intellectual, emotional, and spiritual superiority has not
eradicated his anthropocentric view that human evolution must progress
by the unrestrained exploitation of subhuman life.

Despite the wishful thinking of many antivivisectionists, the silent
suffering and the anguished screams of laboratory animals *have* saved
human lives, reduced human suffering, and prevented and cured diseases.
But this welcome boon to mankind is not the essence of human progress
or evolution. It is simply care and maintenance of physical life. That
human ills can be effectively ameliorated through prior cruelty to animals

is true from a self-centered point of view. From the evolutionary perspective, where the interrelation of all forms of sentient life comes into view, progressive well-being depends upon the highest form protecting and caring for the lower with compassion, mercy, and understanding. Innocent life has rights that we, who are not innocent, have not yet understood. But, one might say, if the spiritual potential of physical life is to be realized, surely it is only common sense to use all possible means to maintain individual life as long as possible. Granted, insofar as such means are conducive to spiritual enlightenment. The continued acceptance, however, of immoral means by doctors and patients disfigures their goals, increases their ethical apathy and insensitivity, and becomes at last a gross deflection from the Good toward which all human life is evolving.

Our present knowledge of anatomy, physiology, genetics, and pathology cannot, of course, be unlearned. But regardless of the true benefits accruing from its application in medicine, we have no justification whatever for continuing to wrest still more knowledge out of lower sentient life by torture, mutilation, and death.

All the biomedical knowledge we now possess has not in any way made man more moral. And since much of it was acquired through the agony of countless millions of innocent lives, and since *Homo sapiens* would have survived without it, its acquisition has no doubt done more evolutionary harm than good. For man comes first—and he has degraded his potential and retarded its realization by more than five hundred years of scientific atrocities against animals. The scientific age still sees no valid reason for abolishing this practice. But abolish it we must, because evolving human life puts increasing demands upon the self-restraint and self-sacrifice of its members. Man evolves through the suffering and death of individuals. To choose to oppose these inevitabilities through the continued infliction of cruelty upon animals is evolutionary stagnation, if not regression.

In Denmark the first chair of behavioral physiology was recently established for Dr. A. Mosfeldt Laursen, whose experimental investigations of mental diseases and insight into the handling of laboratory animals have gained wide recognition. Although there is no general agreement about the therapeutic value of violent mutilation and injury of the brains of the mentally ill, Dr. Laursen's animal experiments have convinced him that surgically induced brain lesions can be effective in eliminating some of the fear and terror so often associated with mental diseases.[4] Through the widely used method of implanting electrodes into specific areas of the brains of anesthetized animals, he has studied the conscious responses of cats to doses of electric current varying from weakly stimulating to permanently injurious.[5] At the same time, he has developed special methods for keeping his laboratory animals relaxed and trusting in order to attain the best experimental results. I would say that any "expert in behavioral problems" who chooses to gain the confidence and trust of healthy animals so that he can mutilate and torment them shows a deplorable lack of understanding of human behavior. As one of Dr. Laursen's own countrymen, P. Agersted, so well put it in challenging the motivation of animal experimenters:

> Animal suffering benefits mankind. What is done is done for
> the sake of humanity. Apparently none of these scientists
> realize that they could just as well use this motive for
> stopping painful animal experimentation. . . . For many, many
> more people than is generally supposed suffer at the thought of
> what goes on in laboratories, and still more would become ex-
> tremely agitated and uneasy in their minds if they knew of the
> atrocities of the extreme forms of animal experimentation.[6]

Surely this thought, centering attention upon the increasingly intolerable *mésalliance* between contemporary scientists and sentient animals, deserves serious consideration by all those who are engaged in the prevention and cure of mental diseases.

Dr. White's contributions to neurological research have added the mammalian brain to the other organs that have been successfully isolated and transplanted. Although he does not claim the feasibility of transplanting the human brain, he hopes someday to maintain it in an isolated state, and he expects this scientific feat, together with his animal experiments, will lead to a more effective treatment of diseases of the brain and to a greater understanding of its nature and function. Despite some opposition to his work, he enthusiastically carries on in the conviction that his studies represent inevitable biological achievements. With equal conviction, I believe that they are not biological achievements at all, because any true study of life, being a part of the spiritual ascent of evolution, must be moral in both means and ends. I further believe that no human achievement in the vast region of mind, soul, consciousness, and subconsciousness can be expected except through the directives of a spiritually enlightened conscience.

Lacking these directives, White's compassion for human mental suffering and his pursuit of scientific knowledge of mental phenomena have led to flagrant interference with the consciousness of animal life and a lamentable increase in the total suffering of creation. He has produced living chimeras—disembodied canine brains transplanted within the carotid-jugular circulation of recipient dogs, and disembodied monkey brains kept alive and functioning in an isolated state.[7] The scores of remnants of mutilated creatures that he has kept alive in the laboratory have made the world a worse place for all of us to live in. In choosing his goals and his means, he has denied his evolutionary responsibility to distinguish good from evil and has ignored his faith. For whatever his final authority for his choices, it cannot have been Christianity.

Dr. White has forgotten that the purest form of Christianity and all other higher religions preach mercy, love, nonviolence, and gentleness and that these qualities have been the hallmarks of mankind's spiritual leaders in their relations with sentient life. He is apparently unaware of the growing number of Catholics who are confidently working to end the church's silence on animal experimentation. They know that she cannot be expected "to sanction everything she has not yet formally condemned."[8] Despite such efforts, the perspectives and possibilities of our scientific age continue to blind many Christians to the incongruities between the moral core of their religion and the decisions of science. By cutting ourselves off from the superior knowledge of our spiritual heritage we fail to see life whole and continue to flounder in ethical confusion and decadence. A theocentric reaction is bound to set in. The intellectual revolt of the young may already presage a spiritual renaissance in which the summit of evolving life will no longer tolerate scientific atrocities against its lower forms. Man is an evolutionary as well as a social animal, and evolution is not a matter of chance. Man needs "to think with the whole of his past."[9] He must at last see, with Plotinus, that as creation aspires toward the Good, it needs increasing unity and harmony in its relationships.

Transplantation biology is concerned with what science considers to be inevitable evolutionary relationships of creatures and their parts. It has partially surmounted the formidable natural obstacles of immunological intolerance and rejection through the suffering of untold numbers

of animals. While experimental fusions of their living parts to intact
animals have received publicity, it is not generally known outside professional circles that much of the practical success of transplantation
biology stems from studies of the mutual physiological effects of the
surgical fusion of whole animals in pairs. This procedure, parabiosis
(life alongside life), is now a routine laboratory technique and is sometimes even extended "to unite several animals in enforced togetherness."[10]
Accepted as a biological necessity, laboratory parabiosis is, in fact, a
biological outrage and a violation of the natural relationships of living
creatures. In the name of evolutionary sanity, let us leave these things
and center our attention upon those relations that can be meaningful
for creation.

For the continued existence of mammalian species, biological evolution requires the sexual association of individuals in pairs. The further
Homo sapiens advances into his psychosocial phase of evolution, the
greater his need for relationships other than those based upon animal
sexuality. As it has been wisely said, "centuries of carnal embracement,
yet man is no nearer to understanding man."[11] Our crying need at the
moment is for a relationship that will give all men, regardless of birth,
education, or faith, a unified sense of rectitude in their endeavors. We
need to come together to communicate more perfectly and to understand that, however many imperfections, sins, and egoistic motives and
desires we possess in common, we remain most firmly related by the
highest that is within us—by those sparks of love, compassion, goodness,
and righteousness that come from the spiritual realm. If these divine sparks
were to coalesce, we would be able to make right choices, and the inter-
relations of man with man, and man with animal, would be in accord
with the Good to which we are being drawn. Psychosocial evolution is
now demanding the emergence of spiritual parabiosis—life alongside
life—with the highest caring for the lower with the same mercy, tender-
ness, and understanding it bestows upon itself.

Evolving life can therefore no longer tolerate the biological injustice
of inflicting agony upon animals to ameliorate and prolong the physical
existence of human lives. Brief respites from suffering and death made
possible by the ruthlessness of scientists against lower life contribute
nothing whatever to the spiritual ascent of mankind. Evolving life has
need instead of gentle souls like St. Francis and Gandhi to show us how
to come together to live lives of nonviolence, in joy and peace with the

whole of sentient creation. For the meek, strengthened and made wise
in their decisions by divine sanction and their spiritual heritage, *shall*
inherit the earth.

The choice to abolish the sentient laboratory animal is an evolutionary
inevitability and a moral imperative. Were Dr. White to join the forces that
are already striving to bring it about, true biological achievement would
be his.

Antivivisection: The Reluctant Hydra by **Robert J. White**

The humanity which would prevent human suffering is a deeper
and truer humanity than the humanity which would save pain
or death in the animal.

—Charles W. Eliot

The quotation above from that distinguished intellectual and former
Harvard University president, written decades ago, continues to crystallize
clearly the basic position of medical science toward the employment of
animals in research and teaching. I would state it more simply: the alleviation of human suffering justifies the sacrifice of lower animals. Because
this statement is as valid today as it was then, and yet has so little impact
on the public conscience, I am almost reluctant to shed the mantle of
clinical and professional detachment and take up the cudgels against that
ill-defined, elusive Hydra—the antivivisection movement. To a degree, my
inertia is also derived from my conviction that medical science has always
seemed to assume a low-profile posture in justifying the utilization of
lower animals for research and education (as it has so often done with
other public health issues); it has invariably waited until one of those
vigorous cyclic antivivisection campaigns, using the most advanced techniques in news management, has reached its apogee before attempting to
combat the pernicious effects on public and congressional opinion. And
then, unfortunately, it has employed almost exclusively its own scientific
journals as the instruments for presenting its position to an already prej-
udiced audience. While the scientific community has lobbied successfully
in congressional committees against restrictive legislation directed at medical research, it has neglected to present to the American public its case
for the continuation of animal experimentation with sufficient force and
clarity to eliminate the ever present danger of government control of biological research through the limitation of animal availability and experimental

design. The intelligent citizenry of this country must be educated not only regarding the already multiple advantages of medical research but, what is more important, the absolute necessity of continued proliferation of biological research.

Man, in a sense, has unwittingly painted himself into an ecological corner, and without the opportunity of biological testing in lower animals he may be unable to extract himself from his polluted environment. Acknowledging man's equally wanton disregard of animal life, as he has slowly but inevitably poisoned this planet (to say nothing of our careless attrition of individual species to the point of extinction), I do not intend that this essay should be, by any stretch of the imagination, construed as an indictment of the broad humanitarian movement; quite the contrary, for many of its objectives, particularly in the ecological field, are not only most laudable but fully subscribed to by many within the scientific community. Rather, my proprietary interest here is to emphasize need for animal experimentation in neurological research. As a consequence, my confrontation is exclusively with those societies, collectively known as the antivivisection movement, whose single unifying principle is the almost religiously held tenet that it is morally wrong to use lower animals in medical research and teaching. Professor Saul Bevolson, in tracing the historical development of the antivivisection movement in this country, demonstrates that the movement, while spawned and nurtured by the humanitarian establishment, is, in reality, separate in organizational structure. Dr. Maurice Visscher has felt the necessity of characterizing the antivivisection movement as a spectrum with certain gradations of moral and ethical absoluteness with regard to man's right to sacrifice lower animal life for scientific knowledge and medical advancement. Thus, this philosophical spectrum is anchored at one end by the abolitionist who sees no justification under any circumstances for the employment of the nonhuman animal for scientific study, and at the other extreme by the regulatory antivivisectionists who would place external controls (obviously governmental) on medical research by limiting the type and number of animals utilized, and demanding review of the experimental methods with particular reference to purpose and duplication. Make no mistake, in spite of their highly publicized concern for the housing and veterinary care of research animals, the true thrust of these organizations is directed toward the eventual elimination from medical investigation and research of all nonhuman subjects.

As a concerned scientist and as a practicing neurosurgeon, I am simply unable to plumb the depths of a philosophy that places such a premium on animal life even at the expense of human existence and improvement. It would appear that this preoccupation with the alleged pain and suffering of the animals used in medical research may well represent, at the very least, social prejudice against medicine or, more seriously, true psychiatric aberrations. Regardless of the social or psychiatric shortcomings of the antivivisectionists, it has always amazed me that the biological profession is forced into a position of periodically preparing defense briefs on animal experimentation (unfortunately appearing only in scientific journals) as a result of the Herculean efforts of these societies, while the meat-packing industry, which slaughters millions of animals annually, seldom if ever finds it necessary today to defend its activities.

As I write this article, I relive my vivid experiences of yesterday when I removed at operation a large tumor from the cerebellum and brain stem of a small child. This was a surgical undertaking that would have been impossible a few decades ago, highly dangerous a few years ago, but is today, thanks to extensive experimentation on the brains of lower animals, routinely accomplished with a high degree of safety.

The human brain is the most complex, the most superbly designed structure known. Before it, all human scientific and engineering accomplishment pales. Our understanding of its intimate functions, such as intelligence and memory, is extremely limited. Even the more easily characterized capabilities of sensory reception and motor activity are only now being elucidated. Without the use of the experimental animal, particularly a species whose central nervous system is similar to that of man, we simply cannot decipher the mysteries of cerebral performance. Without this knowledge of brain function, we will never be able to develop new and improved methods for the treatment of neurological diseases, so many of which now must be placed in an incurable category. Even today the surgery of the brain is in its infancy, and on many occasions the critical tolerance between success and failure in human cerebral operations is narrow. Yet this gap can be significantly increased through properly oriented research. These serious considerations moved Dr. Harvey Cushing, the eminent brain surgeon, to remark, "Those who oppose the employment of animals for such purposes . . . leave us the only alternative of subjecting our fellow man, as a lesser creature, to our first crude manipulations."

In a more personal sense, I have a score of my own to settle with these misguided societies that for decades have been attempting to confuse the public about the true purpose of animal experimentation by depicting the medical and veterinary scientist as the most cruel of men, seeking every opportunity to visit pain and suffering on defenseless laboratory creatures. The more aggressive of these organizations, which are committed to the total abolition of animal research, have recently installed me as their *célèbre terrible,* monster-scientist, perpetrator of abominable crimes. And thus I join the distinguished company of such legendary scientists as Claude Bernard, Louis Pasteur, Lord Lister, Victor Horsley, and Alfred Blalock! Dr. Catherine Roberts herself has already prejudged my work and me by earnestly stating, "The details of his experiments are so horrifying that they seem to reach the limits of scientific depravity." Fortunately, my researches do not stand alone in her sweeping condemnation of medical science, for in the same article she described organ transplantation and profound hypothermia as "life-degrading scientific achievements." I am sure that she, as well as other staunch antivivisectionists, would be willing to include in this list: open-heart surgery, control of infection, surgical metabolism, and shock studies, since literally thousands of animals were sacrificed in the development of these life-saving techniques. In a sense, condemnation of these achievements amounts to condemnation of the most meaningful advances in medicine and surgery in the last thirty years.

What of our own experiments, which have evoked such vituperative treatment at the hands of the antivivisection press? Here are the "shocking" details.

In 1964, we were successful for the first time in medical history in totally isolating the subhuman primate brain outside of its body and sustaining it in a viable state by connecting it with the vascular system of another monkey or with a mechanical perfusion circuit that incorporated engineering units designed to perform the functions of the heart, lungs, and kidneys while simultaneously circulating blood to and from the brain. We were overjoyed, since scientists had attempted to construct such a model surgically for the last one hundred years without success. As late as the 1930s Dr. Alexis Carrel, the Nobel laureate, with the collaboration of Colonel Charles Lindberg, had been able to support the viability of almost all body organs in an isolated state with simple perfusion equipment that forcefully propelled nonsanguineous nutrient fluid through the blood vessels of the separated tissue. Only the nervous system, because of its complexity and delicacy, escaped their magnificent scientific capabilities. Parenthetically, it should be mentioned that Carrel had his problems with the antivivisectionists of his time.

With further refinements in operative technique, perfusion/structural design and blood processing, we were able to demonstrate normalization of intrinsic electrical activity and metabolic performance of the isolated monkey brain for extended periods of time. We now had the methodology to unlock many of the subtle mysteries surrounding cerebral function that heretofore had resisted all attempts at solution because of the difficulties of neurogenically and vascularly isolating the entire brain *in situ.* What is perhaps of greater importance in terms of understanding and treating neurological disease, we could now easily impose on our brain models abnormal clinical states such as infarction, circulatory arrest, infection, and malignancy with absolute control of environmental circumstances and with a real hope of elucidating their effects on brain tissue alone. Once the characteristics of these states were defined, these same models would be of inestimable value in developing new and meaningful therapeutic regimens aimed at eliminating these clinical disease states.

As we set about exploring and documenting the capabilities of the isolated brain in an atmosphere not unlike the conditions described for the fifth level in Michael Crichton's book, *The Andromeda Strain,* we gradually became aware of a growing public interest in the preparation, an interest that intensified after our success in transplanting the brain in the experimental animal in 1966. A succession of competent medical journalists visited our laboratories and subsequently prepared a number of highly informative and reasoned articles dealing with our investigative efforts. I personally have always approved of this kind of interchange. In spite of our best efforts to assist in the preparation of the textual material, however, an unreviewed and unauthorized article written by Orianna Fallachi appeared in *Look* (November 28, 1967), in which this well-known interviewer attempted to humanize the monkey by depicting it as a small child. This single article (or lengthy excerpts from it) has now enjoyed worldwide publication and translation. Besides her treatment of the monkey as a small patient, Miss Fallachi's detailed description of the preoperative preparation (including the induction of anesthesia) and her vivid portrayal of the isolated brain model apparently struck a sympathetic and responsive chord among the membership of the antivivisection societies in this country as well as throughout the world. Like Mary Shelley, Miss Fallachi had created a Doctor Frankenstein and an up-to-date monster, at least as far as the antivivisectionists are concerned. True, this tale has its amusing—if not outlandish—elements, but its overall effect is tragic, since Miss Fallachi's creations are not only as factitious as Mary Shelley's, but in reality the direct antithesis of the Frankenstein legend.

Admittedly, the nervous system is the most difficult body organ system to investigate, not only because of its intrinsic complexity but also because, somewhere within its billions of cells and fibers, pain and suffering are represented. For this reason, the neurophysiologist is, on occasion, unable to avoid producing some discomfort in his animal when he is specifically studying pain in any or all of its complicated ramifications within the neural system. Actually, the isolated brain model is completely denervated by virtue of the fact that all pain pathways have been surgically severed; consequently, this brain model enjoys a completely painless existence by all known physiological criteria.

Since the isolated brain is incapable of perceiving these modalities, one can only wonder at the creditability and objectivity of the antivivisection prose, which has been so uncomplimentary in its descriptions of this subhuman research model.

The nervous system—the repository, so to speak, of pain and suffering, but, more important, of the qualities and capabilities that uniquely distinguish an organism—is most critical to this discussion since direct surgical or electronic manipulation or chemical modification of this system in the experimental animal offers to the antivivisectionist the most logical area for condemnation of biological research. At issue here would not be the indiscriminate infliction of pain and suffering (these experiments are basically free of pain), but rather purposeful alteration of the innate behavior of the organism in order to advance our knowledge of emotion, memory, and intelligence, with the final phase again being the interpretive extrapolation of this information to the human and to human mental functioning. As yet we have heard little from the antivivisectionists regarding the inappropriateness of these experiments with reference to animal welfare. It may be, however, that their historical fixation on the "twin sins" of pain and suffering in neurological investigation has blinded them to the realities of modern experimental research. Just as I must vigorously dissent from the antivivisection philosophy (and the belief of certain physiologists) that the production of some pain, no matter how minimal, is never justified, so too I cannot conceive of the development of a valid argument opposing behavioral research, if only for the simple reason that mental illness cannot successfully be treated until mental performance is understood.

To circumvent the employment of nonhuman animals in medical research, the antivivisection movement has recently turned for assistance to science itself. It has been suggested that many of the physiological and biochemical studies conducted on animals could be programmed for computer analysis and thereby reduce and eventually eliminate the need for the living experimental preparations. Actually, computers, since their inception, have been used in biological research and, with their growing complexity, have markedly extended the frontiers of investigation. If anything, computer availability has contributed to the increasing demand for animals for research.

An equally unrealistic approach to the elimination of animal experimentation has been based on the cell culture work of Professor Sureyat Aygun, director of the Bacteriological Institute of the University of Ankara, and a leading antivivisection proponent. The theory here is that, with proper culture techniques, cells or embryos could eventually be developed into entire organ systems. The technological advances and expense necessary to accomplish such a program to replace present-day animal research facilities are unachievable. There is no more need to seek alternatives to the use of lower animals for medical research than to search for nonflesh substitutions for meat in our diets. While it may well be true that ecological "facts of life" could eventually require the elimination of certain endangered species from both the laboratory and commercial market, there is nothing to suggest that some suitable species cannot be substituted. Even Dr. Albert Schweitzer recognized in his own unique philosophical scheme of things that scientific experiments with animals were necessary for the alleviation of human ills.

The American public demonstrates its overwhelming support of medical research by annually contributing millions of dollars through direct federal financing and private subscription; yet this same public is tragically unaware that progress in medical science is continually threatened by the antivivisection movement. At the urging of a small but determined group of antivivisectionists, the United States Congress is constantly considering legislation that, if enacted into law, will seriously restrict the freedom of individual scientists participating in medical research, in the same way that laws have so seriously hampered similar research in Britain. Since, through research grants to qualified individuals and institutions, the federal government provides the major financial support for medical investigation in this country, all laws affecting the conduct of such research are of paramount importance to the health of the entire citizenry. Unless American medicine and its allied biological professions cast off their mantles of detachment and undertake the responsibility of educating through established lines of communication our citizens to the necessities of medical research, the antivivisection movement may eventually win the day.

In the final analysis there is no way that I can personally resolve or even arbitrate the impasse that exists between the theology of the antivivisection movement and the immutable stance of practicality maintained by biological research, since like R. D. Guthrie, I believe that the inclusion of lower animals in our ethical system is philosophically meaningless and operationally impossible and that, consequently, antivivisection theory and practice have no moral or ethical basis.

Dr. Roberts Replies:

My thanks to Dr. White for his contribution to this debate. Since our rebuttals must be held within definite limits, I shall first point out a few misconceptions and errors of fact in his paper that are not fully covered in mine and then pass on to a more general refutation of his arguments.

1. He says that antivivisectionists are preoccupied with the "alleged" pain and suffering of laboratory animals. This statement is misleading. To allege is to assert without proof; yet biomedical journals abound in observations of experimentally inflicted pain and suffering in animals upon which antivivisectionists can base their claims.

2. He writes that behavioral research involving electrical, chemical, or surgical interference with the nervous system to acquire knowledge of animal emotion, memory and intelligence for extrapolation to human mental functioning is "basically free of pain." This statement is incorrect. Experimental alterations of animal behavior, whether for medical, pharmacological, or physiological purposes, are frequently associated with what scientists choose to call "discomfort." A. Mosfeldt Laursen's experiments on feline behavior referred to in my paper can hardly have

been painless. Electrical stimulation elicited salivation, lip-smacking, head and shoulder twitching, mewing, sniffing, hissing and gagging; intensifying the current to produce brain lesions led to apathy and diminished fright. To take another example, E. D. Weitzman and G. S. Ross, also working on the electrical manipulation of the nervous system, described with masterly objectivity the screams of tortured animals as "high-pitched vocalization" in a paper with the revealing title, "A Behavioural Method for the Study of Pain Perception in the Monkey."[12]

3. Erroneously concluding that pain and suffering tend to be absent from behavioral research, Dr. White is led into the further error that anti-vivisectionists are of the same opinion and are therefore loath to condemn it. This misconception is based on ignorance of the facts. In 1967 H. F. Harlow's psychological research on anthropoid emotion based on protracted solitary confinement of Rhesus monkeys[13] was criticized for both the suffering involved and the irrelevancy of applying the results to man.[14] Today, in this time of ecological crisis, there is a growing awareness that the suffering man inflicts upon animals comprises many forms; religious circles, in particular, are discussing the rights of animals to participate in activities natural to their kind—rights that, even with adequate food and shelter and freedom from disease and physical pain, are denied them under the artificial conditions of the laboratory. Even some biologists have protested against the cruelly frustrating confinement of livestock in factory farming but so far have characteristically failed to condemn the similar plight of the confined laboratory animal.

4. It is only surmise that antivivisectionists are generally unconcerned about the slaughter of animals for meat production. Many antivivisectionists, subsisting on a salutary fleshless diet, are actively demonstrating how unnecessary the carnivorous state is for man.

5. Although Dr. White correctly points out that antivivisectionists may differ over means and goals, he is not correct in implying that they are fully agreed that the biologist's freedom should be curtailed by legislation restricting the use of laboratory animals. Opposition to this view was raised some years ago: " . . . further restrictive legislation would only prevent many scientists from doing what they now earnestly desire to do";[15] " . . . the medical scientist who employs experimental animals will one day have acquired sufficient subjective humaneness to realize that the most desirable world, now and forever, is built upon spiritual insight—and it will then be his own sense of moral responsibility, rather

than external restriction, which will reveal to him when it is time to stop."[16] These thoughts fell upon barren ground at the time, but the intellectual upheavals of the past five years have produced a radically new mental environment more favorable to the growth and dispersal of ideas centered upon the problem of good and evil. And here we come to the basic issue under debate: the present state of the scientific conscience. With respect to biomedicine, Dr. White holds that it is in a healthy, flourishing state, in no need of improvement. I hold that it is in crying need of profound renewal and reform. His refusal to include either sentient animals or antivisection arguments in his ethical system echoes the supposedly immutable claim of established biology that its further advance depends upon the continued exploitation of subhuman life. Based upon ignorance of the evolutionary forces now at work, this claim reflects a state of conscience out of step with the new biology already in the process of creation.

Open discontent with established biology as an adequate science of life is mounting—a development closely related to our present ecological interests in the reality and potential of life in all its associated forms. The frustratingly inadequate reality of contemporary human life, pointing directly to man's unrealized potential, is leading to ever greater ethical dissatisfaction with human endeavors that seem to impede our approach toward the ultimate reality of the Good. Scientific endeavor in an ailing scientific age is naturally wide open to criticism. Recognizing that modern science is now on the defensive and sympathizing in varying degrees with the attacks upon its irrelevancy, amorality, and immorality, experimental biologists are coming together to question the automatic expansion of science, to plan worldwide moratoria on research, to weigh the threats of science against its promises, to define the scientist's moral responsibility, and to discuss scientific methods as well as goals. Some, in moral protest, are dropping out of the scientific establishment altogether. For the first time in the history of science, biologists are earnestly examining their consciences and questioning the kind of biology that Dr. White is defending. As yet, their number is small, their aims uncertain, their methods hesitant. They are nevertheless creators destined to succeed. For the creation of a new biology that sees life in terms of human values and the choice between good and evil is a part of the evolutionary ascent.

The new biologists, no longer satisfied with the supreme authority of established science, are striving for a higher ethical vision and a purer conscience than their predecessors had. They will hardly find it in the dogma that the ends justify the means, whether it be held by revolutionary colleagues intent on changing the established order by force and violence or by scientific colleagues intent on acquiring new knowledge by any effective methodology. The new biologists will be unable to approach life as did Claude Bernard, Alexis Carrel, or other scientists who chose to profane mercilessly the innate potentials of sentient beings in the belief that all biological ends and means deserve evolutionary sanction. Condemnation and rejection of such scientific ethics may not suffice for biology's complete change of mind and heart; some sort of associated regret or remorse—what the Greeks called *metanoia*—for biological violations already committed may also be required. So far animal experimenters have shown little inclination to admit that their vision and conscience have been at fault. Whether Carrel's growing religious insight finally caused him to repent his experimental research, I do not know; his mature views on the future evolution of man[17] show no more understanding of the true man-animal relation than do his very revealing early letters to Guthrie,[18] and thus express a lack of perception at variance with the new biology.

For the new biology, perceiving that the realization of man's potentials is forcing him into a new relation with subhuman life, is seeking spiritual counsel. Much of what it seeks lies in our neglected heritage of theocentric humanism where enlightened men of the past strove to know themselves and to become real through moral aspiration. The new biologists will also find spiritual truths about evolving life in unexpected contemporary places. As the theologian, G. F. Woods, has written,

> The quest for moral perfection is far more than a quest for
> private excellence. It involves the attainment of right rela-
> tionships with God and with our fellow men. And it includes
> a right relation of re-created humanity to the natural world.[19]

To secure this right relation the new biology must renounce both the Carrelian and the Teilhardian evolutionary visions of unlimited quantitative expansion of science by all conceivable means. The new biology must have a higher and purer theocentric vision: In gentleness, mercy, humility, and self-restraint it must limit its advance to qualitative expansion.

Nothing can stop its further emergence as the human race approaches reality by bettering itself and its relations with the rest of sentient creation. The new biology is part of the conscience of evolving life reorientating itself toward the Good and turning ignorance into self-knowledge so that man can spiritually surpass himself in accordance with the divine will. The ethical system of established biology is a gross deflection from the Good and is destined to be replaced by biological righteousness. Sentient animals in the laboratory are not there to stay.

Dr. White Replies:

I was fascinated by Dr. Roberts' paper, finding it a revelation of a sensitive scientist's inner self and her personally evolved theological and philosophical matrix of belief rather than merely the expected sterile recitation of the well-known "sins" of vivisection. True, her employment of the Platonic concept of *Summum Bonum* (the Good) seems to be overly simplistic and clearly self-defeating in her attempt to construct a theological edifice with which to blunt and smother the onslaught of biological science and technology; still, her recognition of the need for scientists to come to grips with the far-reaching effects of their researches, particularly human life, must be complimented. I must also admit, however, to a certain sense of *déjà vu* in reading this presentation since the substance has been similarly developed in her previous publications.

To assist myself in arriving at a reasoned judgment of this particular Roberts manuscript, I took the liberty of forwarding a copy to the Jesuit theologian, Father Nicholas A. Predovich, of John Carroll University in Cleveland, for a learned opinion regarding the religious implications of Dr. Roberts' thesis, since my expertise in theology extends only to the theology of ancient Egypt. In addition, I permitted myself the luxury of taking the document with me to the Soviet Union last fall in hopes that my commentary might at least be distinguished by having been composed at twenty-five thousand feet in Soviet airspace and under a certain psychological and physiological stress, since I do not enjoy flying in Russian aircraft during adverse weather conditions.

Before attempting to review the paper, I must state that the evidence at hand strongly argues that Dr. Roberts' true purpose in seeking this "exchange of opinions" was not with a view toward settling the issue of vivisection but was rather of a grander design, to provide herself with another distinguished forum from which to amplify her personal religious philosophy and again offer it as a solution to the problems developing for mankind from the ever increasing number of scientific discoveries. But these are problems of human existence and survival, not of animal survival. Consequently, her entire thesis seems hardly germane to the subject of vivisection, and one is hard pressed to uncover the link between her pseudoplatonic theology and animal experimentation. Perhaps both Dr. Roberts and I owe the readers of this journal an apology for having consumed so many pages in discussing a topic of such little relevance today.

To clarify the "ground rules" of our individual literary efforts, I must take issue with her in regard to an alleged agreement between us to address ourselves to animal experimentation in the "widest evolutionary, social, ethical, and religious perspectives," since it is obvious from my presentation that I was and am unable to conceive of animal experimentation in terms of human values. There simply is no historical, evolutionary, biological, philosophical, social, or theological justification for applying principles of human morality and ethics to nonhuman creatures. Admittedly, the entire scientific community does not universally ascribe to my opinion. Nevertheless, R. D. Guthrie has recently demonstrated the impossibility of including animals in our human ethical system.

Since Dr. Roberts' thesis rests so heavily on her personally derived Platonic theology, I have taken the liberty of quoting directly from Predovich's critique of her religious and philosophical theories as set forth in his communication to me.

In reviewing Dr. Roberts' manuscript, Father Predovich is disturbed by the lack of a clear definition of what she means by the word *life*, since it obviously forms such an integral part of her argument. Indicating the importance of distinguishing between an *univocal* and *analogous* concept of life, he writes:

If Dr. Roberts has a *univocal* concept of life, then all forms of life such as vegetative, sentient and rational should be preserved and fostered as much as man can make them. If life is only one thing, then what makes the vegetable and the animal different from man? If we must conclude that life is an analogous concept, that is, somewhat the same, yet totally different in the plant and in the animal and in man, then shouldn't we, as rational beings, see that different principles will apply differently for each of the forms of life?

Surely one recognizes the univocal concept of life as peculiarly Schweitz-
erian, and yet even Dr. Schweitzer admitted to the necessity of animal experimentation for the betterment of mankind.

I was disturbed by Dr. Roberts' concept of conscience and her denial
of man's personalistic character, and so was Father Predovich. He continues:

> To speak in terms of conscience and the human being using his
> conscience, confuses the issue and makes conscience purely a
> mechanical process based on one's own insight into the reality
> that is labelled evolution. Rather, conscience looks to the whole
> of reality, to history, to the insights of other human beings, and
> is formed from all of this. Conscience is a process that results
> from integrating many things. It does not appear that C. Roberts
> would agree with this notion of human conscience.
>
> In spite of appearances, this paper by Dr. Roberts lacks insight
> into the human condition as *personalistic*. Homo sapiens seems
> to be treated like a scientific phenomenon rather than an ex-
> istential "I-Thou" reality, which he is. If, as Martin Buber
> proves so well, man is destined to deep, free, open, interpersonal
> relationships with other men, then obviously, even in the evolu-
> tionary process, man's greatest effort will be to effect, to help
> grow, to urge into becoming such interpersonal relationships.
> The preservation of biological species, though worthwhile per se,
> is itself subordinated to the highest form of evolution of man,
> that is, evolution into interpersonal relationships with all men,
> and finally into the total human community with God. This is
> the Omega Point that I think Teilhard de Chardin was talking
> about rather than a mere evolutionary process of a human
> species.

Eventually Dr. Roberts' theological balloon returns to earth with a
predictable thud, since she immediately undertakes to overwhelm us with
her prejudicial descriptions of various animal experiments, notably in the
fields of behavioral psychology and parabiosis. Those tried and trite words,
cruelty, screams, torture, pain, suffering, mutilation, *et cetera,* that form
the litany of the antivivisection language begin to appear with increasing

monotony. I can only assure the readers of the *Scholar* that I have participated for over two decades in animal research in all the areas she so selectively portrays (behavioral, neurophysiological, parabiosis, and organ transplantation), that I have visited institutes for experimentation all over the world, including the Soviet Union and other Iron Curtain countries, and have not witnessed the cruelty or dehumanization that she insists characterizes biomedical animal research. True, some discomfort may be experienced by animals during specific studies, for example, in pain research, but almost invariably the investigator goes out of his way to eliminate all vestiges of suffering, not only because they may affect his scientific results but, more important, because of his innate sympathy for his experimental subjects. Dr. Roberts repeats with relish the often used phrase of antiviviseciton literature, "dehumanization" (of the scientist participating in animal research). This should obviously be classified as a psychiatric syndrome. Fortunately, psychiatric literature and I are ignorant of this spectacular clinical diagnosis—since it does not exist.

I share Dr. Roberts' worry regarding the serious impact on human existence of recently acquired biological knowledge, and, fortunately, she is correct in emphasizing the growing concern within the scientific community itself over the implications of its own research. The awesome capability of biomedical science to modify and qualify human life in the immediate future will be a reality if the same momentum, so characteristic of its present state, continues. The recent works of Albert Rosenfeld (*The Second Genesis: The Coming Control of Life*), Alvin Toffler (*Future Shock*), and Gordon R. Taylor (*Biological Time Bomb*) are devoted to this topic, and while the authors' judgments are somewhat visionary, nevertheless they collectively emphasize that life as we know it today will be radically altered in the very near future. Unfortunately, this truly crucial question has nothing to do with the subject under discussion here—vivisection.

I must remind Dr. Roberts that our advanced technological society and increasing population have produced additional serious health hazards through industrial and human pollution of our air, water, and land, and that the use of animals to establish acceptable levels of biological contamination and to design methods of control and decontamination for humans represents a new dimension of biomedical research that may prove to be utterly crucial to human survival.

In her final paragraph Dr. Roberts kindly invites me "to join the forces that are already striving to bring it [abolishment of laboratory experiments with animals] about," stressing that if I did, "true biological achievement would be [mine] ."

Dr. Roberts cannot be serious in arguing that the elimination of animal experiments carries a priority equal to or surpassing the need for meaningful solutions of the major problems developing or already existent at the sociological-biomedical interface! I am afraid that I cannot join her "moral" crusade, since I cannot even grant vivisection a position of relevancy; but, what is more important, I consider the employment of animals in biological and medical research so critical to continued human existence and survival as to be beyond logical challenge.

Notes

1. C. Roberts, "A New Approach to the Problem of Animal Experimentation," *Animals' Defender* 13, no. 4 (April 1969): 106-14.

2. Letter from Robert J. White, July 25, 1969.

3. C. Roberts, "Animal Experimentation and Evolution," *American Scholar* 40, no. 3 (Summer 1971): 497-503; R. J. White, "Antivivisection: The Reluctant Hydra," *Ibid.*, pp. 503-07; "Dr. Roberts Replies," *Ibid.*, pp. 508-10; "Dr. White Replies," *Ibid.*, pp. 510-12.

4. A. M. Laursen, "Letter to the editor," *Forsøgsdyrenes Værn* 5, no. 3 (1967): 18.

5. A. M. Laursen, "Movements Evoked from the Region of the Caudate Nucleus in Cats," *Acta Phys. Scand.* 54 (1962): 175-84; *Ibid.* 54 (1962): 185-90; *Ibid.* 57 (1963): 81-89.

6. P. Agersted, "Forsøgsdyrene og den Lægevidenskabelige Forskning" [Experimental Animals and Medical Research], Lecture, Danmarks Radio, May 14, 1968.

7. R. J. White, "Experimental Transplantation of the Brain," in *Human Transplantation*, eds. F. T. Rapaport and J. Dausset (New York: Grune, 1968).

8. B. Wrighton, "Justice and the Animals," *The Ark* 45 (April 1952): 4-15.

9. B. Farrington, "Science and the Classics," *Nature* 191 (1961): 1337.

10. C. E. Hall, "Parabiosis," in *Methods in Animal Experimentation*, vol. 2, ed. W. I. Gay (New York: Academic Press, 1965).

11. E. M. Forster, *A Passage to India* (London: J. M. Dent, 1942), p. 116.

12. E. D. Weitzman and G. S. Ross, "A Behavioral Method for the Study of Pain Perception in the Monkey," *Neurology* 12 (1962): 264.

13. H. F. Harlow and M. K. Harlow, "Social Deprivation in Monkeys," *Scientific American* 207 (1962): 136.

14. C. Roberts, "Humanism and the Rhesus," in *The Scientific Conscience* (New York: George Braziller, 1967).

15. C. Roberts, "The Use of Animals in Medical Research—Some Ethical Considerations," *Perspectives in Biology and Medicine* 8, no. 1 (Autumn 1964): 115-16.

16. C. Roberts, "Letter to the Editor," *Perspectives in Biology and Medicine* 8 (1965): 569.

17. A. Carrel, *Mennesket det Ukendte* [Man the Unknown], trans. Elias Bredsdorff (Copenhagen: Gyldendalske Boghandel—Nordisk Forlag, 1936).

18. S. P. Harbison, "Origins of Vascular Surgery: The Carrel-Guthrie Letters," *Surgery* 52 (1962): 406.

19. G. F. Woods, *A Defence of Theological Ethics* (Cambridge: University Press, 1966), p. 131.

11

Defenders of
Established Science

Throughout this book we have stressed the ethical confusion that accompanies contemporary scientific endeavor, and we have called attention to the growing mistrust of established science as a panacea for the crises now confronting life. Most scientists, nevertheless, see the unrestricted advance of amoral science as wholly necessary for man's further evolution.

Established science is pursued without any ethical interference from nonscientific authority. Based upon the anthropocentric vision of man at the center of a godless universe, the life sciences see all ethical systems and moral values as autonomous products of man's brain. Ethics, they believe, is merely subjective opinion about man's conduct and behavior which must necessarily change to keep pace with his intellectual development; lacking final authority, it must be divorced from scientific advance. Science is regarded as an objective search for the objective truths of the universe carried out by scientists who have divested themselves as completely as possible of the ethical norms of their spiritual heritage.

Belief in the necessity of scientific objectivity and amorality has accelerated the enormous advance of science in the twentieth century, but in the process scientific amorality has been partially replaced by scientific immorality. Unhindered by ethical restriction of any kind, the life sciences have taken mighty strides, and their newly acquired results have been unhesitatingly associated with the possibilities of changing life through chemical, surgical, and genetic manipulation. But since human life possesses ineradicable ethical norms, it is now beginning to rise up in protest against its own manipulation designed by those who deny the existence of a divine ethic. No wonder that in attempting to apply their knowledge, students of life are encountering an endless succession of seemingly insoluble ethical problems! So far biologists and medical scientists who, in the pursuit of their professions, need to choose between good and evil have seemed generally unable to make an ethical choice. The scientific conscience, degenerate and decadent, is not equal to the task. Ethical confusion reigns. Established science is thereby being forced into a wider cognizance of essential questions raised by critical voices from within and without. Is the unrestrained advance of science an unconditional benefit for mankind? How far shall science go in manipulating life? Is evolving life progressing toward a higher goal? Any evolutionary vision of the future which arises out of our scientific age bears, consciously or unconsciously, upon these questions, and the degree of spiritual enlightenment that shines through the answers helps in an evaluation of the vision as a whole.

Spokesmen for biology and medicine, who are answering these questions by exhorting conventional science to carry on, express, naturally enough, the prevailing views within scientific circles. Being nearly devoid of spiritual enlightenment, these views are wholly inadequate from an evolutionary point of view, for they are based upon the illusion that biological and biomedical knowledge can be applied ethically after having been acquired unethically. Today this is an impossibility. The scope and intensity of contemporary biological advance precludes any lasting good from emerging out of it before there has been a shaking of the foundations severe enough to eliminate the spiritual darkness and ignorance in which contemporary biology and medicine are enmeshed. Can anyone seriously contend that biologists who objectively seek the truths of life by inflicting suffering and death upon living creatures can at will shift their roles to wise, loving, compassionate leaders whose ethical intuition reveals how they can best help and guide their fellow men?

We have already considered the evolutionary vision of Robert White, who, with crystal clear intent to further experimental transplantation surgery, argues that the objective methods and goals of conventional science constitute a wholly adequate moral standard for evolving man. Working for the avowed benefit of mankind on cephalic transplantation in monkeys, Dr. White and his associates have described some of their successful results in these terms:

> All four of the cephalic exchange transplantation preparations survived; their periods of vitality ranged from 6 to 36 hours. In three to four hours, each cephalon gave evidence of its awareness of the external environment by accepting and attempting to chew or swallow food placed in its mouth. The eyes tracked the movement of individuals and objects brought into their visual fields and the cephalons remained basically pugnacious in their attitudes, as demonstrated by their biting if orally stimulated.[1]

Pugnacious? Those poor, pitiful, dismembered beings—isolated heads kept alive and conscious by surgical attachment to decapitated bodies, reacting as best they can to the brutal and depraved hands of modern science. And again:

> Within 4 hours of transplantation the cephalon (as well as the recipient) awakened, displaying normalization of cranial nerve function and characteristic responsiveness. While no preparation has been maintained beyond 24 hours, their neurological, behavioral and electroencephalographic function during this period have been graded as excellent.[2]

Excellent? In the name of the highest good in man, who dares to speak of any kind of excellence in association with this manipulation of life? Where is the moral condemnation of his colleagues? Where is the moral condemnation of religious bodies and individuals? Why has there been no massive ethical opposition to the atrocities of experimental transplantation surgery? Because contemporary man, filled to overflowing with egoistic darkness and sin, believes he may stand to gain from it. Nothing could be further from the truth.

Admittedly, the evolutionary views of Robert White represent an extreme position. As this professed Christian himself admits, not all biologists would agree that "there simply is no historical, evolutionary, biological, philosophical, social, or theological justification for applying principles of human morality and ethics to nonhuman creatures." Nor would all biologists be expected to endorse his statement that "the inclusion of lower animals in our ethical system is philosophically meaningless and operationally impossible and that, consequently, antivivisection theory and practice have no moral or ethical basis." But even without accepting *in toto* White's justification of animal experimentation, and even when showing increasing interest in a more humane treatment of laboratory animals, biologists who are concerned with the progress of evolving life still fail generally to recognize that the continued use of sentient animals in biological and medical research is in itself an evolutionary and ethical problem of the highest order. They seem to acquiesce in Robert White's dark assertions that the man-animal relation cannot be conceived in terms of human values and that vivisection is not relevant to the truths of religion and theology. In a godless, anthropocentric age most scientific visions of the future naturally arise from the narrow perspectives of scientific humanism: Man, seeing himself as the summit of reality at the center of the cosmos, is blinded to the hierarchy of being which stretches from the subhuman to the superhuman.

A widespread belief of contemporary biologists is that the dilemma of modern science is primarily one of social responsibility. In contrast to the pangs of conscience of the drop-outs from biology and other "scientific hippies" whose distrust of the scientific establishment is still more intuitive than articulate, scientists who are concerned with the future of their profession tend to minimize the moral responsibility of the individual scientist in favor of social responsibility based upon the rational choice of the majority. There is nothing fundamentally wrong, they say, with the way in which scientists today acquire scientific knowledge. What is wrong is the demands of society for its application. Ergo, society is exhorted to develop a stronger sense of social responsibility as scientific advance, uninhibited and unrestrained, pursues its merry way. But of the scientific conscience confronted with the moral responsibility to respect sentient life and to establish a harmonious, compassionate, and righteous relation with it, there is usually not a word—nor a thought.

When there is talk of conscience at all, it most often revolves around scientific goals, not means. Ethical problems attendant upon genetic engineering, transplantation, brain death, pharmacological control of human behavior, sperm banks, artificial prolongation of human life, and so on are being discussed, but nearly always anthropocentrically as problems which affect human reality alone. A few years ago in the United States the Institute of Human Reproduction and Bioethics held a symposium on conscience and choice. Its main concern, according to press reports, was the question about what man is doing to himself. I do not suppose that the biologists attending the symposium, however deeply they might be concerned with the ethical dilemmas of modern science, were thinking in terms of what the present *mésalliance* between scientists and animals is doing to the human race, for scientists are not yet generally aware to what degree the scientific exploitation of sentient animals is impairing and profaning the quality of human life. They are not yet aware that biology's increasing use of violence toward subhuman life is a flagrant obstacle to life's spiritual evolution toward the divine.

In 1970 the Menton Declaration, drawn up and endorsed by biologists in many countries, proposed among other things a moratorium on all technological innovation which is not essential to human survival. More recent reports prepared and accepted by scientists and bearing the ominous titles of "Blueprint for Survival" and "The Limits of Growth" also challenge the so-called blessings and inevitability of the unrestrained expansion of economic growth, industrialization, and technology. The latter envisages a stable "no-growth" world, in which there is less desire for material goods, where the birth and death rate have been equalized, and where there is more time, energy, and desire for more intellectual and cultural pursuits. As far as they go, these endeavors seem ethically sane. They do not, however, go far enough. There has been little thinking within scientific circles about slowing down the growth of biological and medical research; most biologists exclude the uninhibited growth of science from the category of dangerous growth processes. Rational humanism tends to see growth processes as dangerous only when they concern excessive multiplication of physical life on this planet and its accompanying material demands. Intellectual growth and development that is based upon the acquisition of new scientific knowledge and its practical application is still held to be desirable from the standpoint of human evolution. It follows that it must continue without end and by all conceivable means.

This is not to imply that the spokesmen for the uninhibited advance of the established life sciences see the conventional pursuit of scientific knowledge merely as evolutionarily inevitable. Their visions are often prompted by sincere desires to acquire new knowledge in order to relieve the physical and mental sufferings of men. This idea, however noble and praiseworthy, arises out of the narrow perspective of anthropocentricity, which is no longer an adequate attitude toward the whole of evolving life. Unconcerned as they are with the human-divine relation and the human-animal relation, scientists do not consider the evolutionary possibility that biomedical research may be compelled to transform, limit, and restrain itself—not out of the danger of collapse from practical economic reasons or declining interest in science as a profession, but solely because man is growing spiritually. And whatever anthropocentric humanists may believe at the moment, there is no limit to this growth. Here we are confronted with a reality with which rationality and computers cannot deal. We are confronted with the right orientation of the soul, with ethical choices between good and evil, and with the establishment of a harmonious and righteous relation between man and other forms of sentient life. This will require that the further acquisition and application of scientific knowledge be ethically restrained. When biologists and medical scientists agree that there are certain things they must not know and must not do, the spiritual transformation of established biology and medicine will have begun, and the world can look forward to a development of immeasurably greater benefit than could be afforded by scientific breakthroughs of the conventional kind.

Contemporary biology and medicine, forced into a defensive position by their critics, are not yet thinking very seriously in terms of self-imposed restriction and transformation. Yet biologists are thinking through as never before the *raison d'être* of their further pursuit of knowledge. Unquestionably, the ultimate defense has come from France.

Chance and Necessity

Jacques Monod's *Chance and Necessity* [3] is an attempt on the grand scale to justify the unrestrained advance of modern biology. A thought-provoking analysis of the relation between established science and evolution and ethics, it has awakened intense interest, not least because of Monod's claim that the cure for the sickness of modern man lies in a new *Weltbild* arising out of the truths of molecular biology.

These truths, according to Monod, make it no longer possible for rational man in a scientific age to tolerate an ethic based upon the antiquated moral criteria of the traditional philosophies and religions. Such criteria, derived from vitalistic and animistic views of man striving toward a definite evolutionary goal in accord with an objective ethic forced upon him from without, were seen by Monod as dangerous illusions which can only worsen our present fear, anxiety, and misery. Were we instead to listen to the voice of contemporary biology telling us to let go the moral values whose roots it has already destroyed, we could at last take our destiny and ethic into our own hands to create an idealistic, socialistic, scientific humanism, honestly accepting the fact that man is alone in a universe out of which he fortuitously arose. Religion, Monod insisted, is merely a human invention to which man still clings with foolish tenacity to allay his fears and deny his accidentalness; ergo, there can be no change for the better until he decides once and for all to let go.

A vivid experience of more than fifty years ago comes to mind. When I was a small child an older member of the family and I, on a busy street in San Francisco, were trying to catch a streetcar for the Ferry Building. I jumped on first. Feeling at once the insecurity of my position, and frightened at seeing my aunt running beside the moving vehicle, I was tempted to jump off again. At this moment I can still hear her reassuring cry, "Hang on, Cath, hang on!" I did, and we made the ferry without mishap. Many times since, in far more serious situations, I have hung on and shall do so now. For there is nothing in Monod's scientific rejection of traditional religion and philosophy that could induce me to let them go—and least of all the facts of molecular biology. On the contrary, *Chance and Necessity,* with its claims that objective scientific knowledge is the only source of truth and that such knowledge has already destroyed the roots of traditional morality, is a stimulating intellectual and spiritual challenge. One incentive for meeting it was already provided in 1967 by a highly critical reviewer of *The Scientific Conscience* who prophesied that "A century from now we shall all be scientists, and revere the laws of molecular biology as much as Dr. Roberts reveres Plato."[4] Convinced at the time that this prediction was wholly erroneous, I still hold that scientific knowledge is not, and never can be, the most authentic kind of knowledge for evolving man. Regardless of what Monod and other molecular biologists and bio-anthropologists believe, it has in no way destroyed the roots of traditional moral values. All that modern science has done is to obscure them temporarily. Nor is it capable of doing more: the roots of traditional morality, arising out of spiritual knowledge of the divine ethic, are imperishable.

To attempt to refute Monod's evolutionary and ethical arguments in their entirety would, however, require a counterargument exceeding both

my competence and the scope of this book. Here we are primarily concerned with the *mesalliance* between scientists and sentient animals and
its effect on the development of science and the evolution of man. Certain statements about this problem in *Chance and Necessity* must nevertheless be seen against their contextual background.

No modern evolutionist, of course, can deny that throughout their
evolutionary history living organisms have been subject to the laws of
chemistry and physics, nor that recent advances in molecular biology
have enormously increased our knowledge of cellular growth and reproduction to give us new insights into the physical mechanism of inheritance
and evolution. However obscure the technical details may appear to the
nonspecialist, we must all accept as indisputable scientific truths that the
chromosomal gene consists of DNA (deoxyribonucleic acid), that the
DNA molecule is the fundamental biological invariant and the bearer of
genetic information, that it consists of a double chain of nucleotides in
meaningful sequence, that it is under compulsion to reproduce itself and
to transmit its nucleotide sequence to the amino-acid sequence of a pro-
tein molecule, and that these replicative and transmissive processes are
among the fundamental characteristics of life. We must also accept in
good faith that if any random change occurring in the segments of the
DNA molecule as well as any fortuitous disturbance or error occurring
in the mechanism of replication and transmission is acceptable to the
individual's "teleonomic system," it will be selected, replicated, and
transmitted, and that such inherited variations, together with the genic
recombinations arising out of sexual reproduction, have resulted in the
genetic and phenotypic diversity of evolving life. We must further agree
that at the cellular and molecular level the living organism does appear
as an autonomous machine automatically building itself up through
molecular interactions dependent upon chance and necessity. These biological facts do not, however, compel anyone to accept Monod's conclusions: (1) that the nature and quality of the diverse forms of evolving life
now on earth are primarily due to the selection and transmission of
random imperfections, (2) that human evolution cannot be proceeding
toward any predestined higher goal, and (3) that man is alone responsible
for his ethical system.

The alternative view which invokes the existence of a divine reality
guiding evolution and ethics cannot be logically disproved by science. It
is therefore unscientific to eliminate it by disclaiming its validity in the

absence of proof. In his memorable essay on human immortality William James spoke about the illogicality of scientists who make a "denial based on the flat ignoring of a palpable alternative,"[5] and his words apply to the author of *Chance and Necessity*. Personally unable to find objective truth in spiritual knowledge of the divine and disbelieving the fact that ethics is indissolubly bound to the human-divine relation, Monod believed himself logically entitled to reject man's religious-spiritual heritage *in toto*. But by any rational standard he was not entitled to dismiss any religious knowledge in which the knower sees evolving life as an ascent toward a higher spiritual-ethical state unless he could demonstrate that the knower suffers from a delusion. And this Monod certainly did not do. While no one can deny the sincerity with which he considered his own *Weltbild* authentic and the only acceptable one in an age of science, one must deplore the illogicality and the lack of spiritual insight and vision that went into its creation.

Monod, it is true, clearly recognized that the scientific age has other problems than overpopulation, food supply, pollution, and disease. He saw science as part of evolving man's relation to the universe and was aware of the immensity of the problems arising out of this consideration. He advocated the unrestrained advance of conventional science not only to alleviate our immediate crises but also because he believed this to be the only way to understand the world and man's place in it. He therefore found it necessary to advocate a strengthening of the scientific outlook that sees the progressive acquisition of rational, objective knowledge about the world as evolving man's best guide. Scientists must continue to lead the way, he claimed, by liberating themselves still more completely from their religious-spiritual heritage. By refusing to blend any kind of traditional ethics with their pursuit of knowledge, they will find the truth which will enable man to realize his potentials of intelligence and authenticity. For no higher potentials are conceivable for a rational species evolving according to the blind laws of chance and necessity in a changing environment equally devoid of purpose and meaning. This scientific attitude toward life is the true attitude, Monod claimed, and he based his claim upon the belief, as Malaoni Martin has expressed it,[6] that "science encompasses all knowledge."

Monod did, however, put two limits on scientific knowledge. One limit pertains to knowledge of the functions of the central nervous system and the other to knowledge of the origin of life itself. Apart from these limitations, he argued throughout the book that the basic truths of evolving life are being sought and found by biology's never ending acquisition of new objective knowledge. Yet throughout he was unnecessarily obscure about the meaning he attached to the word "objectivity," applying it in different senses to science and to the external world science is investigating. The objectivity of science he sees as a confrontation between scientific experience and logic, in which the subjectivity of the scientist is reduced to a minimum. In striving to become an unengaged, unemotional, insensitive, and amoral seeker of knowledge of external reality, the scientist acts as a passive receptor of sense perception, which, when acted upon by his logical mind, permits him to bestow objective validity upon the knowledge he has acquired of the external world. Such objective knowledge of science is, according to Monod, man's only source of truth. But in also describing nature as objective, Monod did not use, as would be expected, the word to denote reality having an existence in its own right independent of the senses and mind of the scientist but, as far as I understand him, to denote an existential reality which lacks final cause or purpose. Inanimate nature, being produced by the free play of physical forces, is without recognizable goals and is therefore, according to Monod, "objective." But since living organisms appear to be endowed with evolutionary goals, which he calls "teleonomic projects," he encountered a serious difficulty between the teleological nature of evolving life and the postulated objectivity of the nature which science investigates. He was forced to conclude that if science is to advance, it can only do so by accepting the postulate of nature's objectivity.

Despite his assertion that the scientific outlook is always new and open, Monod himself could not even see the evolutionary process apart from biological knowledge. For him evolution *is* the physical and mental expression of the genetic information inherited by the stream of life through molecular interactions which are permitted by the laws of chance and necessity. "All teleonomic structures and performances correspond to a certain amount of information, which must be transmitted in order that the structure can be realized and the performances executed."* I cannot agree. While the development of the central nervous system, which made possible symbolic language and abstract thought, has obvi-

*All quotations from *Chance and Necessity* have been translated from the Danish edition and therefore cannot show exact correspondence with the authorized English edition, which I have not seen.

ously been of enormous evolutionary significance, it does not follow that life's spiritual activity, which, by any standard, is its greatest performance and that which imparts meaning to human evolution, depends solely upon the function of anatomical structures which are the product of autonomous physical development.

This idea is what Monod appeared to maintain. While not denying the existence of the human soul (spirit), his scientific objectivity forced him to consider as illusory the dualism of body and soul (mind and spirit). Scientific thought cannot, after all, permit what men call soul to be other than a function of the central nervous system of the body. But since Monod regarded the functions of the central nervous system to be beyond the limits of the objective knowledge which for him represented the *only* truth, he concluded that the illusion of our dualism is so closely associated with our being that we must ever be content to live in this emotional and moral error—a conclusion revealing that the limited perspectives of science fall far short of the grander perspectives of religion.

It is surprising that atheists who pride themselves on their scientific minds being more susceptible to the persuasion of logic than intuition find it logical to ponder the origin and evolution of life by confining their thoughts almost exclusively to the earth's biosphere. To maintain that evolution, explainable by chance defects in life's mechanism for maintaining its invariability, is nevertheless "miraculous" would seem to require some kind of rational consideration of the miracle in its setting in time and space. Has not the existence of the sun, the other solar systems, and the galaxies any relevance to life on earth? Are the heavenly bodies to be attributed to chance as well? Or does the modern biologist find it convenient to neglect their existence out of fear that his logical mind may force him to go beyond contemporary biological, astronomical, and cosmological theory to postulate an uncreated creative force responsible either for the eternity of physical being or its formation out of a void? Biologists who shy away from the ultimate spiritual mysteries of the universe for which there can be no objective scientific explanations based upon "systematic confrontations between logic and experience" are grossly neglecting the cosmic background for life on this planet. In consequence, their evolutionary and ethical arguments, unmindful of first causes and unsupported by any sense of the cosmic whole, are not only narrow, distorted, and incomplete, but also wholly inadequate for a crises-filled world on the threshhold of a spiritual awakening.

Nor is Monod's scientism wholly logical. To maintain, as he did, that because we lack spiritual truth and have no means of attaining it, we must continue to live with our illusion of the duality of body and soul is an illogical assertion. For Monod, who relied exclusively on objective knowledge for truth, could not know objectively that the duality is an illusion. He had, in fact, no scientific knowledge whatever of the matter and therefore by his own arguments had no truth of it. His postulate that the duality is false can only be based upon wishful thinking: No scientist can claim on the basis of scientific knowledge that the soul is an expression of the consciousness of physical structure, that it resides in the brain, and that it is obliterated at the death of the brain. Such unwarranted claims may even be the result of agnostic or atheistic fear of not yet being wholly liberated from religious authority.

Sir Alister Hardy, in his very important two-volume work on evolution from a theistic perspective, suggests that together with the physical stream of evolving life there "may flow a paraphysical element which is no more, and no less, mysterious in its nature and relation to the physical than is consciousness to the physiology of the body" and further suggests that in the evolution of nonhuman animals there may exist "not only a telepathic spread of habit changes, but a general *subconscious* sharing of form and behavior pattern. . . ."[7] He sees a possible relation between human telepathy, a phenomenon which Monod neglected, and both Plato's world of ideas and Jung's concept of the collective unconscious and stresses the importance of psychical research and of scientific studies of religious experience in order to come closer to the mystery of evolving life:

> If it can be generally accepted that individual minds may be in touch with one another through channels other than those of the normal bodily senses, this could give back a reasonable faith in the possibility of communication with something beyond the self to those who have lost it on false materialistic grounds.[8]

More will be said later about Hardy's views. He is quoted here to emphasize the fact that the extreme paucity of scientific knowledge about the body-mind-soul complex and the conscious-unconscious-subconscious states should make it rationally imperative for scientists, be they theists, atheists, or agnostics, to admit as a theoretical possibility the existence of some kind of nonphysical reality external to our physical bodies upon which life's spiritual evolution wholly or partly depends. They have at least no justifiable grounds to ignore the testimony of the mystics— Christian and non-Christian, past and present—any more than contemporary testimonies of religious experiences that defy materialistic explanation. What, for example, can modern biologists say about the charismatic awakening in Indonesia and America? Whether this phenomenon is to be characterized as truly spiritual must in the final analysis depend upon personal experience; yet, it is being claimed that spiritual energy is being received and transmitted by which physical and ethical imperfection is dispelled. If this is so, what is evolving life now confronting? Who can dogmatically deny the possibility that in our environment there is an unknown form of spiritual energy whose "purpose" is to aid life's ascent toward a loftier state of spiritual-ethical being? A molecular biologist who categorically refuses to admit this evolutionary possibility and who "objectively" employs biological knowledge as scientific weapons to demolish all ideas about spiritual evolution is fighting a hopeless fight without realizing it.

Monod even postulated an ingenious scientific mechanism to account for the acceptance and dissemination of new ideas. He suggested that man's need for meaning and purpose in life is written in his genetic code; he is thus forced to seek "explanations," whether philosophical, religious, or scientific. There is, of course, no more scientific evidence to support this claim than there is to support Monod's other claim that only scientific explanations are valid. But, one is tempted to ask, since the religious idea of the human-divine relation, together with all forms of associated religious experience and behavior, is universal, is it not one of evolution's most successful "teleonomic projects"? If so, and if, as Monod claimed, the human-divine relation is only a lie in men's souls, then it is obvious that with this religious success, evolution has led life astray. Monod is thus forced to preach evolutionary defiance: The panacea for the ills of evolving man is liberation from this eminently successful teleonomic project. One might further ask, What price a teleonomy that deceives us? The answer, of course, is that we have not been deceived. Human evolution *is* a spiritual ascent toward the divine. To reject spiritual knowledge of life in favor of conventional biological knowledge is evolutionary madness. The facts of biology are of course "true," but they comprise only one part of the truths of life, and in the general scheme of things a very insignificant part at that.

In the belief that the objectivity of nature is a postulate incapable of verification, Monod maintained that if it is not accepted, the limits of science would be exceeded. Scientists, to remain scientists, must cast out traditional moral values and ethical systems and assume the objectivity of the nature they are investigating. Otherwise, they will burst the bonds of objective science.

I believe that this is just what biologists must do, and that the present ethical dilemma of science is a preparatory step in the bursting of the bond. So long as scientists allow the means and goals of their profession to be at variance with the divine ethic of the spiritual realm, they impair not only the quality of biology but also the quality of their own lives and the species to which they belong. If biology, the study of life by life, is to become an authentic study, it cannot be separated, as now, from the spiritual knowledge and the ethics that life already possesses. It must begin to become an increasingly subjective experience, in which biologists acquire knowledge of life by spiritually participating in it. They must begin to accept the possibility that the "miracle" of the evolution of life in a changing living and nonliving environment may have meaning and purpose in accord with a supernatural evolutionary design or law which now lies beyond our comprehension. Having accepted this theoretical possibility that nature is proceeding toward a higher goal, biologists would then begin to understand that they must restrain and transform their means and goals for the sake of higher truths. It is this self-imposed ethical restraint, intuitively recognized as having its source in a transcendent objective reality, which can ensure the advance of biology into a true study of life.

In exhorting biologists to continue, without limits, their research by established methods to acquire objectively the objective knowledge of life that is its only source of truth, *Chance and Necessity* is in flagrant opposition to the needs and demands of contemporary revolutionaries. For all their faults, excesses, and inexperience, many of the younger generation have clearly seen what Monod did not: that it is spiritual enlightenment, rather than science and technology, that will save the world. They would, no doubt, nod in approval to these words:

> The book of Genesis and its great pictorial illustrations, like
> the frescoes of Michelangelo, remain a far more intelligent
> account of the nature and origin of the universe than the
> representation of the world as a chance collocation of atoms.

For the biblical cosmology continues to express—however inadequately—the significance of the fact that the world exists and that man has emerged from it, while the scientific picture denies any meaning to the world, and indeed ignores all our most vital experiences of this world.[9]

It must be remembered that not all young students of life are flocking to institutions of learning to learn the latest facts of molecular biology. Some of them are dropping out of biology altogether. Courses of study offered by the scientific establishment are not in greatest demand by students today. Some of them, recoiling in distaste from biology's monstrous treatment of sentient life and from its artificial life-controlling and life-prolonging goals, are in open revolt against conventional science. Others are embracing with open arms the first religious ideology that comes their way, or are traveling thousands of miles eastward to find in oriental spiritual-ethical truths satisfying nourishment for their souls. Still others are devising various kind of ecological projects in sincere attempts to reintroduce ethical harmony between man and the rest of creation.

Monod's "ethic of knowledge" lies upon a wholly different plane of thought and activity. His knowledge, being scientific in the traditional sense of the word, could not, in fact, cope with the problem of choosing between good and evil. And it is precisely *this* knowledge that Monod, by his own admission, lacked. "Who," he asks, "shall decide what is evil and what is good?" The answer, of supreme significance for evolving life, is a spiritual one that cannot be provided by established science.

Monod was quite aware that contemporary science has no answer to this question. At the same time, if I have understood him correctly, he did not consider it a very important question. Far more important for him was the decision never, under any circumstances, to combine our knowledge about the sensible world with any ethical system. This decision is necessary, he insisted, because ethics, being "nonobjective," is outside the realm of knowledge of the truth. He exhorted modern man instead to maintain a *relation* between objective knowledge and non-objective ethics simply by recognizing this distinction between them. This step was seen as an ethical choice by which man somehow arrives directly at an "ethic of knowledge", which is his only authentic moral guide. Monod's ethics appears to be in a deplorable state. One of the chief reasons for this is his erroneous assertion that the scientific view is always new and open. It is not. It is tightly closed to all knowledge that is not scientific.

The incompatibility of Monod's ethics with the spiritual awakening now beginning can be illustrated with certain views in *Chance and Necessity* relevant to the use of animals in biological research.

Monod stated that although research on nonhuman brains can never penetrate directly to the consciousness of the animal, we are yet so far from the limits of knowledge about the functions of the central nervous system that we must naturally continue all kinds of brain research with all means at our disposal. "One cannot," he says, "have logical objections to man analyzing the central nervous system of an animal."[10] That there could be ethical and evolutionary objections to scientific analyses involving the infliction of suffering and death upon captive animals either did not occur to him or, if it did, seemed unworthy of mention.

His approval of animal experimentation in the pursuit of objective knowledge is again implied in connection with ethological experiments on animal behavior. He calls them "cruel experiments, which, in truth, it is unthinkable to carry out on people, on children. Thus, out of respect for himself, man must not allow himself to investigate certain structures which are a part of his own nature and essence."[11] But the denial of the basic rights of sentient creatures and the infliction upon them of pain and death, being part of the established ethical code of objective science, needs neither revision nor questioning. So much for an "ethical system" based upon scientific knowledge alone. Man is entitled to do with nonhuman life what he thinks best, for, according to the concluding paragraph of *Chance and Necessity,* "Mankind knows at last that it is alone in the immense, unfeeling universe out of which it fortuitously arose."[12]

A more anthropocentric proclamation could not be imagined. But we are not alone, neither in life nor in death nor in what follows. When scientists decide to orient their souls toward the divine source from which they came and to which they are destined to return, the life sciences, advancing in ways hitherto undreamt of, will start playing their true role in the evolution of the human race.

Notes

1. R. J. White, L. R. Wolin, L. C. Massopust, N. Taslitz, and J. Verdura, "Cephalic Exchange Transplantation in the Monkey," *Surgery* 70 (1971): 136-37.

2. R. J. White, L. R. Wolin, L. C. Massopust, N. Taslitz, and J. Verdura, "Primate Cephalic Transplantation: Neurogenic Separation, Vascular Association," *Transplantation Proceedings* 3, no. 1 (1971): 603-04.

3. J. Monod, *Tilfældigheden og Nødvendigheden. Et Essay om den Moderne Biologis Naturfilosofi* [Chance and Necessity: An Essay on the Natural Philosophy of Modern Biology], Danish translation by H. P. Lund of *Le hasard et la nécessité* (Copenhagen: Fremad, 1971).

4. J. Maddox, "Double Vision," *Book Week* (1967): 4, 17.

5. W. James, *The Will to Believe and Other Essays in Popular Philosophy and Human Immortality* (New York: Dover, 1956), p. 19.

6. M. Martin, "The Scientist as Shaman," *Harper's Magazine,* March 1972.

7. A. Hardy, *The Living Stream: A Restatement of Evolution Theory and Its Relation to the Spirit of Man* (London: Collins, 1965), pp. 40, 257.

8. A. Hardy, *The Divine Flame: An Essay Towards a Natural History of Religion* (London: Collins, 1966), p. 228.

9. M. Polanyi, *Personal Knowledge: Towards a Post-Critical Philosophy* (London: Routledge & Kegan Paul, 1958), p. 285.

10. J. Monod, *Tilfældigheden og Nødvendigheden. Et Essay om den Moderne Biologis Naturfilosofi* (Copenhagen: Fremad, 1971), p. 134.

11. *Ibid.,* p. 139.

12. *Ibid.,* p. 163.

_12

Scientific Discontent

In Chapters 9 and 10, both of which were written a few years ago, as well as in other places in this book, I have related, directly or indirectly, the problem of animal experimentation to the academic revolt, seeing in its opposition to established authority and its striving for ethical enlightenment a means of bettering the relation between the scientist and the animal. Personal contact with young academic rebels and participation in one of their London meetings on modern science had given me grounds for supposing that their efforts must soon lead to an organized attempt to right some of the flagrant wrongs within the life sciences, including the scientific exploitation and misuse of sentient animals. The course of events since then has shown that I anticipated too rapid changes. The problem of the plight of the laboratory animal has been generally neglected by most of those who actively opposed established biology. Nor can it be said that a new biology restrained and guided by spiritual-ethical truths is as yet a *fait accompli*. There nevertheless remain grounds for optimism. For even though the academic revolt per se has lost its original force and vigor, the religious-spiritual awakening continues to grow—and in step with it, a mounting discontent with the progress of the life sciences from within.

There is, in truth, a new wind blowing in biology and medicine. As the physicists before them, a growing number of biologists and medical scientists are becoming aware that the pursuit and application of *their* knowledge is a matter of conscience. True, the triumphant voices of those scientists who are determined to guide human evolution by means of genetic, surgical, and pharmacological interference with individual lives are still to be heard. Equally audible are those scientists who, while professing a deep concern for man's scientifically controlled future, fancy that the authority of their biological knowledge makes them natural leaders to whom the world must turn for advice. Most of the conferences of the past decade on science, ethics, and evolution have tended to end on a hopeful note: Despite all attendant problems, the participants have looked forward to new scientific breakthroughs as evidence of inevitable human progress. The wind that is now blowing is more chilling. New voices, uncertain rather than confident, are concerned about the growing mistrust of science; they are questioning the visions and actions of their more distinguished colleagues, demanding that the full implication of scientific advance be made public, and requesting aid and advice in guiding the further advance of biology and medicine from circles outside science. In a word, the explosive development of the life sciences has already created a kind of Teilhardian noosphere, before which its creators stand discomfited and intimidated. Teilhard de Chardin saw the unrestricted expansion of human knowledge and intelligence as the necessary means to an evolutionary end and thus welcomed the uninhibited progress of biology. Today the actual and potential horrors of a runaway science of life make it increasingly difficult to share his enthusiasm for the automatism of biological advance.

So far no panacea for our existing and foreseeable ills seems to be in sight. There is no generally accepted answer to the question of whether the human race is capable of guiding its further evolution or whether it is evolution itself which is guiding man toward his predestined goal. Nor is there any agreement as to where the blame should be placed for our present state of ethical chaos in the biological sciences. Does it lie with the individual scientists for their dreams and the steps they have taken to realize them? Does it lie with the five-hundred-year-old scientific outlook which regards the uninterrupted attainment of scientific truths of sensible realities as man's prime desideratum? Or does it lie outside scientific circles in that society which chooses to support and encourage scientific advance and to utilize its results as fast as they are attained?

So in teleological uncertainty, intellectual unrest, and moral disquiet scientists all around the globe are spurred to action. In England the British Society for Social Responsibility in Science has been founded, and wide interest has been shown in the possibility of establishing a kind of Hippocratic oath for scientists. The Menton Declaration, signed by thousands of biologists all over the world, proposed both a moratorium on certain technological innovations and a program of massive scientific research to solve the problems of pollution, hunger, overpopulation, and war that threaten the survival of mankind. In Denmark the Ministry of Cultural Affairs recently issued a 363-page publication on cultural policy, in which Danish scientists have expressed their views about scientific progress. We read:

> The doctor's means of interfering [with human life] have become so extensive that in practising his profession, he is now coming in conflict with other basic values, and it cannot be his duty alone to decide how these conflicts are to be solved. . . . [Society] must come to a decision as to the direction in which medical science shall proceed. . . . In order to guide biological progress humanists, doctors, politicians, lawyers, technicians—all social groups—must take an active interest in these problems. Otherwise the world could be gradually changed into a population of individuals under the influence of medicine, including the awful results of artificially transformed human beings.[1]

This statement of the uncertain and helpless state of contemporary biologists and medical scientists is a faithful representation of the new wind that is blowing. It is also more than an admission that something is terribly wrong in biology and medicine. It is a declaration of moral impotence, revealing that the contemporary scientific conscience is, in truth, gravely ill.

Conscience, as we have defined it, is the recognition that one can distinguish between good and evil and is thus obliged to make moral choices. And it is precisely moral choices which biologists and medical scientists are now openly admitting that they are unable to make alone. Where will guidance come from? Moral uncertainty is a widespread feature of our scientific age, with its predilections for agnostic and atheistic humanism. Denying the authority of any form of external divine law, and equating evolution with continual change regardless of its direction, the world is hard pressed to find any criteria for making moral choices. Modern rational humanism, dominated by the scientific outlook, finds it difficult to distinguish between the moral, the amoral, and the immoral. As a result, one of the things most lacking in the world today is a feeling of rightness about the course of human life. To regain such a feeling will require the replacement of the enervated scientific conscience by a vigorous and robust conscience which refuses to submit to the exclusive authority of science. For the world is still dominated by an obsolete scientific outlook which proclaims that man, the summit of life, most actively participates in his own evolution by the scientific pursuit of biological knowledge, and that this anthropocentric end justifies all the means he can devise.

The scientific conscience has not yet recognized the ethical interplay that exists between the ends and the means of science. So far self-criticism within biology and medicine has been directed mainly against scientific ends. Naturally enough, there has been growing opposition to applying new scientific knowledge in ways which are leading to the chamber of horrors so vividly portrayed by Gordon Rattray Taylor in *The Biological Time Bomb.* [2] Obviously, a scientific conscience which approves, among other things, the modification of human lives through transplantation, drugs, and genetic engineering and on making biological warfare more efficient has every reason to be mistrusted and, as is now happening, to mistrust itself. Many scientific ends are, in fact, becoming questionable for scientists as well as laymen. But, with few exceptions, self-criticism within biology and medicine has so far paid little attention to scientific *means,* despite the fact that the present crisis of conscience in the life sciences bears directly upon the methods which scientists have been employing in the pursuit of their profession.

The methodology of contemporary biology and medicine involves to a large extent the use of animals as experimental objects. What sentient animals have experienced in biological and medical laboratories is more staggering to the mind and senses of anyone concerned about man's future than all the visions which accompany the unending stream of scientific breakthroughs. For, by any standard, this kind of methodology is morally outrageous and the most conclusive evidence imaginable for the impaired state of the scientific conscience. In having accepted the dictum that the ends justify all means, the biologists have convincingly demonstrated their inability to choose between good and evil. Can they then seriously expect intelligent and sensitive human beings to have confidence in their moral judgment or social responsibility when they continue to seek the truths of life by inflicting upon highly sentient forms of life the worst kind of physical and mental suffering?

Animal experimentation, regardless of what the biologists now think, is a problem of the utmost significance for the further evolution of life. Biologists are at this moment torturing and profaning untold numbers of living animals in laboratories all over the world. By these acts they are degrading themselves and retarding the human evolutionary ascent. In exploiting sentient beings for the sake of biological and medical knowledge, the scientific conscience is suffering from a sickness unto death. No amount of knowledge gained by these means, even when it is used to ameliorate the human condition, can remove the stain of wanton cruelty toward sentient beings and the denial of their basic rights. And even the biologists who are not directly involved must share some measure of guilt for their tacit acceptance of such practices by their colleagues.

In June 1969 there appeared in the London *Times* a letter on factory farming written by a group of scientists, including biologists of international repute. They strongly condemned the farmer who, in confining animals to a life of frustrating conditions, çruelly ignores their behavioral distress:

> As citizens of a modern nation we are further convinced
> that the practice of keeping animals under severely frustrating
> conditions, with all the signs of incipient or full nervous disfunc-
> tion similar to those of distress in ourselves, must have a numb-
> ing effect on the farmer's own sensitivity.

And further:

> Even as a short-term policy it should not be acceptable or
> excusable to ignore ill-treatment of animals. In the long run
> the tolerance, by a civilized society, of cruelty to animals which
> is recognized as such seems to us to carry the danger of returning
> to the level of the barbarian, to whom animals are things rather
> than fellow creatures.[3]

This was an admirable step forward. At the same time it is difficult to understand why biologists condemn farmers for practices which their colleagues, with completely benumbed sensitivity, began to employ long before factory farming was ever thought of.

More than a decade ago a long series of psychological experiments was begun in the United States on rhesus monkeys for the purpose of investigating what was called the nature of love in primates. The experiments included the use of artificial mother-surrogates and/or solitary confinement for periods extending up to several years. Many of the animals never recovered from the extreme mental and emotional distress they suffered and remained for the rest of their lives in highly abnormal states. A few years ago one of the authors of the letter to the *Times* described some of these experiments as "fascinating" and to the best of my knowledge never spoke of any of them with moral indignation or censure. It must be hoped then that this more recent letter indicates a change in the attitude of biologists toward frustrated animals, and that their righteous condemnation of factory farming already has been, or soon will be, extended to biological research—even if this means considering some of their colleagues to be barbarians. For it is primarily the experimental biologists and medical scientists who regard animals as things, and that to a degree which would be wholly inconceivable to any barbarian.

There can be little hope of fundamental progress in social responsibility in science before both the means and the ends of biology are made moral. The immorality of animal experimentation must be admitted and its practice at last abandoned by the voluntary action of the biologists themselves. Whether alternative methods of research, which so many antivivisection societies are now actively supporting, are available or not is quite irrelevant. The crux of the matter is that a renewal of the scientific conscience must come. The biologist must at last realize that he must refuse to study life's sentient forms if it means inflicting suffering upon them and denying them their basic rights. Biological and medical knowledge attained by such immoral methods can be of no avail to evolution, since it only retards the expression of human righteousness and compassion. No more efficacious step toward restoring confidence in the ultimate aims of biology and medicine could be taken than for biologists to choose voluntarily to restrain and restrict biological progress by employing only those means which are compatible with the moral and spiritual ascent of man.

> For not to know, either awake or in a dream, the nature of
> justice and injustice, and good and evil, cannot in truth be
> otherwise than disgraceful to him, even though he have the
> applause of the whole world.[4]

Plato's view of the human conscience can hardly be bettered. All scientists and laymen alike must eventually learn to distinguish good from evil simply because it is our evolutionary responsibility to do so.

Human evolution, in its fullest sense, is a spiritual ascent which is not guided by the human race at all. It is guided by that divine reality to which we owe our existence and the highest within us, and to which we are proceeding. This does not mean that men are simply being swept along toward their final destiny. Nor does it mean that they are meant to be passive spectators of their own immorality. Unlike other creatures, they have a conscience by which they can make moral choices. They are able to choose a course of thought and action which is either in flagrant opposition to, or in harmonious relation with, the infinite goodness of the reality which is drawing them upward. Little wonder that the noosphere we are creating confounds us! It has arisen out of our expanding consciousness at the cost of our conscience.

To invigorate, to fortify, and to renew the flagging human conscience so that it will be able to distinguish good from evil and act accordingly will give to the world a feeling of rightness about the whole course of life. And who in a scientific age are better suited to take the initiative than those who call themselves students of life? Great things are in store for the living procession when the scientific conscience fully awakens to its evolutionary responsibility. That this will come to pass is inevitable. What is needed now to transform scientific discontent into a positive force is a greater openness on the part of the scientist toward the religious world picture and its spiritual truths.

Notes

1. "En Kulturpolitisk Redegørelse" [A Cultural and Political Statement], Ministry for Cultural Affairs, Report no. 517 (Copenhagen, 1969).

2. G. R. Taylor, *The Biological Time Bomb* (London: Thames and Hudson, 1968).

3. *Times* (London), June 1969.

4. Plato, *Phaedrus,* 277de.

13

A Scientific Heretic

Although Michael Polanyi's evolutionary vision of bringing science and the scientific *Weltbild* closer to the truth is philosophical rather than theistic, there can be no mistaking his theocentric intent. In his great work, *Personal Knowledge,* which was based upon his Gifford Lectures in Aberdeen in 1951-1952, he states that he is attempting "to proceed by continuous steps from the scientific study of evolution to its interpretation as a clue to God."[1] At the same time Polanyi insisted that fundamental changes within established science are desperately needed. As he says elsewhere, "I do not challenge . . . the existence of science as a coherent system of thought: I merely press for its reform in certain respects."[2]

For many years Polanyi's quarrel with the scientific outlook was that its ideal of detached objectivity is a delusion. He maintained that the pursuit of scientific knowledge can be neither impersonal nor passive because the scientist's intellectual passion makes him personally committed to search for the truth. Scientific knowledge of objective reality, he claimed, is a union of the personal with the objective reality of the external world.

In calling his book *Personal Knowledge,* Polanyi distinguished between

the subjective and the personal. The subjective does not involve commitment; it is a state in which "we merely endure our feelings." The personal,
on the other hand, actively enters into commitment. As he states,

> In so far as the personal submits to requirements acknowledged
> by itself as independent of itself, it is not subjective; but in so
> far as it is an action guided by individual passions, it is not objec-
> tive either. It transcends the disjunction between subjective and
> objective.[3]

Were scientific knowledge to be attained in the recognition that it was a
commitment of intellectual passion involving a union of the personal and
the objective, there would, according to Polanyi, be revealed a new vision
of reality. Retention of the ideal of scientific objectivity, on the other
hand, threatens the future of science, and since it is an inherently false
ideal, it impairs man's moral vision as well.

Basic to Polanyi's proposals is his concept of superior knowledge as
"all that is coherently believed to be right and excellent by men . . . the
sum total of what its classics have uttered and its heroes and saints have
done."[4] Superior knowledge thus extends far beyond the domain of scientific knowledge. It is the record of the thoughts and deeds of the most
enlightened human beings, living or dead. Superior knowledge led Polanyi
to a vision of the extension of biology to a study of great men. This is
what he calls "ultra-biology," in which the biologist is personally committed to center his search for knowledge upon things higher than himself. Elsewhere I have discussed this concept:

> Ultra-biology, in brief, is simply biology's ultimate extrap-
> olation: the biologist's study of great men. Far from con-
> stituting a mere cult of hero worship, it is in the mind of
> Polanyi a further extension of the advance of biology, in
> which personal commitment plays an increasingly important
> role. Here a subtle distinction is drawn between the parti-
> cipation of the biologist in the achievements of living
> beings lower than himself and in the achievements of
> living beings superior to himself. While in both types of
> biological study he is committed to the search for truth,

in the former case he is not himself appreciably modified by
the personal knowledge he attains. In the latter case, since
his knowledge is "centering on things higher than himself,"
he is profoundly modified by its attainment. For by submitting to the superior knowledge of his masters, who are
greater than himself, he acknowledges his own inferiority
and is therefore committed to self-improvement by personal
participation in the attainment of truth. Only when scientists
are ready to discard as delusions the ideals of detached objectivity
and elimination of belief and passion, and substitute for them
the more human idea of personal commitment in their search
for the truth, will they be able to justify their activity and to
realize the role of ultra-biology in human evolution. According
to Polanyi, herein lies the hope of a better world.[5]

Polanyi clearly recognized that from an evolutionary point of view both
science and scientists are destined to undergo deep changes. Ultra-biology
is envisaged as a new kind of biology in which biologists will be personally
committed to the attempt to realize their own potentials. In Polanyi's
mind ultra-biology did not however appear to be essentially concerned
with potentiality as a function of the human-divine relation. Even if his
concept of the objective reality of the universe comprises a hierarchy of
being with God at the summit, he looked at human greatness as the realization of lower degrees of potentiality than the illumination accompanying religious-spiritual experience. At the same time certain passages in
Personal Knowledge point directly to Polanyi's fundamental interest in
the future relations between religion and science:

Our vastly enlarged perspectives of knowledge should open
up fresh vistas of religious faith. The Bible, and the Pauline
doctrine in particular, may be still pregnant with unsuspected
lessons; and the greater precision and more conscious flexi-
bility of modern thought, shown by the new physics and the
logico-philosophic movements of our age, may presently en-
gender conceptual reforms which will renew and clarify, on
the grounds of modern extra-religious experience, man's relation to God. An era of great religious discoveries may lie

before us. . , , Today we should be grateful for the prolonged
attacks made by rationalists on religion for forcing us to renew
the grounds of the Christian faith.[6]

Polanyi subsequently modified to some extent his concept of knowledge
by introducing the idea that there exists an even more profound commitment to seek truth than intellectual passion. This is the "tacit component"
by which "we know more than we can tell." Tacit thought is thus associated with inarticulate mental faculties, and if it "forms an indispensable
part of all knowledge, then the idea of eliminating all personal elements of
knowledge would, in effect, aim at the destruction of all knowledge. The
idea of exact science would turn out to be fundamentally misleading and
possibly a source of devastating fallacies."[7] If the existence and significance
of tacit knowledge were recognized, it might, he believes, compel scientists to renounce their present ideal of scientific objectivity. This is a
revolutionary claim that demands a hearing in any discussion of the
impact of science upon evolving life.

In his own Gifford Lectures, Sir Alister Hardy quotes Polanyi at length
with respect to the concept of tacit knowledge.[8] He stresses Polanyi's
suggestion that tacit knowledge is shared by men and animals alike and
that the tacit powers of animals may even be greater than man's. This
view is of course relevant to Hardy's view of man's basic relation to the
animal kingdom through shared mental activity and is fundamental to
his theory that the whole living world is linked up by a divine element
which is part of the natural process. Polanyi's views, according to Hardy,
thus stress the need for more research on animal behavior in order to
acquire a better understanding of evolution.

Here we are discussing Polanyi's views for other reasons, even though
it cannot be claimed that they offer any direct support for our indictment of the unethical goals of biology and medicine nor of their methodology which involves the misuse of sentient animals. Although Polanyi
clearly stated that "the freedom of the subjective person to do as he
pleases is overruled by the freedom of the responsible person to act as
he must," he does not seem to relate this fact to the biologist's confrontation with the choice between good and evil in the pursuit of his profession. In *Personal Knowledge* he has no condemnation of animal experimentation and mentions *en passant,* and then only indirectly, the state
of the scientific conscience:

> My opposition to a universal mechanical interpretation of
> things, on the ground that it impairs man's moral con-
> sciousness, also implies some measure of dissent from the
> absolute moral neutrality of science. Yet though the issue
> is not yet altogether closed, the principle of moral and
> religious indifference prevails throughout modern science
> without facing so far any effective rival to its rule. . . .[9]

He is also careful to point out in *The Tacit Dimension* that he is not advocating submission to the dogma of contemporary religious authority.

Despite these qualifications, Polanyi's thoughts are of the greatest
relevance to the concept of spiritualized biology with which this book
is concerned. Pregnant with spiritual-ethical implications, his views support, albeit indirectly, the theocentric foundation upon which *Science,
Animals and Evolution* rests. In one place Polanyi says,

> Each new branch of biology that was developed to cover the
> increasingly complex function of higher animals sets up addi-
> tional standards, to which the observer expects the animal to
> measure up. And this intensification of criticism coincides with
> an increasing enrichment of relations between the critic and
> his object. We know an animal, as we know a person, by enter-
> ing into its performance, and we appreciate it as an individual,
> in the interests of which these performances have their mean-
> ing. Even at the lowest, purely vegetative level, we accept the
> interests of the animal as the standard by which our own
> interest in the animal is determined. All biology is, in this sense,
> convivial. But this conviviality rises to emotional concern as the
> animal approaches the human level. We then become aware of
> its sentience, of its intelligence, and above all of its emotional
> relations to ourselves.

> Yet however greatly we may love an animal, there is an emo-
> tion which no animal can evoke and which is commonly directed
> toward our fellow men. I have said that at the highest level of
> personhood we meet man's moral sense, guided by the firma-
> ment of his standards. Even when this appears absent, its mere
> possibility is sufficient to demand our respect.

We have here a fact which sets a new major task to the process of evolution: a task which appears the more formidable as we realize that both this moral sense and our respect for it presuppose an obedience to commands accepted in defiance of the immemorial scheme of self-preservation which has dominated the evolutionary process up to this point.

Yet evolution must make sense also of this after-thought to five hundred million years of pure self-seeking. And in a way this problem can be put in biological terms. For this potentiality for obedience to higher demands is largely involved in man's capacity for another peculiarly human relation to other men, namely, the capacity to feel reverence for men greater than oneself. If evolution is to include the rise of man, with all his sense of higher obligations, it must include also the rise of human greatness.[10]

There can be no doubt that in this evolutionary vision, Polanyi is seeing the path that leads toward the Light. For he dwells upon the ascent of man in terms of realization of potentiality dependent upon intuitive recognition of higher obligations than physical survival. His vision rests on the idea of the evolutionary commitment of evolving man to surpass himself by recognizing and participating in that which is higher than himself. And this, he rightly observes, is due to a creative power inherent in the universe "that goes beyond that which we can account for in ourselves." Polanyi was fully aware of the hierarchy of being in the universe and of man's search for truth and the personal participation in it which transforms the seeker. The Pauline scheme "which imposes an obligation to strive for the impossible in the hope of achieving it by divine grace" seemed to him to be the most satisfactory explanation of human striving.

His vision points toward the divine. It may well be that Michael Polanyi knew more about this hidden reality than he was able to tell.

Notes

1. M. Polanyi, *Personal Knowledge: Towards a Post-critical Philosophy* (London: Routledge & Kegan Paul, 1958), p. 285.

2. M. Polanyi, *The Tacit Dimension* (New York: Doubleday, 1966), p. 74.

3. Polanyi, *Personal Knowledge,* p. 300.

4. *Ibid.,* pp. 375, 376.

5. C. Roberts, *The Scientific Conscience: Reflections on the Modern Biologist and Humanism* (New York: George Braziller, 1967), pp. 54-55.

6. Polanyi, *Personal Knowledge,* pp. 285, 286.

7. Polanyi, *The Tacit Dimension,* p. 20.

8. A. Hardy, *The Divine Flame: An Essay Towards a Natural History of Religion* (London: Collins, 1966).

9. Polanyi, *Personal Knowledge,* p. 153.

10. Polanyi, *The Tacit Dimension,* pp. 51-52.

14

The Spiritualization of Biology as an Evolutionary Imperative

This book began by comparing anthropocentric and theocentric views of that gigantic act in space and time we call human evolution, and the point was made that their divergence is primarily a teleological one. Man is either evolving away as a purposeless development of individual units of body and mind whose limited potentials are strictly autonomous, *or* man is being returned to his divine source through the progressive realization of his infinite spiritual potentials. Modern science, basically anthropocentric, denies the existence of any cognitive evolutionary force higher than the human mind. Religion, basically theocentric, is concerned with the action of divine reality upon evolving human life. Both world pictures cannot be true. Wherein lies the truth?

After decades of faith and confidence in the scientific age, evolving man, now overwhelmed by crises without end, is no longer so favorably disposed to science and the scientific world picture. Many voices are saying that the unrestrained advance and application of science, being largely responsible for our predicament, must be redirected or restrained. A few years ago an article in one of America's influential magazines spoke not only of America's rising discontent with scientific achievement and with its growing opposition, both within and without scientific circles, to the rational, materialistic, and objective ideals of science but also of a noticeable turning toward religion and mysticism.[1] Another sign of the times was the Copenhagen newspaper dropped into our letter-box while I was writing this chapter. It contained an article on ethical values in science and art, an article on recent scientific discoveries pointing toward the existence of emotional life in plants and their bearing on philosophy and religion, and an interview with a Danish professor of biology, who, in speaking about the inexplicable mysteries of human life, insisted that to penetrate them, man must turn beyond biology to art and religion. All these signs breed optimism. Is evolving man in a scientific age at last beginning to look in the right direction?

In the belief that however much man has strayed from the path of spiritual enlightenment during the past five hundred years, his ultimate destiny is to become wholly spiritualized and that he is being divinely helped in his ascent by evolutionary forces of cosmic good, I would like now to reiterate and expand the theocentric concept of potentiality in its bearing upon the future of biology. The attempt could not have been made without the inspiration afforded by many minds aware of the inevitable convergence of science and religion. Even with their help, there is no finality in what follows. As new vistas continue to open up, it can be no more than a preliminary response to some of the mysteries of spiritual evolution. Yet in dealing with potentiality as a function of both the human-divine relation and the human-animal relation, my hope is that this contribution, too, will be in harmony with life's compulsory striving toward the Good.

Potentiality and the Human-Divine Relation

In seeking to understand life and its evolution, biologists have penetrated further and further into its physical and chemical structure and hereditary constitution. Passing from gross anatomical form to tissues to cells to genes and finally to molecules, they have shown that in all phenotypic expressions of life from bacteria to man the fundamental biological unit is the DNA molecule. And since deoxyribonucleic acid is the bearer of what is called genetic "information," modern biology sees individual life as the progressive realization of the genetic potentiality it received at birth, and individual death as the irrevocable termination of further self-realization. For the destruction of the body removes the physical basis of human potentiality, which, for scientific materialists, is its only possible basis. From the standpoint of the evolution of the species, all its intelligence, understanding, and creative endeavor, as well as its ethical systems and religious ideologies, appear to them as expressions of the autonomous development of life striving to become as real as its genetic potential will permit. And human reality, they say, has already become godlike: Thanks to his genes, man is now able to manipulate his life span, his intelligence, and his behavior. Seeing this rapid realization of genetic potentiality as a speeding up of human evolution, they conclude that it was in the scientific age that *Homo sapiens* first became worthy of his name.

This is anthropocentric humanism. By it biologists are blinded to the true nature of the human potential. They cannot see its relation to the divine, for they cannot see beyond the limits of the physical reality of life and what they call its associated mental, emotional, and ethical epiphenomena. They cannot even admit the possibility that an individual life on earth is only an interval between the preexistence and postexistence of an evolving spiritual being. Their narrow vision leads them to wholly inadequate evolutionary claims as, for example, that scientific advance has already destroyed religion or that every process of growth has its limits. These claims are patently untrue. Belief in the human-divine relation is still very much alive, and life's spiritual-ethical growth potential is as infinite as the divine reality itself. It is qualitative growth, whereby men become better. It is equatable with the immense journey the individual human soul is making to return to the source of its being.

However rationally and vehemently many biologists continue to assert their atheism and their disbelief in the reality of the immortal soul and the realm of the spirit, they are unable to disprove the fact that at this very moment evolving human life is actually falling under the compulsion of the divine Good. Atheistic biologists who are fighting for their rational, materialistic, reductionistic interpretation of evolving life cannot, however, be expected to remain long ignorant of the spiritual forces that are impinging upon it. With the religious awakening gaining ground, younger biologists confronted with a rapidly changing climate of world thought will find it increasingly difficult to turn their backs upon the spiritual aspects of the life they are studying. How much more sensible, then, for all biologists to listen with an open mind to alternative views about the nature of potentiality which refuse to be constrained by the undeniable laws of chemistry and physics and the indubitable facts of genetics, molecular biology, and physical evolution. Since potentiality is an attribute of the whole hierarchy of life, both its human and nonhuman forms are proper subjects for biological attention. We shall begin with a consideration of human potentiality.

Theocentric humanism recognizes divinity as the ultimate Good and the supreme Reality, existing spiritually as the noncreated First Cause involved in, but also exalted above, the universe it created; whether conceived as God, mind, spirit, law, will, or light, it is acknowledged as the highest good to which life can aspire. Theocentric humanism believes man's destiny is to return to this transcendent source of his being and to become increasingly spiritualized in his ascent; to promote this end he is provided not only with body, mind, and soul, but also with some kind of "impeccable center" of inner divinity—be it called spark, spirit, or the eye or apex of the soul—which, in seeking the light, divests evolving life of its human limitations and provides it with divine purpose. Theocentric humanists hold that the individual human life on earth continues its conscious existence and strivings after the death of the body. Whether or not they all accept the doctrine of preexistence and reincarnation or transmigration of souls, they agree with the religious postulate that evolution in the body is only part of the ascent of man, and that since he cannot lose his spark of inner divinity which is ever striving, consciously or unconsciously, to return to its source, the human potential is in truth immortal and divine.

Theocentric humanism can thus offer the scientific age an alternative view of evolving human life in terms of spiritual rather than genetic potentiality: The essence of human life on earth at any moment in evolutionary time is its nongenic spiritual diversity, and one of the prime tasks of biology, the study of life, is to investigate how spiritual potentialities have been realized and how their realization can be enhanced. Any human population contains saintly and satanic souls, together with all grades between. By studying this diversity biology could help to make all men better. The modern world has long been overridden with a plethora of criminal acts of violence, injustice, and destruction committed by men lacking spiritual enlightenment and its accompanying moral sense. In desperation the world has looked to the life sciences to discover how these deflections from ethical behavior arise and how they can be prevented. What is lacking is an equal, if not greater, interest in the saintly conduct that characterizes spiritually enlightened individuals. If we consider this, as we should, a biological problem, then we are led directly to Michael Polanyi's vision of the extrapolation of biology into ultra-biology, in which biologists, for the sake of human progress, center their attention upon objective reality higher than themselves. And the more attention the biologist pays to these higher truths, the greater his inclination to pursue the most humanly significant problems of life. The whole direction of biology, and medicine as well, would thus receive a spiritual-ethical thrust.

Here we are expanding the concept of ultra-biology into spiritual biology in the conviction that the ultimate objective reality is the divine. And since it is spiritually related to evolving life in ways we do not understand, it follows that the primary goal of studying life is to elucidate the nature of the human-divine relation. In a time of spiritual awakening the search for spiritual knowledge through preoccupation with religious and mystical teaching and experience seems so clearly the "right" thing to do. Why does it refresh and invigorate us? Why do we seek out the spiritual reality that the scientific age has so long denied? One answer may be that we know intuitively that only in the divine can man find the sense of righteousness he so desperately needs for his further evolution.

What becomes significant for the future of the life sciences is that the acquisition of spiritual knowledge is on a wholly different plane from the acquisition of scientific knowledge: it can permanently transform the knower. And since the spiritual is indissolubly associated with the divine Good, the transformation becomes, in the most real sense, an ethical one. This is not to imply that every biologist who investigates the spiritual aspects of life is to become a saint, mystic, or religious prophet, but in studying the highest potentials of man's spiritual diversity, he is automatically provided with an opportunity better to realize his own. For he is being turned toward the spiritual light that is falling upon the world, and he is transformed in the turning.

How the turning comes about is essentially a mystery. The divine light that is falling upon the world from the realm of the spirit does not automatically make us sacrosanct. The holiness of life depends upon the ability to see and absorb the light, but enlightenment is more than passive reception. The realization of spiritual potentiality, made possible through divine guidance and inspiration, must somehow be earned. As far as can be judged, the love, compassion, meekness, purity, and righteousness of the saints, sages, and mystics required a mighty effort on their part to orient the eye of their soul, or divine spark, toward the light that was falling upon them. It seemed to entail a resolve to purify their own mental world by thinking good, positive, cheerful thoughts in all situations—a kind of conscious commitment to turn all earthly experience into nonegoistic spiritual gain. At the same time the resolve appears to be initiated and sustained by superhuman forces. The turning toward the spiritual realm is based on cognizance of "a certain sphere above which the soul could not rise by her own efforts."[2] A particularly beautiful expression of this mysterious relation between divine and human will is found in this Christian fragment:

> I will try this day to live a simple, sincere and serene life,
> repelling promptly every thought of discontent, anxiety,
> discouragement, impurity, self-seeking. . . . In particular
> I will try to be faithful in those habits of prayer, work, study,
> physical exercise, eating and sleep which I believe the Holy
> Spirit has shown me to be right. And as I cannot in my own
> strength do this, nor even with a hope of success attempt it,
> I look to thee, O Lord my Father, in Jesus Christ my Savior,
> and ask for the gift of the Holy Spirit.[3]

The religious experience of turning toward the light, be it Christian or non-Christian, involves the gradual destruction of the lower egoistic self through faith in the existence of higher spiritual reality so that the immortal soul, helped by recollection, can better see. And since the scientific age, despite its ingrained resistance, is being drawn ever closer to the light, it behooves biologists, as sensible and rational human beings, to move in ever greater harmony with the cosmic evolutionary forces that are leading us out of the darkness.

As the spiritualization of biology progresses, objective, dispassionate scientific investigations of religious or mystical experiences can be expected to give way to personal participation in these higher realizations of human potentiality and its accompanying spiritual transformation. Obviously, only those most radically transformed are best qualified to speak, if they will speak, on the nature of the transformation. At these lower, darker levels we can only compare their records with our own, pitifully small in comparison, to indicate the magnitude of religious-spiritual experiences open to biological study and participation.

One who has experienced a high degree of personal transformation speaks, for example, in these terms:

To open the mind need not mean to close the heart, but to
cleanse and clarify it, and that only in the reason of a purified
heart can the mind be truly enlightened. Then, indeed, man's
feet will be once again on "the Way" from which he has
wandered throughout his history so often and so disastrously,
but to which every great teacher has sought to recall him. . . .
Although, therefore, we can learn much from the traditional
teachings about "the Way," it will involve for modern men
and women a distinctive journey towards meaning which
must take account of the situation in which we find ourselves today. The dominant factor in that situation which
was largely lacking in the past is a one-sided development
of the mind in the scientific field and a self-conscious indi-
vidualism in which the exercise of intellectual analysis has,
as I have suggested, almost sterilised spiritual intelligence.[4]

A Christian theologian, also speaking with the authority of personal experience, enlightens us further about spiritual intelligence and participation:

Theological thinking is essentially a spiritual activity in which
we are engaged in a movement that corresponds to the movement of the Spirit and indeed participates in it. It is a form of
kinetic thinking in which the reason does not apprehend the
truth by sitting back and thinking ideas, but is an act or movement in which it participates in what it seeks to know.

. . . through the Spirit we are converted from ourselves to
thinking from a centre in God and not in ourselves, and to
knowing God out of God and not out of ourselves. . . . The
Holy Spirit operates within us, but in order to turn us inside
out. He is at work to realize the Godward side of our life,
and to direct us in all our being and knowing away from
our own subjectivity to the objective Reality of God's
own Being and Word.[5]

In *The Mystical Life* J. H. M. Whiteman speaks of mystical experience
as a transformation through the progressive development of spiritual consciousness. This development, he says, "is no unnatural striving for the

'occult,' no abandonment to subjective feeling states, but the gradual unveiling of all that is most real and heart-fulfilling in our lives here and
now."[6]

What is being unveiled? Whatever it may be, those who cannot see beyond the veil realize intuitively that conscience is somehow involved.
Speaking of what he calls "participation in the perfect humanity of God,"
Whiteman mentions the "spiritual transformation that goes with it,
causing a permanent awakening to righteousness and an anguish of battle
against self-centered desires and worldly persuasions." He speaks also,
as any platonist and theocentric humanist must speak, of mystical experience giving "a new direction to the ethical conduct of our lives in this
world," of the realization of the "potentiality of the individual for good,"
and of "spiritual death" as the "departure from total regard for the Good
and accepting the outlooks and values of the world." The human mind,
Whiteman believes, has a higher and lower part; the higher "is active
within us when our life is governed by the conscience of goodness and
truth (partly, if of truth alone; wholly, if of goodness with truth),"
while the lower mind is "active when that conscience is forgotten or
ignored." This emphasis on the ethical aspect of mysticism is echoed by
H. H. Price, who, in his illuminating introduction to Whiteman's book,
speaks of "the moral disciplines which seem to be the necessary conditions for having it [the mystical experience] and the transformation of
moral character which seems to be the almost invariable consequence
of it."

The out-of-the-body experiences with which Whiteman is primarily
concerned he calls "separation" phenomena, in which the conscious
mind, in varying degrees, is released from the body for different periods
of time. In maintaining that following mystical separation, the mystic
returns to the body "healed and spiritually invigorated for the leading of
a better life in this world," he again points to the ethical association of
the genuinely spiritual phenomena with the divine Good. Is it possible
that the unveiling of this real and heart-fulfilling aspect of human life—
man's recognition and love of divine righteousness—can be successfully
investigated or understood by the dispassionate objectivity of modern
science? There is not the slightest chance that it can. Any study of the
spiritual diversity of life that leads to true enlightenment means that
both the investigator and the investigation become increasingly spiritualized by their approach to the divine.

It has been wisely said that one of the most difficult tasks is to persuade human beings of their own potential divinity.[7] This applies in particular to those biologists who, obdurately clinging to the scientific *Weltbild*, oppose their souls' search for the light of the spiritual realm. Theocentric humanism, attempting to make this realm supremely desirable for man, is suggesting a new orientation of the students of life toward it for the sake of potentiality and its realization. It is trying to persuade them to participate in an evolutionary ascent by which man surpasses himself not anthropocentrically for his own sake but theocentrically for the sake of the cosmic Good.

A widespread belief of the scientific age is that the reality of deity and the spiritual realm, together with all the holiness, sanctity, and mystery we see in it, is man-created, existing only as projections of thoughts from the human mind. Others hold that transcendent reality, being perceptible by the expanded consciousness, exists but only as part of a natural universe, in which there is no place for the supernatural or divine. In denying the objective existence of divine reality and its intervention in evolution, the anthropocentric humanist confidently expects that as science advances, any psychological or psychic phenomena which now tend to support the idea of uncreated "supernatural" reality will have become natural phenomena, neatly fitting into an expanded scientific world view based upon the proposition that evolving life is strictly autonomous.

The theocentric humanist, in contrast, sees deity as the ultimate, transcendent objective reality, from which the spiritual realm arises. Although he believes this realm to be nonspatial, his conceptions of it are often based upon spatial symbolism. He may regard it as a plenum extending from an invisible transcendent perfection down to life on earth; he may visualize it as rays of light emanating from the Godhead, or as a hierarchy of spiritual beings. In any case, it cannot be dissociated from the numinous, which is that part of the divine reality which arouses awareness of itself in the human soul and consciousness. And anyone who is convinced in faith of the reality and divine origin of the spiritual realm knows that it is a vast reservoir of forces and energies that man can, and must, utilize, in his further ascent.

In discussing the turning of biological attention toward man's spiritual diversity, we have so far been concerned with its highest manifestation in the form of religious or mystical experiences in which divine reality is apprehended in an intuitive, suprarational, or extrasensory way. There remains the difficult question of whether the whole range of unexplained human experience designated as paranormal phenomena is also apprehension of divine light from the spiritual realm. Are paranormal phenomena nothing but a creation of the human psyche or, like the mystical experience, are they spiritual in the sense of revealing different degrees of human contact with the divine? The difference of opinion that reigns among theocentric humanists has been nicely summarized by H. H. Price, who, as Sir Alister Hardy[8] points out, looked forward years ago to the help psychical research can give in resolving the conflict between science and religion. In his introduction to Whiteman's book, Price writes:

> It would seem that "psychic powers" (psi-capacities as they are sometimes called) do quite commonly emerge at a certain stage of a mystic's spiritual development. Some mystics, both Eastern and Western, have regarded them with suspicion; and some writers on mysticism, Dean Inge, for example, seem to think that the less said about them, the better. They have been thought of as hindrances in the path of spiritual progress, or even as temptations. A sharp distinction has sometimes been drawn between "the psychical" on the one hand and "the spiritual" on the other; and certainly there is nothing very spiritual about card-guessing experiments or telepathic dreams, or the phenomena of physical mediumship.

He then speaks of Whiteman's claim concerning the existence of successive stages in a psychical-spiritual hierarchy:

> On this view, out-of-the-body experiences, even when they purport to be experiences of other worlds (and not merely of this one, observed from a point of view at which the percipient's physical organism is not at the moment located) would be classed as psychical, not spiritual. In the Hindu Vedantist terminology, other worlds—even worlds of a "heavenly" kind—belong to the sphere of *Maya,* the realm of Names and Forms, whereas spiritual experience takes us beyond that sphere.

> Dr. Whiteman's view is rather different, if I interpret him rightly. He conceives of these out-of-the-body and other-world

experiences as a graded series (an uphill path, so to speak) with *Deificatio,* the highest experience of all, as its culmination.[9]

Whiteman does not, however, seem to regard all graded experiences of this kind as truly mystical or spiritual in the sense of being expressions of the human-divine relation. Although he states there are great difficulties in characterizing them, particularly the transitional phenomena, he believes that some may be properly regarded as psychical or psychological. In general, he regards the psychological state as one which "may come and go," while the spiritual "takes root in us, to survive as a part of our being," a distinction which emphasizes the transforming nature of the truly spiritual experience. Whiteman says further that in a mystical experience one is continuously conscious of the Godhead, whereas in the psychical, which may represent merely the condition of the lower mind, there is no continuous centering of attention upon the divine.

Our vast ignorance of the nature and interplay of mind and soul in both conscious and subconscious states, in the body and without, makes difficult any rationally satisfying distinction between psychical and spiritual phenomena. Whatever knowledge of this matter there may be in my subconscious mind and soul, I can only give conscious expression to an intuitive conviction that a religious distinction is possible: The spiritual is ever associated with the light and goodness of divine reality, while the psychical need not be so. In a spiritual experience some of the reality of the spiritual realm must "take root in us," as Whiteman says, to transform us. Psychical experiences, including those which science calls "paranormal" because they are inexplicable by natural laws, need not be transforming. For the psychical realm, which accompanies the evolution of the human mind must be "lower" and less real than the spiritual realm, which has its origin apart from us. But since the psychical can become permanently linked with spiritual goodness and light in ways evolving man does not fully understand, a study of psychical phenomena obviously becomes a matter of interest to any student of life who is seeking the truths of evolution.

It is not often that theocentric humanists who are interested in psychical phenomena attempt to relate them to biology and evolution. One who has done so is Sir Alister Hardy, whose Gifford Lectures for 1964-1965 are encompassed in a remarkable two-volume work already referred to which, in its entirety, constitutes a theistic plea for the scientific investigation of evolving life in its relation to the divine. In rightly asserting that

life, especially the mind-body relation, cannot be understood by the laws
of chemistry and physics alone, Hardy maintains that it becomes more
understandable if we can believe that "the living stream of evolution is as
much divine as physical in nature." Hardy wishes to persuade a scientific
age to accept this belief, based upon a conception of the divine as an
attribute of an external power whose nature we do not know but which
seems partly transcendent and partly immanent. Divinity is thus "not
strictly supernatural, but paraphysical," and evolving man needs an
" 'extra-sensory' contact with a Divine Power which *is greater than, and
in part lies beyond, the individual self.*" Hardy then asserts that the scientific investigation of nature can "help in the re-establishment of a declining faith" because it would make a scientifically minded public
realize that "a faith in spirituality was not contrary to scientific fact."
He advocates in particular a concentration of scientific investigation of the
mind-body relation in the hope of demonstrating that evolving life is subject to a paraphysical force which he would call divine. In the belief that
the intensification of psychical research could thus destroy the atheistic,
materialistic, scientific world picture, Hardy envisages this kind of expansion of biology as the inauguration of a new age of faith. It would mean,
he believes, the "re-establishment of the idea of God as both a philosophical
and scientific Reality."

In stating his reasons for believing that further psychical research would
be of enormous help in centering attention of the world upon the religious-
spiritual outlook, he writes:

> If psi-phenomena, as they are now often called, do *not* fit
> into the material-physical system then they must have a
> profound meaning for both religion and philosophy; they
> would not only throw light, either directly or indirectly,
> upon the vexed question of the mind-body relationship,
> but would break once and for all the supposed scientific
> grounds for the materialism which now grips the world.
> Their existence would establish that there *is* a dualism of
> material and mental elements. This would alter the whole
> intellectual atmosphere and again admit the reality of a
> non-material, spiritual if you like, part of the universe
> in which the religious yearnings of man could find a
> place; it would be like supplying air to a fire which is now

only dimly flickering for lack of it. The divine flame would
burn with a new light.[10]

While I fully agree with Hardy that biology has a role to play in man's
religious orientation toward the divine, I believe that future relations between science and religion will be somewhat different from those he has
envisaged. This belief arises out of what appears to me to be a shortcom-
ing in Hardy's vision of evolving human life: his neglect of the problem
of good and evil and ethical choice.

Hardy assumes that any paranormal phenomenon which points toward
the existence of a nonmaterial, extrasensory part of the universe is also
pointing toward there where "God must lie." In other words, since psi-
phenomena cannot fit into the material-physical system, they must reveal
the existence of a spiritual realm of divine origin, and it must be the task
of conventional biology to uncover this fact scientifically.

These assumptions seem questionable. Psychical experiences do not
necessarily represent contact with the spiritual realm. "Mental elements"
need not be spiritual elements. At this stage in evolution, man's psychical
realm seems to be no more than a potential link with the light of the
spiritual realm, with only a small fraction of the potentiality having been
realized. The psychical realm may exist, as Hardy claims, as a stream of
mental activity which has accompanied man's physical evolution, but
since man has obviously not come very far in his spiritual ascent, it follows
that both the conscious and subconscious components of his mind-soul
complex are still highly imperfect and very far from the reality of the
spiritual realm toward which they are progressing. His compulsory ascent
toward the Good, essentially religious in nature, has already met great
resistance in the scientific age. Theocentric humanism, which is a conscious awareness of the human-divine relation, has been temporarily ob-
scured by an anthropocentric humanism which rejects divinity. If the
universe contains evil spirits and forces, the world's consciousness and
subconsciousness may have been feeling the full force of their attack. If
Jung's collective unconscious exists, the archetypes of darkness may have
been in the ascendancy. Whether the veil of egoism which blinds us to the
spiritual light is of our own making or not, our psychical world is now
replete with ethical apathy and chaos as well as evil intent. If science is
to reestablish the idea of deity, it will need not only to study the psychical
realm but, more important, to attempt to purify it so that it can become

a more complete and perfect link with the divine. Conventional objective science can never do this.

It is indeed quite difficult to imagine modern science as we know it today inaugurating a new age of faith. Faith has to do with a turning toward the divine Good. If biological investigators of the psychical realm, as Hardy expects, are to help to satisfy man's religious yearnings, I believe they must fulfill two conditions which Hardy neglects: (1) They must be concerned to show what relation exists between the psychical and the ethical, and (2) They must replace their objectivity and ethical apathy with personal engagement and ethical aspiration.

A Danish television program some years back, ambiguously called "Focus on Superstition," comes to mind. It consisted for the most part of interviews with healers of human ills who claimed their skills depended upon hypnosis, magnetism, diet, minerals, herbs, or Jesus, together with fortune tellers, clairvoyants, astrologers, and an eighty-year-old musician who, as a Danish counterpart of England's Rosemary Brown, claimed that her unquestionable musical abilities were due to the constant presence and guidance of Frédéric Chopin. I contest none of these claims. The existence of mysterious powers and curative forces in the universe has long been established and must not be brushed aside by biology or medicine. Both professions have much to learn from the unorthodox. It is, however, worthy of note that the perspectives of the unorthodox who were interviewed that evening appeared to be more psychical than spiritual. Even in the demonstration of religious healing, emphasis was not upon the existence of a supreme Good per se but upon the existence of a higher power that can serve mankind by relieving our sufferings and prolonging our existence on earth. There was little, if any, thought devoted to a divine ethic by which mankind could serve its creator. Nor was there any thought of the very real danger that might arise should any of these paranormal capacities become the property of immature, unscrupulous souls.

As a friend, discussing the problem of the psychical and the ethical, recently wrote:

> The psychical phenomena commonly investigated have a quite
> earthy ring to them, [being associated with] all too human
> longings and emotions. . . . If, as I suspect, the paraphysical
> plenum stretches like an elastic thong between the spiritual

and the material poles of nature, evil may also get in and
play havoc at its lower end. And so, morality first. . . .[11]

Of course! What profit telepathy if men have nothing good to communicate? What profit hypnosis if hypnotizers have never tried to orient
their souls toward the light? We must remember that despite the spiritual
awakening, our situation is still desperate. In a civilization in the throes
of intellectual and ethical chaos, beset on all sides with suffering, want,
pollution, violence, death, and destruction, men everywhere continue to
make choices in flagrant disharmony with life's striving toward the Good.
It follows that the science of life has matters of much higher priority
than the investigation of psychical phenomena to satisfy scientific curiosity. Life's most pressing concern at the moment is ethical enlightenment, to find as quickly as it can the answer to Socrates's question, How
can men learn to distinguish good from evil—and act accordingly? This
question, in which biology is deeply involved, is essentially a religious
question.

Alister Hardy sees clearly the coming convergence of biology and
religion. But in neglecting the problem of good and evil and ethical choice,
the carte blanche he gives established biology is premature. The world does
not stand to profit spiritually by the scientific exploration of life phenomena based exclusively on conventional scientific methodology and attitudes. It must be remembered that the contemporary scientific conscience openly admits that it is unable to distinguish good from evil. If
science is ever to point toward the light of a divine force intervening in
evolution, there must be a conscious turning of scientific attention toward
the religious-ethical aspects of life and a replacement of moral apathy by
moral vision.

What we see is something quite different, generally speaking. Conventional biology based upon objectivity, amorality, or immorality, and
atheism is already engaged in psychical research, where the prefix *psych-*
is invariably used to refer to mind and mental functioning rather than
to soul or spirit, and where "parapsychology" means the study of any
mysterious, inexplicable phenomenon associated with conscious or subconscious states. According to a 1972 survey based upon replies to 1,500
questionnaires, interest in psychical research is, however, now so strong
that the majority within the scientific community favor its further advance
even if this should upset the scientific *Weltbild;* there is even a growing

discontent with the slow progress being made. "There even appears to be a definite feeling that the present pattern of quasi-psychological experimentation is inherently fruitless and needs to be replaced by radically different tactics.[12] Corroboration of this attitude has been expressed by the president of the Society for Psychical Research in London. In alluding to the fact that "all that psychical research has established is the occurrence of various phenomena which cannot yet be understood," he asserted that none of the present theories provide really valid explanations of the phenomena and stressed that what are wanted are verifiable hypotheses.[13]

It is probably correct to say that most investigators of psychical phenomena are scientific materialists who neglect religion and ethics in the pursuit of their profession. This is not to forget those who have hoped to "demonstrate that a spiritual world exists, a world of independent and abiding realities, not a mere 'Epi-phenomenon' or transitory effect of the material world."[14] But it might be helpful to suggest that if, in their present search for new theories, hypotheses, and tactics, they were to open their minds to the possibility that a spiritual realm which, in virtue of its divine ethic, exists on a higher plane than the psychical realm, they would be in a better position to elucidate the nature of both. In denying the existence of divine reality, everything in the universe remains natural for the investigator, and without the supernatural he is reduced to the tedious objectivity and moral apathy of contemporary science. So long as these conditions prevail, investigators of any kind of psychical phenomena can be expected to grope in darkness among insignificant paranormal phenomena and still more insignificant interpretations of them.

If science is to draw attention to religious truths, then, from the theocentric point of view, the ultimate verifiable hypothesis for the investigation of the whole range of paranormal phenomena from card guessing to the mystical union with God would be whether it can transform moral potentiality into moral vision. In other words, will the investigator himself be ethically transformed in the pursuit of his investigations? This does not mean that he must blindly accept the spiritual-ethical basis of the religious *Weltbild* before beginning his work, but he must be so open to it that he will recognize the possibility that the ethical development of the biologist is a fundamental part of biological investigation of the psychical link between the material and the spiritual.

In considering the fact that speculations about the sub- or unconscious component of psychical activity can never penetrate to the essence of the matter, it is not surprising that scientific attempts to do so have led to such widely divergent views as those of Freud and Jung. The former saw the unconscious as a psychological fact, which, as a rational scientist, he used to challenge the whole religious-spiritual world picture. Jung, on the other hand, was drawn all his life to the truths of religion but his scientific outlook prevented him from making them a part of his being. His contributions to human thought were nevertheless extraordinary. From his mind emerged the concept of the collective unconscious, made up of inherited psychical factors called "archetypal categories of the imagination" and which included the God-image archetype. But in denying that his mind could distinguish between God and the unconscious, and that as a consequence he could not know "whether God and the unconscious are two separate entities," he postulated deity only as a psychic truth dwelling within the individual. The possibility that it could also exist as a transcendent reality outside man he did not deny, but if at times he leaned toward this view, he appeared to do so without the conviction of theocentricity. Jung's agnosticism may explain his lifelong aversion to the concept of perfectionism; he saw human evolution in terms of the realization of "wholeness," both good and bad, rather than a gradual approach to the Good of the spiritual realm.

Let us turn again to platonic views of human potentiality. In his concept of immortality and preexistence of the soul, Plato properly carried "psychology" far beyond the limits of any modern field of science which attempts to deal objectively and dispassionately with states of consciousness. Plato knew that the problem is essentially religious and spiritual in the sense of being related to the divine Good and that it involves participation that leads to transformation. Believing that the soul, having existed prior to its earthly life, already has partial knowledge and experience of the higher objective reality of the spiritual realm, he saw that man's acquisition of truth becomes, in part, a recollection by the mind of truth already existing in the soul. How the soul perceives reality in its out-of-the-body state we can only surmise from mystical accounts of orientation of its divine center toward the light. Its powers of perception may be quite different from both sensory and extrasensory perception psychically known to the conscious mind. But perception and whatever transformation accompanied it must survive in the soul after the death of the body, if the true self, that immortal part of us that is embarked upon the immense journey back to the source, has any real meaning.

The far limits of the conscious states attained in this life are generally believed to represent the highest reality of the ego or self, a view that Plato could hardly have accepted. As a Christian mystic writing some 2,300 years after Plato has said:

> We tend to imagine ourselves as a conscious mind which is
> "above" and a sub-conscious mind that is "below the con-
> scious". This image tends to be misleading. The conscious
> mind of man is *exceeded in all directions* by his uncon-
> scious. There is darkness not only below our conscious
> reason but also above it and all around it. Our conscious
> mind is by no means the summit of our being. Nor does it
> control all the rest of our being from a point of eminence.
> It merely controls some of the elements that are below it.
> But our conscious mind may in turn be controlled by the
> unconscious that is "beyond" it, whether above or below.
> However, it should not be controlled by what is below it,
> only by what is above. Hence the important distinction be-
> tween the animal, emotional, and instinctive components of
> our unconscious and the spiritual, one might also say the
> "divine" elements in our superconscious mind.[15]

A Christian platonist, writing about Eastern mysticism and spiritual wisdom, has said,

> The fundamental doctrine of Indian religion is that the self-
> conscious ego, the subject of rights and duties, is not the real
> self. Consciousness is never more than a mirror of reality; it
> creates nothing.[16]

It may have been intended to create something. From the evolutionary point of view, the individual consciousness on earth, being able to recollect only a small part of what the soul has seen of eternal light, is not yet wholly real but only becoming so, in the same way that the whole soul is being spiritually transformed by the light of truth. With the evolution of consciousness, great things would be in store for evolving man. To en- visage these prospects requires acknowledging the objective reality of the soul, the spiritual realm, and the divine, which most biologists are not yet prepared to do. Between Plato and most psychologists and parapsychologists there still remains a wide gap. Plato was a theocentric humanist and a pagan mystic who rightly saw the mind's search for truth in terms of the human-divine relation. For him, the conscious attainment of truth is self-awareness, where "self" is that part of the soul that is oriented toward its divine source. A. E. Taylor in his analysis of the possibly spurious dialogue, *Alcibiades I,* has referred to Socrates' thoughts about the Delphic inscription, "Know Thyself," in this way:

> We can get to know ourselves truly by knowing God. . . .
> Until we know ourselves, we cannot know what is good
> for ourselves, for other men, for the state. . . . The states-
> man must impart *goodness* to his countrymen, and he can-
> not impart what he has not. It must be his first concern to
> get goodness by "looking to God."[17]

Putting goodness into the conscious mind could be a creative act of great evolutionary significance for the whole of suffering creation. Perhaps this is what Plato meant in his preoccupation with the theocentric realization of ethical potentiality. Conscious preoccupation with the problem of good and evil and ethical choice can create good in the world, and the whole of evolving life can thus become more rapidly real. Such a creative act would involve no indiscriminate expansion of conscious states by devious means but a qualitative expansion of the consciousness by the conscience in full recognition that it is an activity of the soul that depends, ultimately, upon superhuman aid.

This, it hardly needs saying, is a far cry from the contemporary interests and attitudes of most investigators of psychical phenomena. We must, therefore, be grateful for the theistic perspectives to be found in Alister Hardy's two books on evolution. Attention should also be drawn to Dr. Nils-Oluf Jacobson's admirable book on parapsychology; in his treatment of a wealth of difficult material, he combines scientific clear thinking with an unmistakable religious-spiritual orientation toward transcendent reality that openly questions the validity of the scientific world picture.[18] Yet when books of this kind, so obviously pointing in the right direction, fail to deal with the divine ethic, it cannot be expected that the general run of investigations of psi-phenomena which are based exclusively upon the scientific *Weltbild* can be remotely involved in the aspiration and orientation of the soul toward the love, compassion, righteousness, and mercy that mark the high points of the human ascent.

Contemporary biologists, being still generally objective and anthropocentric, have not yet fully considered the problem of human potentiality. They have not realized that in this time of unparalleled crises, this is a problem in which they, in their capacity as scientists, must become personally engaged. As Jon Wynne-Tyson has succinctly observed:

> The problems of a country, much less of the world, will never
> be solved or even helped by party politics or institutions,
> but only by better people. By a change of values, not by a
> change of administrators from the same stable as their prede-
> cessors. Unregenerate people can only create an unregenerate
> organization and an unregenerate society. Only better people
> can create a better society. They do not even have to create
> it—it is already there.
>
> Most of the basic truths are what the confused and corrupted
> term simplifications. This is one of them, and I do not apologize
> for it.[19]

Better people are desperately needed within science. Despite the darkness of the moment, it must again be emphasized that there are all grounds for optimism. In ways we do not know, the spiritual light is getting through to us to a degree hitherto unknown during the five-hundred-year history of the modern scientific age. It is spurring us on to ever more difficult resolves to divest ourselves of our egoistic veils so that the eye of our souls can better see the light. Even in this partial darkness we can already discern the heavenward thrust of human potentiality, and in doing so, we seek still more light.

The light falls, now as before, upon us all. The problem of the spiritual diversity of evolving life comprises nonhuman as well as human potentiality. Man, capable of perceiving some of the light, is learning that his future evolution depends upon the role he will play in the evolution of the lower forms of life making up his environment.

Potentiality and the Human-Animal Relation

The scientific age, pondering the bewildering number and diversity of living forms, has attempted to bring order into chaos by assuming the spontaneous origin some 2 to 3 billion years ago of a living cell as the progenitor of all that has ever lived and by conceiving a tree of life with multitudinous branches representing the evolutionary sequence of plant and animal forms. The most highly organized vertebrate animals, the Mammalia, include the Primates, in whose suborder, Anthropoidea, man places monkeys, apes, and himself. *Homo sapiens* and his immediate forebears are said to be some millions of years old.

Consciousness and sentience have long been regarded as a property of animal mind, which in turn has been associated with the progressive evolutionary development of the central nervous system culminating in man's own greatly enlarged forebrain. Recent experiments, however, have disclosed the wholly unexpected result that a primary sensory system at the cellular level seems to exist in the plant kingdom as well. Using the psychogalvanic reflex instrumentation employed in the lie detector, Backster[20] has claimed that Philodendron plants exhibit phenomena similar to extrasensory perception in man. They are said to react violently to human thoughts about them, registering pain, fear, anxiety, and relief, and are even conscious of injury or death inflicted upon other organisms in their vicinity.

No one knows what we are dealing with here. It has been suggested that some unknown universal field of force exists as a "life signal connecting all creation." If this be so, is it part of the "natural" order of things for which atheistic scientists will one day provide a natural explanation? Or does it originate in the spiritual realm to support Sir Alister Hardy's view that psychical experiences point toward divinity? Since the assertion that all psi-phenomena in man are expressions of his response to divine intervention in evolution seems doubtful, the same uncertainty must hold for similar phenomena associated with nonhuman life. Telepathic transfer of thoughts from one mind to another, quite possibly occurring, as Hardy suggests, far more frequently during evolution than is generally supposed, may well have contributed to physical survival in both the plant and animal kingdoms but not at all to the spiritual ascent, except in the sense of helping to ensure the continued existence of living matter destined to become spiritualized. A universal stream of consciousness connecting all life could be thought to exist apart from the spiritual realm when the latter is believed, as here, to include the cosmic Good. John Vyvyan has said:

> The psyche, which is a metaphysical system, arises naturally out of the mediating process between stimulus and response. It is brought into being, in the first place, to ensure that the response shall be appropriate. . . . From the assumption that "minute mind-like activity accompanies all the processes of living matter," it follows that even the most elementary lives have this psychical potentiality.[21]

Yet this elegant formulation is not equivalent to saying that the whole of evolving life necessarily receives spiritual stimuli. Conceivably, elementary lives, even though they be psychically related by a common consciousness, are *not* capable of apprehending the spiritual light falling upon the world. Knowing so little about the human soul, we know still less about the nonhuman soul, if it in fact exists. For the most part, nonhuman lives appear to react to whatever stimuli they receive by choosing the right response, where "right" for them is that choice which best ensures their continued well-being and existence. So far there seems no evidence, not even among the wild anthropoids which most resemble us or the dogs, cats, and horses which are most closely associated with us, that any non-human consciousness perceives "right" in the same way that man does. For man is capable of conceptual abstraction and of recognizing the divine ethic and submitting to it. This involves surpassing himself by permeating his lower egoistic self with love for the cosmic Good. No plant or animal, as far as we know, is capable of anything like this. If all lives perceive spiritual light, man's perception must be so much clearer that it is qualitatively different from that of the rest of creation. It is a predominantly ethical awareness of his evolutionary commitment to self-transcendence, and this must impart to evolving man at least some degree of spiritual uniqueness.

It must be admitted, at the same time, that any assertion of man's spiritual uniqueness is based in part upon ignorance of the inner life of nonhuman species. The Greeks believed that every living organism, human and nonhuman, possesses a potential of supreme excellence characteristic of the group to which it belonged. They called this highest attainable good *areté*. Both wild and domestic animals often radiate an unmistakable *joie de vivre* which must have its origin in an inner life of superior excellence. If they have not reached perfection in their lives, they appear at least to be realizing their *areté* to a higher degree than is man and in doing so are helping to strengthen and sustain the whole evolutionary process. Some years ago I expressed the thought that

> A bird can strive no further than to live in complete harmony with its environment. This is to fulfill its "rightness" and to realize its highest potentiality. But for man to live and prop-agate as a healthy, vigorous animal in blissful harmony with his environment represents only a fraction of human areté. The supreme excellence of which he is capable stretches further heavenward than that. Unique among all organisms in his awareness of the realm of the spirit, he strives to approach it, and only in the striving can he realize his potentialities and become as human as he is able.[22]

Although I remain convinced that human *areté* represents a higher state of reality than animal *areté* and one that is much more difficult to attain, I am no longer sure that *Homo sapiens* is the only species aware of the realm of the spirit.

If our knowledge of plants and animals depends upon our own limited sensory and intellectual equipment which precludes personal experience of their conscious and subconscious activity, can we ever hope to know whether evolving nonhuman lives also have immortal souls that are making an ethical ascent toward the realm of the spirit and beyond? Biology will need to consider this question. It is obviously related to the contemporary ecological view that evolving life is, in fact, an ascending whole whose human component has somehow lost its way. And since the whole of life is now threatened by ecological disaster, we can hardly afford to disregard the voices who claim that our only hope of finding again the upward path is to reestablish a closer and better relation with the rest of nature. If man is to do this, he will need to know much more about the intellectual and spiritual potentials of nonhuman lives than he does now. The life sciences, in other words, must concern themselves with nonhuman as well as human *areté*.

Of the inner life of animals we know very little, but we do know some-thing. We have, for example, countless records of domestic animals ex-hibiting friendship, love, and devotion—even to the point of self-sacrifice—toward each other and toward man, suggesting that their *areté* comprises some kind of primitive spiritual-ethical consciousness. Observations of wild animals point in the same direction. That higher animals may even participate in spiritual activity is suggested by some observations of a biologist who lived for a period in South American jungle canopies:

> Shortly before dawn the canopy comes to life. There are those animals that start to stir while the supra-canopy mists are still thick. These are many kinds of monkeys and birds. They don't go anywhere and they don't do anything until the first rays of the sun emerge from below the rim of the horizon. Even then they may stay still and, in some cases, there may then come an almost absolute silence. And here I propose to stick my neck way out and say that I agree with certain Brahmins in India and West Africa who assert that the animals are at that time "praying." I cannot get over the sight of a huge troop of magnificent black-and-white guereza or Colubus monkeys that I once witnessed thus engaged on the very tops of a canopy giant; all sitting quietly facing the rising sun, with heads slightly bowed and arms folded on knees. Not a sound came from them for many minutes, and nobody stirred except a few youngsters, who were then cuffed and scolded. The whole jungle was utterly silent. No insects chirped or clicked; nothing rustled. Then suddenly a crazy bird—probably a Pied Hornbill—let out a raucous yell and the whole world began to stir.[23]

Even second-hand, such experiences of close contact with undisturbed nature are profoundly thought provoking, forcing one to ponder the similarities and differences between the potentials of man and other species. If an advanced stage of spiritual-ethical awareness of compulsory self-transcendence is a distinctly human attribute which confers unique-ness upon man, it hardly needs saying that his ability to recognize and love the divine ethic has never been a guarantee that he will comply with it. As we have already stressed, man is also unique in being a species capable of sin. The reverse is equally true: Animals and plants are unique by virtue of their innocence.

If they are incapable of immoral acts, then it is equally true that nature thinks no evil. This seems incontestable. When animals prey upon one another, taking their food with violence, they do so in limited measure and with self-restraint, rarely desiring more than necessary for well-being and survival. All their fighting and bloodshed stands no direct comparison with the egoistic acts of man. Animals do not spend their lives plotting and scheming, from minute to gigantic scales, acts of wanton destruction, greed, violence, cruelty, and injustice for the sake of self-centered goals so contrary to the natural order that their very existence as human thoughts violates the concept of evolution and obstructs the evolutionary process.

Nature thinks no evil. This may be part of the knowledge of the inner life of nonhuman creatures that man needs to improve his relations with them. If we assume—and there is no reason for not doing so—that the psychical world of animals is made up of their thoughts and dreams, then this realm, in contrast to man's, must be wholly devoid of evil intent and insusceptible to evil forces. The psychical world of nonhuman nature must accordingly be purer than that of man. Does this mean that it can better perceive the spiritual light that is falling upon the world, that it is in closer association with the spiritual realm and the divine? We do not know. A wise man has said that "animal innocence intimates to us the meaning of holiness."[24] It is tempting to think that the religious awakening's growing concern for nature may have its origin in an unconscious longing to return to our proper environment, to live again in close association with elementary lives that in the deepest part of their being are wholly innocent. *Nature thinks no evil—and does no evil.* How blessed is man to have an environment of purity!

But being himself impure, man, as nearly everyone is now aware, has spent his civilized life controlling, ravaging, and destroying his environment, and in the last five hundred years he has deliberately tried to obliterate the mutually beneficial relations that were established between nature and his ancient forebears. What is not generally recognized is that this *mésalliance* with nature has reached its monstrous culmination in the biological revolution of our times. The life sciences and medicine, proudly divesting themselves of every shred of moral aspiration and vision in order to expand their frontiers at breakneck pace, are now placing their coarse, brutal hands upon untold millions of representatives of defenseless, nonhuman species in defiance of all religious exhortations to compassion, love, gentleness, mercy, and nonviolence. Little wonder that scientists have failed to penetrate the essential secrets of life's *areté* and its evolution. They have forgotten the reality of the spiritual realm and the divine ethic.

It is curious that those who have attempted to close the gap between the scientific and the religious world views by stressing the need for biological investigation of the psychical and spiritual aspects of evolving life have not always paid due regard to the appallingly immoral treatment of evolving life by scientists. Although Alister Hardy fully realizes that the essence of evolving life can only be understood in religious terms, he does not seem to realize the full consequence of this fact: that life can never be understood by science before a renewal of the scientific conscience has set in. He considers, on the contrary, that the objective means of conventional science are beyond moral reproach and therefore fully adequate for the investigation of the higher potentials of life.

I disagree. I believe that such investigations comprise a search for sacred knowledge which cannot be attained—and should not even be sought—without some form of active participation on the part of the seeker. If biology is to point toward the light of a divine evolutionary force, then the biologist's psyche must be directed toward the divine ethic. This is a problem which Hardy ignores. Nowhere in his two volumes does he discuss the biologist in his confrontation with the problem of good and evil, nor has he any word of reproach for the bestiality with which science has treated and still treats sentient life. If the scientific age is to be persuaded by science that the universe is theistic, then science must adopt a theistic attitude toward life. This can hardly be reconcilable with Hardy's view that

> The scientific method, that is quantitative study and experiment, *can* be applied to the behaviour of living animals, treating them as living wholes, just as it can be applied to the behaviour of electrons, atoms, and molecules. . . . Because science cannot yet explain the mind-body relation, it does not prohibit us from using the scientific method to study animal behaviour just as legitimately as we can use it for the study of the reactions of atoms and electrons. . . .[25]

It will surely be closer to the view of a fifteenth century theist: "All reason and natural search ought to follow Faith, not to go before it, nor to break in upon it."[26] It is my deepest conviction that it is quite wrong by all theocentric standards to advocate the unrestricted use of conventional scientific methods in the further study of animals and their psychical activity. The violence, cruelty, and injustice which have hitherto accompanied so many objective studies on animal behavior, far from supplying us with evidence for a theistic universe, have only darkened the scientific conscience and removed man farther from theism.

These comments on Sir Alister Hardy's proposals for establishing a link between science and religion are not meant to detract from the intrinsic value of his evolutionary vision. Based as it is upon a lifetime of thought about nature and the numinous, it is a theocentric vision for which the world should be grateful. My opposition to it is directed mainly toward Hardy's reliance upon the ability of conventional science and the contemporary scientific conscience to reestablish the idea of the divine in the world without becoming radically changed in the process. I believe this to be an impossibility. The scientific conscience openly admits that in the objective pursuit of science it cannot, and must not, distinguish good from evil. Biologists of this kind suffer, as a friend has aptly written, from "moral weakness" and "malfunctioning of minds and/or souls."[27] They cannot continue to study living creation with the scientific method and expect it to respond with spiritual truths. But if they were to confront the living world out of a theocentric resolve to evolve harmoniously with it, they would provide the first ethical proof that biology, as Hardy rightly maintains, has a role to play in man's reorientation toward the divine.

Rudolf Steiner, like Hardy, recognized the inadequacy of the materialistic world picture of modern science, and his evolutionary vision, based upon his own interpretation of Christianity, likewise included the gradual convergence of science and religion. Steiner's profound interest in paranormal phenomena was largely based upon personal experience, and he tended, like Hardy, to equate the supersensible and the spiritual, regardless of whether ethical enlightenment was involved. It is, therefore, interesting that in his concept of spiritual science, which he defines as "the study of the spiritual processes in human life and in the cosmos,"[28] Steiner failed as completely as Hardy to dissociate himself from the ethical apathy and confusion that permits the ruthless scientific exploitation of animals.

Steiner's curious view about the evolutionary status of animals is also interesting in this connection. In the belief that the different kingdoms of nature have evolved at very different rates and that for the sake of the

general course of evolution, some beings at different stages must remain
behind, he considered contemporary animals to represent the waste
products of human evolution:

> In the course of our earthly evolution we have left of our worst
> to the animals, and they stand around us as tokens of how we our-
> selves came to our perfection. We should not have got rid of the
> dregs if we had not left the animals behind.[29]

In direct opposition to the contention of this book that nature thinks no
evil, Steiner speaks of the "vices" of animals, considering how fortunate
we are that we no longer possess the cruelty of the lion or the slyness of
the fox. At the same time he insists that man's debt to the animals is
great: Since they remained behind so that we might rise, we must treat
them with the utmost kindness and consideration. He also believes that
in the very remote future in some new cycle of evolution, the animal
kingdom will realize its higher potentialities. But long before this comes
about, he is confident that there will come "a better relationship between man and the animal kingdom than there is now, particularly in
the west. There will come a treatment of the animals whereby man will
again uplift those he has pushed down."[30] But Steiner, as far as I know,
never helped to bring about this new relation by exhorting his contem-
poraries to think of the plight of laboratory animals or by admitting that
the scientific conscience which is responsible for their plight is very far
indeed from perfection.

Contemporary anthroposophists seem equally blind to the *mésalliance*
between science and animals. Johannes Hemleben, a German anthro-
posophist, biologist, and theologian, has written an excellent critique of
modern biology and evolutionary thought entitled *Biology and Christianity*.[31] While I profoundly agree with many of his anthroposophical arguments against the unethical goals of contemporary biology, his failure to
oppose biological methodology reveals to me a lack of ethical insight.
To become spiritualized, science must recognize and repent the fact that
the explosive development of modern biology and biomedicine has been
based upon an increasingly ruthless and brutal treatment of nonhuman
sentient life. Hemleben's attitude echoes a statement of Steiner, made in
1902, that the conventional methods of natural science can, and must,
be extended to the spiritual realm since "in its own sphere, its mode of

thought holds good and its methods are unassailable. . . . We shall only be acting in the spirit of natural science if we study the spiritual development of man as impartially as the naturalist observes the sense world."[32] This argument, so similar to Hardy's, is ethically untenable. Natural science, seeking to understand all aspects of life, is not only the impartial observation but also the impartial manipulation of the living. The scientific approach to nature is made in a spirit which has had disastrous consequences for nature and for man. The mode of thought and the methods of the life sciences, especially in the fields of biology and medicine, are outrageously immoral, just as they were at the turn of the century. Hemleben and Steiner have condemned cruelty to animals in general terms, and Hardy has done so more specifically,[33] but neither in *Biology and Christianity* nor in any of the works of Steiner and Hardy with which I am acquainted have I found any direct condemnation of the cruelties of animal experimentation, which, as they all knew, have been tolerated by nearly all students of life.

The theosophists, despite their unorthodox views about the course of animal evolution, seemed to see the matter much more clearly. According to John Vyvyan's masterly account of the antivivisection movement, after Anna Kingsford, an ardent antivivisectionist of the nineteenth century, became president of the London branch of the Theosophical Society, her views on vivisection gradually

won a permanent place in theosophical thought, and all its leaders have expressed substantial agreement with them. It is a coincidence that the Theosophical Society should have been founded by Madame Blavatsky and Colonel Olcott in New York in the same year, 1875, in which Frances Cobbe and Dr. Hoggan launched their Society for the Protection of Animals Liable to Vivisection; and yet, in a sense they were sister movements, and have remained in mutual sympathy.[34]

H. P. Blavatsky was extremely outspoken in her condemnation of the methodology of nineteenth-century biology and medicine:

But if these humble lines could make a few readers realize the real value of St. Paul's noble words, and thereby seriously turn their thoughts to all the horrors of vivisection—then

the writer would be content. For verily when the world feels
convinced—and it cannot avoid coming one day to such a
conviction—that animals are creatures as eternal as we ourselves, vivisection and other permanent tortures, daily inflicted on the poor brutes, will, after calling forth an outburst
of malediction and threats from society generally, force all
Governments to put an end to those barbarous and shameful
practices.[35]

Four years later she reached an even deeper insight:

Indeed when reflecting on . . . the awful horrors of vivisection, we may sometimes be inclined to feel more sorrow for
the vivisector than for his pain-racked victim, for the awful
pangs of remorse that sooner or later will seize on the former,
will outweigh a thousand times the comparatively momentary
pain of the poor dumb sufferers.[36]

However great the immediate need for abolition of painful experimentation in the laboratory, the present *mésalliance* between biologists and
animals does not depend exclusively upon the infliction of pain. It depends
also on the utter disregard for the basic rights of animals. Many contemporary biologists, and antivivisectionists as well, feel that so long as
pain is banned from the laboratory, there can be no limit to the number
of animals science employs or the kind of treatment it subjects them to.
Ethically and evolutionally this point of view is inadequate. Just and
harmonious relations with higher animals cannot be established in the
belief that it is morally right to inflict on them painless mutilation or
death under anesthesia, or to force them to live out their lives under the
unnatural conditions of the laboratory, or to deprive them of association
with their own kind. Higher animals, just as men, have need of unconfined
movements, of forests, streams, hills, meadows, sun, stars, and rain. Neglecting the basic interests of nonhuman life cannot long continue within
scientific circles. A feeling of genuine repentance for having done so for
so long may not be far off. The spiritual awakening is gaining theocentric
momentum to strengthen and sustain evolution.

That the scientific world, still almost wholly anthropocentric, is at the
moment openly confused and uneasy about the status of modern evolu-

tionary theory is no coincidence. A leading scientific journal, opening its pages to a discussion of the problem, contains an article pointing out that there are now many "anti-Darwinists" and even "theistic evolutionists" in scientific circles,[37] and at least one recent contribution from outside science may be adding fuel to the fire.[38] Present uncertainty about Darwin's vision presages the spiritual awakening's growing opposition to the idea of a purposeless, nondirected evolution based upon natural selection, survival of the fittest, and blind chance and necessity.

Biologists may soon be returning to evolutionary views which most sharply diverged from the utilitarianism of Darwin, in particular the mature views of A. R. Wallace, which have not yet been taken seriously by the scientific community as a whole. As Loren Eiseley has pointed out, Wallace lived to see evolving life from an increasingly religious perspective and could not accept the view that ethical behavior has a utilitarian origin. In one eloquent passage Eiseley writes:

> Perhaps there is something appropriate, in the end,
> about the fact that Wallace was a searcher after birds of
> paradise and that he was a butterfly hunter among the islands
> of the Coral Sea. He loved beauty, and among the many
> rarities he came to cherish was the potential moral beauty of
> man. He found it among simple people and it never passed
> away from his heart.[39]

To his colleagues who were effectively silencing the clergy, Wallace dared to disclose his belief that "some higher intelligence may have directed the process by which the human race was developed."[40] Darwin objected strenuously to this disclosure, even though he realized that natural selection was no wholly satisfactory explanation of the evolution of man.

In 1959, the centenary of the publication of *The Origin of Species*, Loren Eiseley said about human evolution, "of its nature and causation even the modern biologist is still profoundly ignorant."[41] Since biologists still admit that they are very much in the dark, it would seem that they would have nothing to lose, and most probably much to gain, by turning their attention to still other unorthodox evolutionary theories, which, although not rejecting Darwinism in all its aspects, diverge even more sharply from it than did the religious speculations of Wallace. I refer again to H. P. Blavastsky and Rudolf Steiner, whose views on evolution have

been taken much less seriously than the unorthodox views of Wallace.
This is not surprising. Books written about divine ancestors of man living
on other planets, of life's future journey to Jupiter, of invisible globes
and astral bodies, and of the ape's descent from man lay themselves open
in an age demanding scientific proof of every factual assertion to abrupt
dismissal as harmless or harmful fairy tales created by imaginations run
wild. Without in any way claiming that all theosophical and anthroposophical evolutionary doctrines are true, and in harboring an ineradicable
antagonism toward dogmatic assertions about the origin and subsequent
evolution of life which appear to be only hypotheses, I am, nevertheless,
convinced that it would be profoundly shortsighted for biology to dismiss
them as wholly untrue.

Blavatsky's views of the creation and evolution of life claim to be derived from the ancient spiritual wisdom of the East, and she looked forward, as do contemporary theosophists, to an uncovering of the basic
unity and truth underlying all religions. Steiner, in contrast, saw Christianity as the central fact of human evolution. Both, however, were convinced that if science is to find the truths of life, scientists must not
only concern themselves with religion and philosophy but must also
attempt to develop their own latent powers of extrasensory perception.
As clairvoyants, Blavatsky and Steiner were themselves able to realize
psychic potentiality far exceeding that realized by most human beings.
And they both elaborated visions of human evolution of surpassing moral
beauty, permeated through and through by recognition of man's divine
potential and its progressive realization through his return to the spiritual
source of his being. Whether or not their cosmogonal doctrines and their
visions of the course of past evolution on earth are true, we do not know;
it may one day be revealed to us. At present we can say that in terms of
its foreseeable benefit to mankind, the nobility of their visions of the
future course of human evolution dwarfs anything that contemporary
science has to offer. Both of them deserve serious consideration by a
scientific age that is floundering in intellectual and moral confusion.

In the 1920s there appeared in Denmark a work on evolution[42]
similar in a number of respects to the basic doctrines of theosophy and
anthroposophy. Still largely unknown outside of Scandinavia, it claims
to be a communication from the supersensible world, received by a
medium who did no more than record the truth that was passed on to

her about creation and evolution and about the leading roles that Christ and a repentant Satan played in the epic struggle between the forces of light and darkness. Despite dogmatic claims of the existence of spiritual globes, astral bodies, anthropoid evolution in reverse, and the necessity of completely revising Christian doctrine, it, too, is permeated by spiritual-ethical insights into man and nature that compel attention and respect. Like theosophy and anthroposophy, it is an account of man's spiritual ascent which cannot by any ethical standard be dismissed as irrelevant to a world in which both evolutionary theory and Christian doctrine are uncertain of themselves.

At the moment biologists who see no reason to accept a divine ethic for distinguishing good from evil are inundating the world either with acts of violence against nature or with dispassionate critical analyses of the status of science and its relation to society. How barbarous the former, how cold and sterile the latter! If biologists wish to study life truly and authentically, they need to participate in the righteousness, purity, and strength of its holiness. What is thus required of biologists who would understand the spiritual diversity of the whole of evolving life is personal engagement on an all-out scale, for they, too, must evolve. The moral vision that will enable them to do so must come. Each of us has a divine spark, and the spiritual light that is falling upon us all cannot fail to elicit a theocentric redintegration of the scientific conscience whereby science will recognize the truth of the religious world picture. The advance of biology and medicine can then be expected to be effected, more and more, by men who seek knowledge of life that ethically transforms. A contemporary philosopher and theocentric humanist has wisely said,

> The knowledge of nature is inextricably bound to moral
> and spiritual laws and the purity of the seeker after this
> knowledge. It seems as if Hinduism like so many other
> traditions had felt intuitively that the only safe way to
> penetrate the mysteries of nature and to cultivate physics,
> in the universal sense of the term, is to become saintly and
> to seek the saintly life.[43]

What does it mean for a student of life to become saintly? White-coated biologists who, for the sake of outrageous scientific goals, are at this moment employing equally outrageous scientific means to try to wrest out of subhuman life its inner secrets, have never raised this question. Now that it is raised, let us try to answer it.

To become saintly and to seek the saintly life is part of the inevitable spiritualization of biology and medicine. It would mean first of all a turning aside in abhorrence and repentance from the ruthless violence, brutality, and injustice which conventional biology chooses to employ against lower sentient life. This currently used methodology is also a wholly unsafe way to advance the life sciences. Acts of violence and injustice backfire. This is evident all around us today in our enormous ecological problems and in the mounting ethical confusion of those who are attempting to solve them. Biologists, to become saintly, must find ethical sanity. They must recognize the inadequacy of the contemporary scientific conscience that cannot distinguish good from evil. And having learned the distinction, biologists who seek the saintly life must themselves abolish, before they are forced to do so by restrictive legislation, the evils which they are committing against life.[44] When a biologist recognizes that love and compassion for defenseless sentient beings represents a higher order of things than scientific knowledge about them, he will no longer consider animals merely as things, and what is more, he will have become a student of life with some of the truth of life within him. Will his refusal to mistreat animals and neglect their basic rights mean that biological and biomedical advance must slow down and eventually stop? Not at all. It would mean, on the contrary, a more rapid progress in the qualitative study of life.

For becoming saintly begins with self-denial and self-restraint. The more advance in this direction, the greater the recognition of growing inner strength to be used for the good of others. Biologists can be no exception. In seeking the ultimate truths of life by personal participation, they will have to limit and restrict their advance, thus initiating a new kind of relation between themselves and the objects of their study. This will be a profound transformation. A biology which now violently mistreats and wantonly destroys sentient lives in the delusion that scientific progress justifies all means will become a biology gently seeking out subhuman lives in the resolve to help them. The spiritualization of biology is more than putting an end to morally reprehensible practices. As biologists become more saintly, they will proceed beyond this to more positive thought and action. They will become concerned with the potentials of the whole of evolving life.

What is the ultimate purpose in realizing individual human potentiality? It is surely not individual gain alone. The more real an individual becomes— the more *areté* he attains—the better will he understand that he is rising in order to help others to rise, and that all *must* rise for the sake of the cosmic Good. Can it then matter, if it is ordained that all shall eventually rise, how quick the individual rising? Yes, for a rapid realization of potentiality helps to restore righteousness, harmony, and love to the world to strengthen and sustain the whole evolutionary process. Contemporary biology and contemporary religion, converging, cannot fail to make this goal their own.

And in doing so, biology would center its efforts on realizing the potentials of both the student of life and the life he studies. The resolve to promote the attainment of human and nonhuman *areté* becomes an ethical commitment for a biology in the process of spiritualization and for the biologist who is becoming saintly.

A few years ago, in a moment of spiritual insight, an American historian, Lynn White, proposed St. Francis as the patron saint of ecologists. The proposal was made in the belief that this Christian's great contribution was to point to the true Christian view of man's relation to nature. St. Francis, he said, "tried to substitute the idea of the equality of all creatures, including man, for the idea of man's limitless rule of creation."[45] One wonders if St. Francis pondered the question of how high the animals can come spiritually in this life and in evolutionary development. Nikos Kazantzakis, in his novel about the saint, has something relevant to say in these words of Brother Leo:

> The sun had come out; the rain had stopped. Trees and stones were laughing, the world glistening, newly washed. Two black-birds in front of us shook their drenched wings, looked at us and whistled as though taunting us. Yes, that's what they were doing: taunting us. But Francis waved his hand and greeted them.
> "These are the monks of the bird kingdom," he said. "Look how they're dressed!"
> I laughed. "You're right, Brother Francis. Really, in a monastery near Perugia I once saw a blackbird which had been trained to chant the 'Kyrie eleison'! A true monk."
> Francis sighed. "Oh, if only someone could teach the birds

and oxen, the sheep, dogs, wolves and wild boars to say just those two words: 'Kyrie eleison'! If only the whole of Creation could awake in this way each morning, so that from the depths of the forest, from every tree, every stable, every courtyard you would hear all the animals glorifying God, crying 'Kyrie eleison'!"

"First let's teach men to say those two words," I said. "I don't see why the birds and animals need learn them. Birds and animals don't sin."

Francis stared at me with protruding eyes. "Yes, what you say is correct, Brother Leo. Of all living things man is the only one that sins."

"Yes, but on the other hand, Brother Francis, man is the only one who can surpass his nature and enter heaven. The animals and birds can't do that."

"Don't be too sure," protested Francis. "No one knows the full extent of God's mercy. . . ."[46]

Are animals evolving in the same direction as man, destined in the fullness of time to surpass themselves spiritually on their way toward union with the ultimate spiritual reality? Or are the animals, having already reached their own kind of spiritual perfection, unable to evolve higher? We do not know. But if all matter is destined to become completely spiritualized, the essence of nonhuman *areté* may be indistinguishable from that of human *areté*. If, then, even the slightest possibility exists that animals, as well as men, are taking part in the spiritual ascent, we have no choice but to try to help them here and now in their earthly life to realize their higher potentials.

According to legend, St. Francis showed, perhaps better than anyone else, that animals can respond in extraordinary ways to human joy, love, understanding, and compassion. The animals sought him out, desiring what he had to give them. Many of us, in far lesser ways, have had relations with an animal—perhaps a dog or a cat—that mutually binds us in a way that can only be called spiritual. And the animal, participating in the relation and appearing to derive immense joy from it, behaves in a way suggesting that it understands and comprehends far more of life than a scientific age deems possible for a canine or feline brain. Is this a transfer of spiritual energy from us to them—or from them to us? Are they capable in extrasensory and suprarational ways of receiving from us some of the light that we, in similar ways, have received from the spiritual realm? Does the mutual joy of a spiritual relation between a human and an animal disclose a mutual exchange of energy that can transform both participants? Does theocentric animalism exist side by side with theocentric humanism? Before he died, St. Francis may have found the answers to these questions. Biologists will need to seek them by adopting a more Franciscan attitude toward life. Nonviolence, gentleness, joy, compassion, and love are part of saintly conduct, and by saintly conduct evolving man can help lead others higher up the mountain.

Those who are trying to create a better world are attempting, among many other things, to better the human-animal relation by exposing the fallacy, accepted blindly by so many Christians, that animals exist *only* for the sake of men. In rightly opposing this view by showing that it has no biblical foundation, Lynn White and others are countering with an alternative view of evolving life as a developing whole made up of a brotherhood of living beings. In stressing man's relation to animals and playing down the diversity among living creatures, they are using the concepts of democracy and equality. Such profoundly well-meaning efforts to better the relations between man and the rest of creation do, however, seem to have gone somewhat too far, for to proclaim that man is in no way unique is a distortion of spiritual truth. Man's conscious awareness of his conscience, the divine ethic, and his self-transcendence as a realizable human potential *does* set *Homo sapiens* apart from other creatures. And precisely because of his spiritual uniqueness, he has a responsibility to help lower beings to ascend that exceeds any responsibility to them based on a sense of physical relation through common descent. The first responsibility is more spiritual than the second. In my mind there is no doubt which weighs more heavily.

In assuming the existence of a spiritual hierarchy of being, there at once emerges an idea wholly undemocratic and, at the same time, wholly necessary for the evolutionary ascent: noblesse oblige. This is no illusory concept to bolster the human ego. The spiritual hierarchy of being extends not only from microorganisms to man but also beyond man to the spiritual realm. In the religious scheme of things, the higher are ever helping the lower to realize potentiality for the sake of the cosmic Good. Man, in helping, is himself being helped by those nobler than himself. E. F. Schumacher, whose name is well known in circles actively engaged in creating a better world, has elucidated from a religious point of view the human-divine and the human-animal relations:

> An irreligious age looks with amused contempt upon the hallowed statements by which religion helped our for-bears to appreciate metaphysical truths. . . . Man, the highest of his [God's] creatures, was given "dominion", not the right to tyrannise, to ruin and exterminate. It is no use talking about the dignity of man without accepting that *noblesse oblige*. For man to put himself into a wrong-ful relationship with animals, and particularly those long domesticated by him, has always, in all traditions, been considered a horrible and infinitely dangerous thing to do. There have been no sages or holy men in ours or in anybody else's history who were cruel to animals or who looked upon them as *nothing but* utilities, and innumerable are the legends and stories which link sanctity as well as happiness with a loving kindness towards lower creation.

It is interesting to note that modern man is being told, in the name of science, that he is really *nothing but* a naked ape or even an accidental collocation of atoms. "Now we can define man," says Professor Joshua Lederberg. "Geno-typically, at least, he is six feet of a particular molecular sequence of carbon, hydrogen, oxygen, nitrogen, and phosphorus atoms." As modern man thinks so "humbly" of himself, he thinks even more "humbly" of the animals which serve his needs: and treats them as if they were machines. Other, less sophisticated—or is it less depraved?— people take a different attitude. As H. Fielding Hall reported from Burma:

> To him [the Burmese] men are men, and animals are animals, and men are far the higher. But he does not deduce from this that man's superiority gives him permission to ill treat or kill animals. It is just the reverse. It is because man is so much higher than the animal that he can and must observe towards animals the very greatest care, feel for them the very greatest compassion, be good to them in every way

he can. The Burmese's motto should be *noblesse oblige.*
He knows the meaning, if he knows not the words.[47]

Another Christian, viewing the human-animal relation, has expressed
himself with equal eloquence and religious truth:

So, whether we consider science, politics, commerce, the
churches, or the man in the street, there is truly a mountain
of assumptions to be rejected, of opinions to be changed and
hearts to be touched and converted, before we come in sight
of a fair deal for the animals. There is no short cut to our
goal, but some ways are more direct than others. The most
direct, I would suggest, is an unremitting demand for moral
integrity in the adaptation of means to ends. Men have for
some time now been losing their hold on absolute standards
of right and wrong. These have weakened or faded away
along with belief in God and immortality, leaving conscience
unsupported in the flux of situations and circumstances.
The upshot is that welter of "permissiveness" in which western
society now seems to be rotting away. The only remedy, of
course, is to restore the absolute standards; men must know
beyond dispute that some things may never be permitted under
any pretext. If such a thing as the torture of a sensitive being
may be permitted as a means to any end, however good, then
the pass is sold, religion has lost its meaning and civilization
has received its death-sentence. It is all over with morality,
all over with beauty, truth and goodness as human ideals:
for all these depend on principles which are immutable and
eternal—principles which, once a man has accepted them, he
must die rather than violate. *Noblesse oblige:* and surely
foremost among nobility's obligations (to say nothing of the
Christian gospel) are reverence for life and compassion with
suffering. These supreme values of civilized humanity may
never be sacrificed to anything inferior. If man is indeed
the noble creature he claims to be, and was meant to be,
he must eventually repudiate the foul methods which have for
so long disgraced his pursuit of those lesser goods: knowledge,
health and affluence.[48]

St. Francis, I believe, was fully aware that noblesse oblige; and in trying to fulfill this spiritual obligation, he was not trying to set up a democracy based on the equality of living creatures. In the spiritual sense,
democracy and equality have meaning only when the final spiritualization
is attained through return to, and union with, the divine. In proceeding
toward this remotely distant goal, evolving life is characterized by an
enormous spiritual diversity, whose higher limit is the human commitment to help in increasing love, compassion and self-sacrifice all others
on the path of self-transcendence. It follows that at this stage of evolution the human potential for good is correspondingly greater than that
of the nonhuman potential. Of course, we are brothers and sisters, units
of matter alive together during this earthly existence, but man, capable
of sin and of ethical choice and of evolutionary vision, can rise higher in
this life than his nonhuman relatives and is thus qualified to be the leader
of the spiritual ascent toward the source of all being.[49]

It is entirely fitting that Kazantzakis dedicated his book on St. Francis
to "the St. Francis of our era, Albert Schweitzer." This saintly Christian,
whose famous precept, reverence for life, emerged out of a profound
philosophical search for the truths of religion, was well aware of the
hierarchical nature of the spiritual diversity that characterizes contemporary living forms. He also seems to have known full well that the whole
of life is progressing toward the attainment of supreme excellence, although,
as far as I know, he does not refer to the Greek concept of *areté*. As
Henry Clark has made clear in his absorbing treatment of Schweitzer's
ethical mysticism,[50] Schweitzer considered the human potential more
worthy of realization than the nonhuman; at the same time he recognized
that any truly ethical man is committed to assist in the realization of both
kinds of potentiality:

What shall be my attitude towards this other life? he asks.
It can only be of a piece with my attitude towards my own
life. If I am a thinking being, I must regard other life than
my own with equal reverence. For I shall know that it longs
for fullness and development as deeply as I do myself. Therefore, I see that evil is what annihilates, hampers, or hinders life.
And this holds good whether I regard it physically or spiritually.
Goodness, by the same token, is the saving or helping of life,
the enabling of whatever life I can to attain its highest development.[51]

Albert Schweitzer could not fail to become preoccupied with the problem of good and evil and ethical choice, and probably no Christian of the twentieth century has pointed more directly to the prime cause of the dissolution of the modern world:

All progress in knowledge notwithstanding, we have experienced in the past few decades a stagnation of our civilization which manifests itself in every area of life. There are even numerous signs of a genuine retrogression. The sickness displays manifold symptoms, but the root cause is to be found in this condition: nothing in our civilization, including religion, is providing enough ethical ideals and energies. It has lost the great aim of the moral perfection of all mankind, and it is hemmed in by the walls of national and sectarian ideals instead of encompassing the whole world in its vision. Its greatness and its goodness pretend to be self-sufficient, whereas they ought to put themselves at the service of that general ethical perfection which, in accordance with the preaching of Jesus, one may call the Kingdom of God. These values of civilization only possess genuine ethical worth to the extent that they do serve this end.[52]

In his own striving to come closer toward ethical perfection, Schweitzer, living close to nature in the African jungle, realized the impossibility of completely avoiding the harming or killing of all lower forms of life. He also realized that it was ethically necessary for him to bring to the attention of the modern world a wholly new feeling for all animals based upon reverence for life. Whether or not Schweitzer was opposed to every form of scientific exploitation of animals I do not know, but the world should not forget that one of his last public statements, made only a few months before he died, was a greeting to the members of the World Coalition Against Vivisection at their congress in Zurich in July 1965. At that time he wrote,

We will fight against the spirit of primitive cruelty, with which we treat animals. Teachers of religion and philosophers have never interested themselves in our attitude towards animals but have only been interested in men ... but animals suffer in the same way as men. A true and deep humanism

cannot allow us to let them suffer. This view has come late
to us. It is our duty to see to it that it is valued all over the
world, and we must take this duty, which has been so long
neglected, seriously.

> With the kindest greetings to the participants in
> the congress against vivisection
>
> Yours faithfully
>
> Albert Schweitzer[53]

Schweitzer was well aware that man's loving, gentle, and compassionate
treatment of all forms of life is a necessary part of his own ethical ascent.

> Ethics alone [he writes] can put me in true relationship
> with the universe by my serving it, cooperating with it, not
> by trying to understand it. . . . Only by serving every kind
> of life do I enter the service of that Creative Will whence
> all life emanates. I do not understand it; but I do know
> (and it is sufficient to live by) that by serving life, I serve
> the Creative Will. It is through community of life, not
> community of thought, that I abide in harmony with that
> Will. This is the mystical significance of ethics.[54]

This truly Franciscan attitude of mind and heart carried his life and
thought beyond mere opposition to evil practices. He was directly engaged
in the positive task of helping to realize potentiality wherever he found
it. In the depths of his being, Schweitzer, like St. Francis, must have
known that noblesse oblige. A biology in the process of spiritualization
will need to follow humbly in the footsteps of these two men, separated
by seven long centuries and the vast stretch of sea and land between
Assisi and Lambarene but both belonging to a spiritual kin that transcends
the confines of time and space.

In the course of human evolution many souls have known that the
truest and best relation man can establish with animals is but a reflection
of his awareness of the human-divine relation as the central fact of his
existence. In their theocentric orientation these souls sensed that the
divine ethic is absolute, unchanging, and eternal in all situations: they
knew, accordingly, that ethical man must treat sentient beings with love,

righteousness, gentleness, mercy, and compassion in order that all of us can rise to surpass ourselves.

To expect modern biology and medicine to accept the religious world picture is no utopian dream. The spiritualization of biology is an evolutionary imperative from which science can never claim exemption. For science is an activity of scientists who, just as other human beings, have spiritual potentials to realize in this brief period on earth between birth and death. Until now scientists have been limiting the true progress of their profession by imposing upon themselves false ideals of objectivity, amorality, and atheism. Loren Eiseley has truly said that "the reality we know in our limited lifetimes is dwarfed by the unseen potential of the abyss where science stops."[55]

Science must not, and cannot, stop here. What appears to be an abyss is, in fact, the spiritual realm in which there is to be found a path of infinite potentialities leading to the divine Good. It is the most difficult path men can travel, but evolution requires that they make the journey and lead the way for others. The spiritual awakening has begun, and an increasingly syncretized science and religion will find the moral vision to give a disordered world a firm foundation of righteousness, harmony, serenity, and peace. The spiritualization of biology is only an extrapolation into what it must become: the ethical study of life by life to convert evolutionary potentiality into reality for the sake of the cosmic Good.

Notes

1. "Reaching Beyond the Rational," *Time,* April 23, 1973.

2. R. Steiner, *Christianity as Mystical Fact and the Mysteries of Antiquity,* trans. H. B. Monges (New York: Anthroposophic Press, 1947), p. 189.

3. Quoted by D. Caradog Jones, "Fellowship of the Spirit" (August 1973).

4. H. I'Anson Fausset, *The Lost Dimension* (London: Stuart & Watkins, 1966), pp. 71-72.

5. T. F. Torrance, *God and Rationality* (London: Oxford University Press, 1971), pp. 174, 177.

6. J. H. M. Whiteman, *The Mystical Life: An Outline of Its Nature and Teachings from the Evidence of Direct Experience* (London: Faber and Faber, 1961), p. 109.

7. "Poles of Self-Knowledge," *Theosophy* 60, no. 7 (May 1972): 193.

8. A. Hardy, *The Living Stream: A Restatement of Evolution Theory*

and Its Relation to the Spirit of Man (London: Collins, 1965), pp. 238-39.

9. H. H. Price, "Introduction" in *The Mystical Life,* J. H. M. White-man (London: Faber and Faber, 1961), p. xii.

10. A. Hardy, *The Divine Flame: An Essay Towards a Natural History of Religion* (London: Collins, 1966), p. 177.

11. Harold Wakeford Cox, personal correspondence.

12. C. Evans, "Parapsychology—What the Questionnaire Revealed," *New Scientist* 57 (January 25, 1973): 209.

13. C. W. K. Mundle, "Strange Facts in Search of a Theory," *Proceedings of the Society for Psychical Research,* January 1973, quoted in *The Aryan Path* 44, no. 4 (April 1973): 192.

14. *Ibid.*

15. T. Merton, *New Seeds of Contemplation* (London: Burns & Oates, 1961), p. 107.

16. W. R. Inge, *Mysticism in Religion* (London: Rider, 1969), p. 52.

17. A. E. Taylor, *Plato: The Man and His Work,* 7th ed. (London: Methuen, 1960), p. 526.

18. N. O. Jacobson, *Liv efter Døden? Om Parapsykologien, Mystikken og Døden* [Life After Death? On Parapsychology, Mysticism, and Death] (Copenhagen, 1971).

19. J. Wynne-Tyson, *The Civilised Alternative: A Pattern for Protest* (Fontwell, Sussex: Centaur Press, 1972).

20. C. Backster, "Evidence of a Primary Perception in Plant Life," *International Journal of Parapsychology* 10 (Winter 1968): 329-48.

21. J. Vyvyan, *Sketch for a World-Picture: A Study of Evolution* (London: Michael Joseph, 1972), pp. 67-68.

22. C. Roberts, *The Scientific Conscience: Reflections on the Modern Biologist and Humanism* (New York: George Braziller, 1967), p. 79.

23. I. Sanderson, with D. Loth, *Ivan Sanderson's Book of Great Jungles* (New York: Messner, 1965), p. 255.

24. M. C. D'Arcy, *Humanism and Christianity* (London: Constable, 1971), p. 37.

25. A. Hardy, *The Divine Flame,* p. 30.

26. Thomas a Kempis, *The Imitation of Christ,* trans. G. F. Maine (London: Collins, 1957), p. 276.

27. Harold Wakeford Cox, personal correspondence.

28. R. Steiner, *Theosophy: An Introduction to the Supersensible Knowledge of the World and the Destination of Man,* 3rd English ed. (London: Rudolf Steiner Press, 1970), p. 15.

29. R. Steiner, *The Manifestations of Karma: Eleven Lectures Given in Hamburg, 16th to 28th May, 1910,* 2nd ed. (London: Rudolf Steiner Press, 1969), p. 53.

30. *Ibid.,* p. 55.

31. J. Hemleben, *Biologie og Kristendom* [Biology and Christianity], trans. H. Madsen (Copenhagen: Borgens Forlag, 1971).

32. R. Steiner, *Christianity as Mystical Fact and the Mysteries of Antiquity,* trans. H. B. Monges (New York: Anthroposophic Press, 1947), pp. 6, 8.

33. Hardy was among the scientists referred to in Chapter 12 who protested in a letter to the London *Times* against the cruelties of factory farming, and in his book, *Great Waters* (London: Collins, 1967), he unequivocally condemned as unnecessarily cruel the harpoon gun used by Norwegian whalers.

34. J. Vyvyan, *In Pity and in Anger: A Study of the Use of Animals in Science* (London: Michael Joseph, 1969), p. 140.

35. H. P. Blavatsky, "Have Animals Souls?" reprinted from *The Theosophist,* 1886, in *The Theosophical Movement* 40 (1970): 251.

36. H. P. Blavatsky, "Cruelty to Animals," reprinted from *Lucifer,* 1890, in *The Theosophical Movement* (June 1967): 342.

37. A. T. J. Hayward, "Creation in California," Letter to the Editor, *Nature* 240 (December 29, 1972): 577.

38. N. Macbeth, *Darwin Retried: An Appeal to Reason* (Boston: Dell, 1973).

39. L. Eiseley, *Darwin's Century: Evolution and the Men Who Discovered It* (London: Gollancz, 1959), p. 324.

40. *Ibid.,* p. 312.

41. *Ibid.,* p. 285.

42. *Vandrer Mod Lyset! Et Budskab til Menneskeheden fra den Oversanselige Verden* [Toward the Light! A Message to Humanity from the Supersensible World], issued by Michael Agerskov (Copenhagen: Folmer Hansens Forlag, 1920), 5th impression (Gl. Viby, Sjælland: Strubes Forlag, 1972).

43. S. H. Nasr, *The Encounter of Man and Nature: The Spiritual Crisis of Modern Man* (London: George Allen & Unwin, 1968), p. 90.

44. After this chapter had been written, there came to my attention the very interesting fact, reported by Farooq Hussain (*New Scientist,* January 25, 1973, p. 183), that the American neurophysiologist, John Lilly, had voluntarily given up his extensive research on dolphins because "his scientific work could not be justified when it was at the expense of the dolphins—'I was running a concentration camp for my friends.' "

45. L. White, "The Historical Roots of Our Ecologic Crisis," *Science* 155 (1967): 1207.

46. N. Kazantzakis, *God's Pauper: St. Francis of Assisi,* trans. P. A. Bien (Oxford: Bruno Cassirer, 1962), pp. 109-10.

47. E. F. Schumacher, *Small Is Beautiful: A Study of Economics As If People Mattered* (London: Blond & Briggs, 1973), pp. 98-99.

48. B. Wrighton, "Noblesse Oblige," *The Ark* 41, no. 2 (August 1973): 8-10.

49. After reading these lines, Martin Andic added: "Leader or not, I can treat them with love, justice, and reverence that is their due as creations if not images of God." A lovely spiritual footnote.

50. H. Clark, *The Philosophy of Albert Schweitzer* (London: Methuen, 1964).

51. A. Schweitzer, "The Ethics of Reverence for Life," *Christèndom* 1, no. 2 (Winter 1936): 225-39.

52. A. Schweitzer, *Die Geschichte der Leben-Jesu-Forschung,* concluding statement. In *The Philosophy of Albert Schweitzer,* trans. H. Clark, pp. 199-200.

53. *"Albert Schweitzer, Humanismens Store Forkæmper, Er Ikke Mere"* [Albert Schweitzer, The Great Champion of Humanism, Is No More], *Forsøgsdyrenes Værn* 3, no. 3 (October 1965).

54. A. Schweitzer, "The Ethics of Reverence for Life," *Christendom* 1, no. 2 (Winter 1936): 225-39.

55. L. Eiseley, *The Night Country* (New York: Scribner, 1971), p. 215.

Epilogue

More than five years have passed since Chapter 14, on the spiritualization of biology, was written in the quiet and isolation of a semirural area in Denmark. Since then many excellent books have appeared which also deal with man's ethical response to nonhuman life, with his relation to divinity, and with the incipient convergence of contemporary science and ancient spiritual wisdom. To conclude with critical responses, for example, to A. Linzey's *Animal Rights* (London: SCM Press, 1976), S. R. L. Clark's *The Moral Status of Animals* (Oxford: Clarendon Press, 1977), Peter Singer's *Animal Liberation* (New York, The New York Review, 1975), Hans Ruesch's *Slaughter of the Innocent* (New York, Bantam Books, 1978), as well as to Arnold Toynbee and Daisaku Ikeda's *Choose Life* (London: Oxford University Press, 1976), E. F. Schumacher's *A Guide for the Perplexed* (London: Jonathan Cape, 1977), and Fritjof Capra's *The Tao of Physics* (New York: Bantam Books, 1977) would of course bring *Science, Animals, and Evolution* more abreast of the times and place it more firmly within contemporary thought.

Yet the times, if profoundly stimulating, are extraordinarily confusing as well. The spiritual groping of the present is still toward an essentially unarticulated goal. Now, back in Berkeley in this spring of 1979 after an absence of more than thirty years, I am vividly aware of the presence of

spiritual energy, but it is against a background of criminality, pollution,
sexual permissiveness, drugs, energy waste, and the mindless and heart-
less expansion of one of the great universities of the world into such
fields as nuclear armament and genetic engineering. As the numerous
sects, cults, and other spiritual groups in this part of the world vie with
one another and with established religions, it is becoming a matter of
urgency to choose the right spiritual path. Some are convinced that they
have made the right choice while others, in theistic, atheistic, or agnostic
anxiety, are seeking they know not what. Spiritual energy is being dis-
sipated because we cannot agree about the nature of the relationship between the human and the divine. The religious awakening has indubitably
begun, but the uncertainty and discord that accompany it show the need
for a common goal and perspective to reveal the basic identity of all
personal strivings.

Any attempt to explain the contemporary human situation is based
on the age-old desire to see life whole and then to have the last word
about it. No one mind is capable of this. Bombarded as we are on all
sides with New Age thoughts (many of which, we tend to forget, are
very ancient), where is the eclectic who can choose exactly those threads
required for the weaving of the cloth that is most needed now? Some
hold that since widespread spiritual bewilderment cannot be avoided at
this time, it is useless, and very presumptuous, to attempt to bring order
into agnostic chaos by envisioning both present and future as a single
spiritual process following an evolutionary path that leads from Here to
There. If, however, one is in the grip of a conviction that carries with it
a pervading sense of the inevitability of a nobler, purer life than that
which man is now experiencing, then such an intuitive belief in good
things to come must at least be offered for acceptance or rejection,
as I have done in the present volume. What concluding thought could
now be added to the foregoing presentation in the hope of leaving the
reader with the idea of one unified goal and perspective which, in spite
of widely different degrees of enlightenment and enormous diversity of
opinion and belief, we are all consciously beginning to share? Perhaps
only this single thread: Our inner spiritual work to help ourselves and
others is not purely autonomous behavior because self-transcendence
is a compulsory act of evolution whereby life, in every moment of its
existence, is being drawn There from whence it came. Who does the drawing? The divine hierarchy of good that is above our consciousness and

above our already realized spiritual potentials. In ways we do not understand, *Homo sapiens* is now being provided with spiritual energy to liberate itself from the egoistic preoccupation and ethical apathy that obscure the path back to its source. If men could but rise together above the misery of the times and the mist of religious confusion and dissent, they would see evolution as indissolubly bound to every thought about ego and ethics and enlightenment.

With this spiritual perspective we would be able to help one another in a joyous ascent, as it is meant to be, and living species everywhere would reap benefit beyond words. The secular rising to meet the sacred, the material becoming spiritualized, and a sense of rectitude expanding in every human heart is no longer wishful thinking. Where are the biologists who will begin to study life in harmony with the evolutionary truths the New Age is already revealing?

Bibliography

American Friends Service Committee. *Who Shall Live? Man's Control Over Birth and Death.* New York: Hill and Wang, 1970.

Armstrong, A. H. "Plotinus," pt. 3. *The Cambridge History of Later Greek and Early Medieval Philosophy.* Edited by A. H. Armstrong. Cambridge: University Press, 1967.

Backster, C. "Evidence of a Primary Perception in Plant Life." *International Journal of Parapsychology* 10 (1968): 329-348.

Blavatsky, H. P. *Isis Unveiled: A Master-Key to the Mysteries of Ancient and Modern Science and Theology,* vols. 1 and 2. A facsimile of the original edition of 1877. Los Angeles: The Theosophy Company, 1968.

———. *The Secret Doctrine,* vols. 1 and 2. A facsimile of the original edition of 1888. Los Angeles: The Theosophy Company, 1964.

Broch, J. O. *Det Kunstige Menneske (The Artificial Human Being).* Oslo: Minerva Forlag, 1969.

Carrel, Alexis. *Mennesket det Ukendte.* Danish translation of *Man the Unknown.* Copenhagen: Gyldendalske Boghandel-Nordisk Forlag, 1936.

Clark, Henry. *The Philosophy of Albert Schweitzer.* London: Methuen, 1964.

D'Arcy, Martin C. *Humanism and Christianity.* London: Constable, 1971.

Déchanet, J.-M. *Christian Yoga.* English translation of *La Voie du Silence.* London: Burns & Oates, 1960.

De Ropp, Robert S. *Drugs and the Mind.* New York: St. Martin's Press, 1957.

——. *The Master Game: Pathways to Higher Consciousness Beyond the Drug Experience.* New York: Delta, 1968.

Eiseley, Loren. *Darwin's Century: Evolution and the Men Who Discovered It.* London: Gollancz, 1959.

——. *The Night Country.* New York: Scribner, 1971.

Elkinton, J. R. "Beards, Flowers, Drugs, and Love." *Annals of Internal Medicine* 67 (1967): 1341-1343.

——. "The Literature of Ethical Problems in Medicine, I-III." *Annals of Internal Medicine* 73 (1970): 495-498, 662-666, 863-870.

——. "Medicine and the Quality of Life." *Annals of Internal Medicine* 64 (1966): 711-714.

Evans, C. "Parapsychology – What the Questionnaire Revealed." *New Scientist* 57 (1973): 209.

Evans-Wentz, W. Y., ed. and comp. *The Tibetan Book of the Dead.* London: Oxford University Press, 1960.

Farrington, Benjamin. "Science and the Classics." *Nature* 191 (1961): 1337.

Fausset, Hugh I'Anson. *The Lost Dimension.* London: Stuart and Watkins, 1966.

Forster, E. M. *A Passage to India.* London: J. M. Dent, 1942.

Frislev, Erna, trans. *Evangeliet om det Fuldkomne Liv eller De Tolv Helliges Evangelium.* Danish translation of J. G. Ouseley, trans. *The Gospel of the Holy Twelve.* Copenhagen: Strubes Forlag, 1971.

Godlovitch, Stanley and Rosalind, and J. Harris, eds. *Animals, Men and Morals: An Enquiry into the Maltreatment of Non-Humans.* London: Gollancz, 1971.

Hall, C. E. "Parabiosis." In *Methods in Animal Experimentation,* vol. 2, edited by William I. Gay. New York: Academic Press, 1965.

Harbison, S. P. "Origins of Vascular Surgery: The Carrel-Guthrie Letters." *Surgery* 52 (1962): 406.

Hardy, Alister. *The Divine Flame: An Essay Towards a Natural History of Religion.* London: Collins, 1966.

——. *The Living Stream: A Restatement of Evolution Theory and Its Relation to the Spirit of Man.* London: Collins, 1965.

Hemleben, Johannes. *Biologi og Kristendom* [Biology and Christianity]. Danish translation from German. Copenhagen: Borgens Forlag, 1971.

Hoffer, Abram, and H. F. Osmund. *The Hallucinogens.* New York: Academic Press, 1967.

Huxley, Aldous. *The Doors of Perception.* London: Chatto & Windus, 1954.

——. *Heaven and Hell.* London: Chatto & Windus, 1956.

Inge, W. R. *Mysticism in Religion*. London: Rider, 1969.

Jacobson, N-O. *Liv efter Døden? Om Parapsykologien, Mystikken og Døden* [Life After Death? On Parapsychology, Mysticism and Death]. Danish translation from Swedish. Copenhagen, 1971.

Jaeger, Werner. *Paideia: The Ideals of Greek Culture*. Vol. 2. *In Search of the Divine Centre*. Translated from German. Oxford: Basil Blackwell, 1957.

James, William. *The Will to Believe and Other Essays in Popular Philosophy and Human Immortality*. New York: Dover, 1956.

Kazantzakis, Nikos. *God's Pauper: St. Francis of Assisi*. Translated from Greek. Oxford: Bruno Cassirer, 1962.

Kennan, George F. *Democracy and the Student Left*. London: Hutchinson, 1968.

Lacey, P. A. "Quakerism Looks to the Future." In *Break the New Ground: Seven Essays by Contemporary Quakers*. Birmingham: Friends World Committee for Consultation, 1969.

Macbeth, Norman. *Darwin Retried: An Appeal to Reason*. Boston: Dell, 1973.

Maslow, A. H. *Religions, Values, and Peak-Experiences*. Columbus: Ohio State University Press, 1964.

Merton, Thomas. *New Seeds of Contemplation*. London: Burns & Oates, 1961.

Monod, Jacques. *Tilfældigheden og Nødvendigheden* [Chance and Necessity]. Danish translation of *Le Hasard et La Nécessité*. Copenhagen: Fremad, 1971.

Muggeridge, Malcolm. *Noget Skønt for Gud*. Danish translation of *Something Beautiful for God*. Copenhagen: Kristeligt Dagblads Forlag, 1971.

Mundle, C. W. K. "Strange Facts in Search of a Theory." *Proceedings of the Society for Psychical Research* (January 1973). Quoted in *The Aryan Path* 44, no. 4 (April 1973): 191-193.

Murdoch, Iris. *The Sovereignty of Good*. London: Routledge & Kegan Paul, 1970.

Nasr, Seyyed Hossein. *The Encounter of Man and Nature: The Spiritual Crisis of Modern Man*. London: George Allen and Unwin, 1968.

Otto, Rudolf. *The Idea of the Holy: An Inquiry into the Non-Rational Factor in the Idea of the Divine and Its Relation to the Rational*. London: Oxford University Press, 1923.

Plotinus. *The Enneads*. Translated from Greek by Stephen MacKenna. London: Faber and Faber, 1956.

Polanyi, Michael. *Personal Knowledge: Towards a Post-Critical Philosophy*. London: Routledge and Kegan Paul, 1958.

――――. *The Tacit Dimension*. Garden City, N.Y.: Doubleday, 1966.

Ravetz, Jerome R. *Scientific Knowledge and Its Social Problems.* Oxford: Clarendon Press, 1971.

Roberts, Catherine. *The Scientific Conscience: Reflecting on the Modern Biologist and Humanism.* New York: George Braziller, 1967.

———. "The Three Faces of Humanism." Tract 14. Lewes, Sussex: Gryphon Press, 1975.

———. "The Three Faces of Humanism and Their Relation to Problems of Science and Education." *Teachers College Record* 80, no. 3 (February 1979): 564-586.

Sanderson, Ivan, with D. G. Loth. *Ivan Sanderson's Book of Great Jungles.* New York: Messner, 1965.

Schumacher, E. F. *Small Is Beautiful: A Study of Economics as if People Mattered.* London: Blond and Briggs, 1973.

Schweitzer, Albert. "The Ethics of Reverence for Life." *Christendom* 1, no. 2 (Winter 1936): 225-239.

Steiner, Rudolf. *Kristus og Menneskesjelen* [Christ and the Human Soul]. Four lectures given in Norrköping, July 12-16, 1914. Norwegian translation of *Christus und die menschliche Seele.* Oslo: Vidarforlaget, 1951.

———. *The Manifestations of Karma.* Eleven lectures given in Hamburg, May 16-28, 1910. Translated from German. London: Rudolf Steiner Press, 1969.

———. *Theosophy: An Introduction to the Supersensible Knowledge of the World and the Destination of Man.* Translated from German. London: Rudolf Steiner Press, 1970.

Taft, A. "Why Has God Allowed Us into Space?" Interview with Wernher von Braun. *Christian Life* (July 1969): 18-21, 42-43.

Taylor, A. E. *Plato: The Man and His Work,* 7th ed. London: Methuen, 1960.

Taylor, G. R. *The Biological Time Bomb.* London: Thames and Hudson, 1968.

Thomas a Kempis. *The Imitation of Christ.* Translated by George F. Maine. London: Collins, 1957.

Torrance, T. F. *God and Rationality.* London: Oxford University Press, 1971.

Vyvyan, John. *In Pity and in Anger: A Study of the Use of Animals in Science.* London: Michael Joseph, 1969.

———. *Sketch for a World-Picture: A Study of Evolution.* London: Michael Joseph, 1972.

Walton, Izaak. *The Lives of John Donne, Sir Henry Wotton, Richard Hooker, George Herbert, and Robert Sandersen.* London: Oxford University Press, 1927.

Watts, Alan W. *The Joyous Cosmology: Adventures in the Chemistry of Consciousness.* New York: Pantheon Books, 1962.

White, Lynn. "The Historical Roots of Our Ecologic Crisis." *Science* 155 (1967): 1203-1207.

White, Robert J. "Experimental Transplantation of the Brain." In Felix T. Rapaport and Jean Dausset, eds., *Human Transplantation.* New York: Grune, 1968.

White, Victor. *God and the Unconscious.* London: Collins, 1952.

Whitehead, A. N. *Science and the Modern World.* Cambridge: University Press, 1926.

Whiteman, J. H. M. *The Mystical Life: An Outline of Its Nature and Teachings from the Evidence of Direct Experience.* London: Faber and Faber, 1961.

Woods, G. F. *A Defence of Theological Ethics.* Cambridge: University Press, 1966.

Wrighton, Basil. "Justice and the Animals." *The Ark* 45 (April 1952): 4-15.

———. "Noblesse Oblige." *The Ark* 41, no. 2 (August 1973): 8-10.

Wynne-Tyson, Jon. *The Civilised Alternative: A Pattern for Protest.* Fontwell, Sussex: Centaur Press, 1972.

Zaehner, R. C. *Hindu and Muslim Mysticism.* London: Athlone Press, 1960.

———. *Mysticism Sacred and Profane: An Inquiry into Some Varieties of Praeternatural Experience.* London: Oxford University Press, 1957.

Index

About the Author

CATHERINE ROBERTS has written extensively and is the author of *The Scientific Conscience,* as well as articles for such journals as *American Scholar, The Antioch Review,* and *Teachers' College Record.*